THE LIFE AND LEGACY OF
ROCHDALE COLLEGE

Henry Mietkiewicz
Bob Mackowycz

McGRAW-HILL RYERSON
Toronto   Montreal

DREAM TOWER: The Life and Legacy of Rochdale College

© 1988 Henry Mietkiewicz and Bob Mackowycz.

First published in 1988 by
McGraw-Hill Ryerson Limited
330 Progress Avenue
Scarborough, Ontario, Canada   M1P 2Z5

ISBN 0-07-549597-X

1 2 3 4 5 6 7 8 9 0   DWF   6 5 4 3 2 1 0 9 8

Printed and bound in Canada

Canadian Cataloguing in Publication Data

Mietkiewicz, Henry.
Dream Tower

ISBN 0-07-549597-X

1. Rochdale College. 2. Free schools – Ontario – Toronto.
3. Toronto (Ont.) – Social conditions. 4. Drug abuse – Treatment – Ontario – Toronto. 5. Hippies – Ontario – Toronto.
I. Mackowycz, Bob. II. Title.

LE3.R63M54 1988   378.713'541   C88-094881-7

To Dorothy
For always being there
with the intellect of Amanda
and the passion of Pinkie.
H.M.

To Frances
Twenty years and it still feels like
we're kids walking home from school.
I share this book with you.

And to my children, Bob and Lesia —
remember grasshoppers: when you can snatch
the pebble from my hand then, and only then,
will you be able to leave the temple.
B.M.

C O N T E N T S

Acknowledgments   xi
1   A Day in the Life   1
2   Do You Believe in Magic?   7
3   The House of the Rising Sun   24
4   Crown of Creation   42
5   Stoned Soul Picnic   68
6   Love the One You're With   83
7   Purple Haze   105
8   Dazed and Confused   129
9   I'd Love to Change the World   146
10   I Fought the Law   164
11   The Beat Goes On   186
12   Riders on the Storm   215
13   After the Gold Rush   239
14   Won't Get Fooled Again   246
15   Right Place Wrong Time   257
16   The Long and Winding Road   279

I pace upon the battlements and stare
On the foundation of a house, or where
Tree, like a sooty finger, starts from the earth;
And send imagination forth
Under the day's declining beam, and call
Images and memories
From ruin and ancient trees,
For I would ask a question of them all

From "The Tower"
W. B. Yeats

THE ROCHDALE BLUES

Well I saw her as she loitered in the lobby
I knew she put her body up for grabs
I figured out that ballin' was her hobby
But I never figured that she had the crabs

CHORUS: I got the Rochdale blues

I followed her as she went up the back stairs
I carefully avoided all the shit
And then she turned to me as if she really cared
But she only asked me if I had a hit

CHORUS: I got the Rochdale blues

I can't forget we spent the night together
I can't forget no matter how hard I try
'Cause all she did was add to my displeasure
And all my dope was used to get her high

CHORUS: I got the Rochdale blues

Well now I got to cut the hash in such small pieces
There's no one here to take a second toke
She left me here with one of her diseases
And my Rochdale baby has gone up in smoke

CHORUS: I got the Rochdale blues

"Red" Rebel
Rochdale Resident

ACKNOWLEDGMENTS

The authors would like to express their gratitude to Alex Mac-Donald, who was instrumental in contacting and arranging interviews with many of Rochdale's "alumni." Most of the photographs in this book also come from Mr. MacDonald's personal archives. An additional word of thanks goes to Morgan Davis for introducing us to Mr. MacDonald, a meeting that started the ball rolling.

Thanks also to David Sharpe for providing access to research material assembled for his book, *Rochdale: The Runaway College;* Judith Merril for her valuable suggestions and advice; Metro Police Inspector Robert Crampton and Staff Sergeant Jack Press for putting us in touch with officers who had worked the Rochdale beat; Gary "Lou" Slaight for his moral support and use of the photocopier; Peter Livingston and David Johnston for believing in the project; Pino Scoleri for help to transcribe interviews; Renate Brickman for typing beyond the call of duty; Reggie Bovaird for being Reggie; and everyone who gave generously of their time to spin some mind-blowing yarns.

C H A P T E R   1

A
Day in
the Life

One snowy March night in 1969, in an auditorium thick with ecstatic moans and four-letter cries, a twenty-two-year-old actress bared her breasts before a wide-eyed audience and brought the revolution to good, gray Toronto.

Her performance in the notorious production of *Futz*—a satire about a farmer's carnal love for his pet pig—marked the first public display of nudity in a dramatic presentation at a mainstream Toronto theatre. With unprecedented bluntness, it challenged a complacent, conservative populace to examine suppressed feelings about such taboos as incest, bestiality and free love. It was also the first substantial indication of the dynamic but disturbing effects of a visionary downtown enclave known as Rochdale College.

If Torontonians were aware of Rochdale at all in early 1969, it was probably as a result of having casually glanced at largely complimentary newspaper and magazine articles, such as those in *Time, Newsweek,* or *Weekend.*

But now, in view of the active support that Rochdale had given to the troupe that staged *Futz,* civic authorities finally began to comprehend the true nature of the social and cultural powerhouse in their midst. It was more than tie-dyed T-shirts, peace slogans, love beads, high-decibel music, shoulder-length hair. Rochdale embodied a revolution in the arts, education, sexuality, drug use and political philosophy. Acting as a magnet for disaffected and disillusioned members of the younger generation, it threatened to catapult a once-insulated community toward the extremes of other cities in the turbulent Sixties.

Outwardly, Rochdale seemed no different from any of the high-rise apartment buildings that had sprouted in Toronto during the construction boom in the Sixties. It loomed over the nondescript corner of Bloor and Huron streets in a working-class neighbourhood known as the Annex. And yet, Rochdale was situated at the nerve centre of the city—if not in a physical sense, then in a figurative one. To the immediate south lay the sprawling central campus of the University of Toronto, the provincial Legislature, a burgeoning Chinatown, the twin, semi-circular towers of the futuristic new City Hall, the Bay Street financial district and the seamy, raunchy Yonge Street strip. To the east sat Varsity Stadium, the Royal Ontario Museum and grungy Yorkville, where hippies and candle-lit coffeehouses were slowly being displaced by an invincible wave of exclusive upscale boutiques. To the north and west crouched the homes and businesses that served the university—fraternity houses, co-op residences, second-hand book stores, record shops, fast-food restaurants, repertory movie theatres, the YM-YWHA—amid a dizzying, ethnic patchwork of blacks, Jews, Italians, Chinese, native Indians, East Indians and, of course, WASPs.

On Thursday, March 6, 1969, the morning after *Futz*'s shocking debut, most citizens remained blissfully ignorant of the giant slumbering on their doorstep. So what if a group of young people had somehow built a $6 million high-rise and, in the spirit of freedom and good will, thrown open the doors to thousands of their eccentric brothers and sisters? There were, after all, more important things in the world to worry about. Richard Nixon, barely two months after his inauguration as president, was hinting about a resumption in the bombing of North Vietnam. Sirhan Sirhan was denying that he had gone to the Ambassador Hotel in Los Angeles the previous June to assassinate Senator Robert Kennedy.

Closer to home, six juveniles were found guilty of mischief in the $2 million damage spree in February at the computer centre of Sir George Williams University in Montreal. Federal cabinet minister Allan MacEachen faced criticism that immigration officers were not only turning back U.S. draft resisters, but informing on them to American border authorities.

Even the good news was enough to divert attention from Rochdale. Apollo 9 astronauts James McDivitt and Russell Schweickart were successfully testing the lunar module that would land on the moon the following July. For the fourth time in his career, Bobby Hull of the Chicago Blackhawks scored his fiftieth goal of the season, while the Boston Bruins' Phil Esposito hit a new single-season record for his sixty-three assists. At the same moment that farmer Futz was proclaiming his love for his pet pig, Amanda, Prime Minister Pierre Trudeau was thanking 1,600 Liberal colleagues at a $50-a-plate dinner in Toronto's Royal York Hotel for their support in his election the previous June.

Rochdale may have acted as a catalyst in the transformation of Toronto, but the raw materials of the Sixties were already in place, even in a city so proud of its atmosphere of caution, order and moderation. Alongside *The Toronto Star*'s review of *Futz* on March 6 was an ad inviting customers to "body paint our beautiful, completely topless girls" at the Mynah Bird on Yorkville Avenue.

Movies, by and large, had entered the new age of frankness and psychedelia with *2001: A Space Odyssey* at the Glendale Cinerama, Zeffirelli's *Romeo and Juliet* at the Park, *Candy* at the Hollywood Cinema South and *The Magus* at The Cinema in the Toronto-Dominion Centre. But, a quaint throwback, the Coronet at Yonge and Gerrard streets still warned patrons that the Peter Cushing film *Corruption* "is not a woman's picture! Therefore: No woman will be admitted alone to see this super-shock film!!" Small wonder that less daring souls were content to curl up at home on March 6 with "Star Trek" (the first run of its third season), "That Girl," "Ironside" and "Bewitched." Canadian nationalists dutifully tuned in to "The Day It Is," "Telescope," "Pierre Berton" and "Perry's Probe."

Rock became the pulse-beat of the younger generation. Toronto AM stations such as CHUM and CKFH still dominated the airwaves in March 1969, as they turned out both the innocuous (Tommy Roe's "Dizzy") and the adventurous (Simon and Garfunkel's "The Boxer," Creedence Clearwater Revival's "Proud Mary" and Sly & The Family Stone's "Everyday People"). Toronto was also beginning to discover the "underground" sound of CHUM-FM, where free-form disc jockeys were playing extended tracks from recent albums such as *Beggar's Banquet* by the Rolling Stones, *Electric Ladyland* by the Jimi Hendrix Experience and *Astral Weeks* by Van Morrison.

The live music scene was also firmly in place, with March appearances by Ronnie Hawkins at Le Coq d'Or, Richie Havens and Gordon Lightfoot at Massey Hall, Janis Joplin at O'Keefe Centre, Procol Harum and Blood, Sweat and Tears at the Electric Circus, and Chuck Berry and the Mothers of Invention at the Rock Pile. Even Jim Morrison, who had been arrested in Miami on March 1 for indecent exposure and lascivious behaviour, played Maple Leaf Gardens with the Doors at the end of the month.

By 1969, Toronto had a thriving music scene, based in bars and clubs like Le Coq d'Or, the Hawk's Nest, the Blue Note, the Colonial Tavern, the Brown Derby and the Friar's. Toronto-based bands such as the Paupers, Stitch 'N' Tyme, Luke and the Apostles and Jon and Lee and the Checkmates were being touted as the next wave of international stars.

Stand on the plaza facing Rochdale on March 6, 1969, and you find yourself dwarfed by an eighteen-storey concrete monolith shaped roughly like a squared-off letter S. From the outside, there appears to be nothing exceptional about the structure—a hulking mass of functional grayness broken only by the checkerboard pattern of orange-curtained windows and the street-level presence of a bank, book store and health food restaurant.

But approach the building and your perspective shifts abruptly. The front door, you'll notice, has had its lock smashed in a spirit of openness and camaraderie—resulting in a stream of underage runaways, wild-eyed speed-dealers and burly motorcyclists mixed in with the long-haired hitch-hikers and road-weary backpackers who happen to be passing through. The lobby is a maelstrom of activity—a group of laughing students in neat turtleneck sweaters and bellbottom jeans on their way out to the U of T, a teenage girl who saunters by without a stitch of clothing beneath her black leather jacket, a man in his late thirties hobbling with a vacant stare and outstretched arms on a zig-zag path toward the elevator, two young women arguing heatedly about the merits of armed revolution, and a smiling man with a grizzled, brown beard hunched in contemplation over an acoustic guitar. Behind and around them, the muralled walls swirl and writhe with the day-glo reds, tawny golds and electric blues of everything from disjointed abstractions to pastoral scenes to fairytale characters.

Smell that? Sharp, sweet and pungent. The girl who just walked by was openly puffing a joint. No big deal, you say? Well, don't forget that if she's caught and convicted, she's almost sure to get a jail term, like smokers in Canada and other countries wasting away in prison for possession of a single joint or even seeds and twigs. (Today, by contrast, a rap on the knuckles, a mild lecture and no criminal record are standard procedure for a first offence.) Now consider that she's not alone. In fact, grass by the bale is smuggled into Rochdale every month and casually consumed, along with a substantial amount of hashish and LSD. Where are the police? A good question—and one that will be repeated by concerned Torontonians with mounting anger in the coming years.

For now Rochdale continues to function as a world unto itself. Residents can drop into the second-floor cafeteria for hot, nourishing meals. Or they can cook for themselves with groceries purchased in the health food store (whole-wheat bread thirty cents, European bread nineteen cents, sardines ten cents). Child-care facilities, still a relative rarity in the Toronto of 1969, are already a fact of life here. And a fully stocked clinic is just days away from opening.

In a cultural sense, Rochdale also has it all under one roof. Just check current issues of the *Daily* (a mimeographed newsletter) for your activity of choice—a free screening of *Huelga*, a documentary about the California grape strike, tomorrow in the second-floor lounge in preparation for the big boycott-grapes rally at the nearby Dominion supermarket; a festival of classical music, folk and jazz this Saturday in the lounge; an informal concert on March 15 by folk singer Murray McLauchlan (admission fifty cents); a meeting to discuss revolution in music, based on transcripts of the lyrics by Bob Dylan, the Mothers of Invention, the Fugs, Phil Ochs and the Doors.

The *Daily* will also give you a quick taste of the ups and downs of life for the building's unorthodox residents. A glance in the Help Wanted box reveals that a draft resister's wife, after visiting her husband in Rochdale, needs help raising money for her fare back to the U.S. ("Even ten cents will help"). Free room and board are being offered to those willing to work at the communications desk in the lobby and keep an eye out for suspicious visitors.

Come, let's board the elevator, which happens to be working today. It's not hard to imagine the elevator ride as a psychedelic version of a trip through Dante's *Inferno*. When the doors slide open, you might find yourself stepping into paradise or one of the terrifying circles of hell. And don't let the graffiti bother you. After all, the elevator is more a means of communication than it is a mode of transportation.

We've come to our destination—no, it doesn't matter which floor. At Rochdale you pick a floor and let the adventure happen. Many of the doors are open, as residents wander happily and uninvited from one apartment to another. Children also toddle cheerfully down the corridor under the watchful eyes of passersby.

Check the sign on that door: "If you want to come in and make love to me, wipe your feet first." Look, there's another: "This apartment is protected by a forty-megaton nuclear device which will be triggered by the entry or attempted entry of any unauthorized person, chicks included. So watch it."

That brings to mind the matter of security. As it happens, this area—and this entire floor, actually—is rather clean and well run. Guests and crashers are welcome, but a set of rules has been imposed, in sharp contrast to the devil-may-care system on other floors. Here all rooms are swept and dishes washed several times daily.

Life isn't all peace and brotherhood at Rochdale, and tonight it gets just a bit rougher. *Futz*'s second performance will proceed as planned at the Central Library Theatre, but this time the police will charge the producers, director and cast under the Criminal Code with giving an immoral performance—opening the way for possibles fines of $500 per person or six months' imprisonment or both. The police will return almost every night for weeks to lay the same charges on behalf of a disturbed and outraged populace.

How could an apartment building dedicated to free love, open drug use, radical politics and educational experimentation spring to life in a city as conservative as Toronto?

It all began when the baby boom ran smack up against one man's dream. . . .

CHAPTER 2

Do You
Believe
in Magic?

Time and again, the link between Rochdale's residents and the building's origins proved to be one of unwitting irony. Even as the inhabitants triumphantly declared their intention to "live for today," they occupied a structure whose name echoed more than a century of working-class tradition. Cries of disdain for financial accountability were proclaimed from the meeting halls of a tower that had been built at a cost of nearly $6 million. Contempt for an unyielding Establishment persisted even though Rochdale's creation depended upon legislation passed by sympathetic federal politicians.

In 1958 an ambitious nineteen-year-old Toronto entrepreneur named Howard Adelman was hired to find some means of satisfying the growing demand for student housing at the University of Toronto. His employer was Campus Co-operative Residences, an independent organization born in the more serene 1930s. Campus Co-op remained virtually unchanged during its first two decades, as it played landlord to a mere one hundred students in five old houses in the university area.

"By the late fifties, they must have been the last places in Toronto with iceboxes instead of refrigerators," Adelman recalls. "They made their own paint out of sour milk, they used camp cots and army felt mattresses, and they lived like they were still Depression-era people. So even though there was a need for housing, they were out of step with the times and had a high vacancy rate."

Even the leaders of Campus Co-op were unable to ignore the harbingers of change. Children born during World War Two were about to enter university, and it was obvious that even more student housing would be required when post-war young-sters—the flood of baby boomers—reached college age in the 1960s.

But the U of T, like so many other universities, claimed to have insufficient funds to meet the housing demand, despite generous new mortgage rates offered by Ottawa to universities to develop student residences. Whatever money the universities could spare was earmarked for construction of on-campus necessities such as classrooms and libraries.

By the same token, the students had begun to feel that the quality of life in their spartan accommodations was sorely in need of improvement. If conditions were to be changed, the residents themselves—not the universities—would have to take charge of the upgrading program. "Students were regarded by society as somehow a race apart," says J. Malcolm Wells, a Campus Co-op tenant who became one of Rochdale's architects. "Among students, there was also the feeling that the residences were too authoritarian and that you were just basically a number on a door off a corridor."

So it fell to Campus Co-op to assume a major role in planning, financing and constructing homes for the incoming generation of college students. Howard Adelman seemed ideally suited to the task. Even in his teens, he had taken a hand in managing a hotel and restaurant, and he had a reputation as an able administrator. Paul Evitts, who later became one of Rochdale's first students and an executive member of its governing council, remembers Adelman as "almost a prototypical yuppie. He espoused a lot of the educational values we were talking about. But at the same time, he was definitely into using the system, and he was quite into money and the good life. His family was involved in the development business and he got a lot of his ideas from being in that milieu."

Author Dennis Lee, who was instrumental in mapping out Rochdale's education program, helped to edit Adelman's book, *The University Game*, in the early Sixties and remembers Adelman as being "super-bright and super-ambitious. He appeared, at the time, to have chosen to take his enormous entrepreneurial skills and put them into something other than conventional money-making. I admired that. But of course, his empire-building impulse was still there. He always had a brash, see-how-far-you-can-push-it quality. It's funny, because he was quite a towering figure in some ways, but there was a sort of cocky twelve-year-old side to him, too."

In turning to Adelman, Campus Co-op was hiring an outside manager for the first time in its history. Says Adelman, "I fell in love with the co-operatives. I mean, it was a lovely place to be, with a really nice community of people. But the difference was, I brought in business planning. We began to buy houses and invest in property. Before we knew it, we jumped to seven houses, then to ten houses. At the time, the houses were costing us $15,000 or $20,000 and are now worth $150,000 to $300,000. The money was borrowed, of course, but that was no problem because Campus Co-op had a lot of equity in its properties and not much debt."

What followed, quite naturally, was the formation of Co-operative College Residences Inc., a non-profit off-shoot of Campus Co-op whose mandate was to develop new housing for students. Although Toronto was the initial focus of attention, the first project to be completed (in 1966) was the University of Waterloo's Hammarskjold House, the first student-built co-op in North America.

Toronto's name might have gone into the record books ahead of Waterloo's, if not for the fact that the U of T had ceased to be merely a disinterested party and, by 1960, was a major irritant. No sooner did the co-op settle on an attractive location than the university expropriated the land for its own purposes. Had the students been allowed to retain the site they originally chose in 1960, they might have wound up with a trouble-free building that was modest in both size (a hundred tenants) and lifestyle (separate outside entrances for men and women). But the U of T repeatedly foiled the co-op's plans, even going so far as to seize a desirable property that had earlier been declared as lying beyond the university's expansion area.

Perhaps to atone for its acquisitiveness, the university offered the co-op a deal involving a site on the west side of Spadina Avenue, between Harbord Street and Sussex Avenue. But Adelman and his colleagues were familiar with the development boom in the outlying regions of Metropolitan Toronto, and they knew that politicians were under increasing pressure to build an expressway uniting the suburbs with the downtown core. If the highway had been completed (plans to finish it were not killed until 1971), a river of automobiles would have emptied onto Spadina, dividing the campus from the land that the university had made available. Co-op College declined the offer and resumed its search.

Adelman and his associates were also lobbying to wring financial concessions from the federal government. In 1960, the

National Housing Act had been amended to allow universities to finance student residences with federal mortgages for ninety per cent of the total project cost, at an interest rate considerably below market rates. Adelman felt that similar terms should be available to student residences built by co-ops—and in 1964, he led a delegation to Ottawa to accomplish just that.

"The co-op did it, but I organized the lobby, and we got alumni to help us. Mind you, none of this was done specifically for Rochdale. It was for student housing in general, prior to any thinking about Rochdale. But we hit cabinet ministers, members of Parliament—everybody.

"Everybody had been giving us encouraging words and we were sure we were going to get what we wanted. Then we went into Paul Hellyer's office—he was minister of defence, I think—and after five minutes he said, 'Look, it's already been to cabinet. They rejected it. It's not as if anybody has any reason to be opposed. It's an all-right idea. They just don't want to be bothered. For this kind of thing, we only react to pressure. So you have to show them that if they don't do it, there'll be a lot of bad publicity. You show that, and you'll get your amendment.' So we did exactly what he said—and we got it!"

Momentum for an educational element was added by heightened resentment against the U of T. The university in the mid-1960s planned to build a small, relatively luxurious college to house the cream of the campus population. These select few—distinguished by high academic standing—were to live in a sheltered environment of courtyard fountains and hushed reading rooms, tucked behind an imposing, ivy-covered brick wall. The institution would be funded by and named after the distinguished Massey family, whose members included Canada's Governor-General Vincent Massey and actor Raymond Massey.

Adelman grumbles, "Naturally, people asked, 'Why the hell are these rich Massey students going to be spoiled, while the poor students get nothing? Why don't we have a college of our own?' "

And so, in 1964, with approximately two hundred and twenty-five students living in seventeen owned and six rented houses in the U of T area, Campus Co-op incorporated its project-to-be as an educational institution. The college was named Rochdale after one of the first recorded co-operatives founded in 1844 in Rochdale, Lancashire, England. "It could have been any one of us who named it," says Adelman, "but it was probably me, because I had written so much about the history of the co-op movement and the first Rochdale. It seemed a very appropriate, almost self-evident name and it recalled the movement's origins."

Clearly, the time was right to build. The only question was: Where? The answer came through architect J. Malcolm Wells who was acquainted with the students' dilemma. With his partner, Elmar Tampold, Wells had helped to design a Toronto project that was developed by Revenue Properties. Revenue, Wells learned, was in a position to develop a site it owned at the south-east corner of Bloor and Huron.

With a site finally chosen and a developer ready and waiting, Co-op College set out to secure a low-interest mortgage from the federal government's Central Mortgage and Housing Corporation (CMHC). A meeting with CMHC officials was convened in February, 1966, in the board room of Simcoe Hall, seat of power at the University of Toronto. Among those present was Jack Dimond, a U of T graduate of humanities who had undergone Jesuit training and graduated from Boston College, but came to Toronto to take advantage of its superior graduate program. In need of accommodation upon arrival in Toronto in 1964, he wound up at Campus Co-op, where he became treasurer in 1965 and president in 1966.

"The basic pitch," says Dimond, "was that the co-op was a fairly stable organization that already had a history of running houses successfully. And in the case of Rochdale, all the co-op planned to do was figuratively stack the houses one on top of the other as a high-rise. CMHC decided to grant the mortgage. Essentially they gave approval in principle to the idea. But one thing that CMHC wasn't concerned about was the educational component, because the building was still being conceived strictly as a high-rise residence. The educational component arose after that."

With CMHC covering 90 per cent of the project's cost, the rest of the money proved to be relatively easy to raise. A second mortgage came from Revenue Properties, which had reinvested a percentage of its equity. Campus Co-op kicked in a portion by mortgaging some of its holdings. The Nu Sigma Nu fraternity signed on in exchange for accommodation for its members when Rochdale opened. In later years, Revenue Properties would also hold a fifth mortgage.

In April, 1966, the first Rochdale Council was elected to supervise plans for the residence. Three months later, CMHC put its stamp of approval on the project and informed the jubilant council it had qualified for a $4.8 million mortgage at 6⅞ per cent interest (standard rates were 9¼ per cent), amortized over fifty years. By March 1, 1969, CMHC expected to receive the initial monthly mortgage payment of $26,000. Finally, in late 1966, construction began on the $5.8 million, eighteen-story concrete tower, with a projected opening date of June, 1968.

Former council members still complain that untold damage was caused by saddling Rochdale with a confusing, top-heavy corporate structure. Although Rochdale's ills clearly stemmed from a great many factors unrelated to finance, the building was hobbled in its infancy by the lack of a simple, efficient and controllable management system.

Flaws in the building's concept and design also began to manifest themselves. With the U of T in control of the best sites in the neighbourhood, Co-op College was reluctant to pass up the property at Bloor and Huron. Unfortunately, the land did not carry the preferred residential zoning of two times coverage—a designation that would have yielded an unassuming, easily administered building whose floor area was only twice the area of the lot. Owing to its location on a busy downtown arterial road, the site was zoned at a whopping seven times coverage.

For Revenue Properties to build at less than the permissible density would have meant making less than optimum use of its investment. But for Co-op College, the consequence was an immediate and unanticipated jump to 840 tenants, which eventually led to staggering difficulties in managing so concentrated a group of free-wheeling residents.

However, given the expansionist tenor of Toronto in the mid-1960s and the mounting pressures on Campus Co-op to house more students, this change in the project's magnitude seemed like nothing short of a godsend. If anything, Rochdale had fallen into closer step with the times. Suddenly, it found itself part of the buoyant bigger-is-better mentality that was mesmerizing North America and enlarging everything from colour television picture tubes to gas-guzzling automobiles to that gargantuan novelty, the shopping mall.

Size was only one critical aspect of the lot's designation. Zoning regulations also decreed that the property had to be the site of an apartment-hotel. This meant that only half the floor space could be used for apartments with self-contained kitchens—hardly a problem for Campus Co-op, since most students tended to cook and eat in a common area. However, Rochdale's managers later discovered that a communal system in a high-rise setting often resulted in an absence of responsibility among residents.

The two types of accommodations—self-contained apartments in the west wing and communal, hotel-type units in the east wing—gave Rochdale a split personality, at least in its early years. The western apartments tended to attract a more stable, responsible, self-sufficient tenant who played an active role in operating the building. Meanwhile, residents in the eastern hotel rooms were generally more transient and less inclined to take an active interest in matters affecting Rochdale.

In addition, the apartment-hotel zoning dictated construction of more underground parking space than was necessary for tenants who were either poor transients or students whose modest income was reserved for tuition, food and rent.

"We had to cut a couple of floors below ground," adds Elmar Tampold, "and the shoring was very expensive. It probably cost to create each car space 25 to 33 per cent of the unit cost. And it probably didn't produce—nor could it ever produce—enough income to pay for that space."

For engineering reasons, the size and configuration of the parking garage also determined the area and layout of the floors and rooms above. "I learned," says Adelman, "that apartments have twenty-one-foot bays because you need that space to park two American cars. So you plan the design of your floor around the bays and the pillars of the parking garage. Other than that, parking wasn't a problem. Even though the students didn't own many cars, the idea was to rent out the space. So the parking could easily have paid for itself if it had been run properly."

Since so much attention was paid to meeting the apartment-hotel requirements, some of Rochdale's occupants later came to believe that a student residence never really figured in the developers' plans. "Revenue Properties, which had assembled the original site, was basically gambling that Adelman wasn't going to be able to pull this off," insists Paul Evitts. "If the financing fucked up or the project fucked up before the first floor was finished, Revenue Properties could step in and take it over and make it into something like the Colonnade [a commercial-residential development]."

Adelman, however, dismisses the notion as nonsense. "It's simply not true that Rochdale was purposely designed to be converted into an apartment-hotel. I don't think that was in anybody's mind."

In its final form, Rochdale consisted of an eighteen-floor west wing and a sixteen-floor east wing connected by a seventeen-floor central core, all atop a two-level underground garage. The first two floors held the front lobby, a few street-level commercial spaces, a cafeteria, office space and some seminar rooms. Each of floors three through eighteen in the western, apartment-type wing contained six one-bedroom units (known as Aphrodites) and one large two-bedroom unit (Zeus). Each of floors three through sixteen in the eastern, hotel-type wing contained six one-bedroom units (Gnostics) and five additional units (Kafkas), each with one double bedroom, one single bedroom and a bathroom. Occupants of the Kafkas shared living room and kitchen space with residents of the central core. Each of floors three through seventeen in the core contained a large, communal set-up (Ashram) consisting of four double rooms, four single rooms and a common living room and bathroom. A major portion of the eighteenth floor was also used as a laundry room. Rents ranged from about $50 to $200 a month.

"The architects actually did the design," Adelman said. "But we programmed the floor, we programmed the mix and the architects came up with different drawings. It was a student decision and we were caught in the model of how we lived in houses. We were trying to build the equivalent of houses within a high-rise, instead of saying, 'This is a high-rise, so let's actually live in a high-rise.' We were always being caught in an old system of thinking."

In a post-postscript to his 1969 book, *The Beds Of Academe*, Adelman himself lists "three clear errors" in design. The first was the discovery that the amount of parking space could have been significantly reduced. Since the number of parking spots was tied to the number of residential units, Rochdale's planners could have connected pairs of single rooms and simply labelled each hybrid a two-room suite. Even though the floor area would have stayed the same, the actual number of units would have dropped.

The second weakness was the decision to equip each Ashram with one huge washroom. A wiser move would have been to construct two domestic-scale washrooms, each being used either for toilet or bathing purposes. This would have made the washrooms more economical to build and easier to clean.

Third, since the Ashram lounge was intended to serve an entire floor, it was easy prey for unauthorized intruders, or "crashers."

During the first few months of Rochdale's existence, many of the residents who gave any thought to their rooms' appearance and furnishings seemed satisfied. Carol Shevlin, who lived in the building with her husband, Tom, in 1969, remembers their apartment as having "lovely red drapes, a couple of student-type beds, a couple of desks—it was completely furnished. Everything had lots of pillows and stuff on it. The kitchen had a wonderful stove, and you could use either the oven or the range top—not both at once."

Others were harsher in their assessment. "It was your basic stereotypically ugly high-rise apartment building," complains Paul Evitts, one of the first people to move into Rochdale. "A lot of the crap around Rochdale was, as far as I'm concerned, people actively trying to make some human use out of the arid environment we got stuck with all the time. I was involved with the design committee that was looking at the use of interior space. We were co-opted—we really were. I would be sitting there on the design committee discovering that, in fact, our choices regarding the interior decor were limited to the colours of the drapes."

Commercial tenants were also affected by design problems. In particular, the SCM Book Room found itself shoe-horned into an awkward, three-level space at the building's north-east corner. Browsers were fond of the excellent location and the cozy atmosphere, but former saleswoman Carol Vine still recalls that the complete absence of windows "caused us a lot of grief. And the ventilation was terrible! I don't think there was air conditioning and there was never any fresh air going through. Bobby [former manager Bob Miller] always used to have to open both the back and front doors for relief."

It's hardly surprising, then, that some of Rochdale's notoriety has clung for two decades to the building's architects. "Rochdale caused us many difficulties," says Malcolm Wells. "And I think there were people who perhaps didn't want to use our services afterwards, because we were the kind of people who had designed buildings like Rochdale. So what was a very exciting business at the beginning got to be rather a nightmare."

One can only speculate that the physical side of Rochdale may have been flawed because so much attention was paid to affairs of the mind—especially the building's most exciting and revolutionary component, education. By 1965, Rochdale was formally calling itself a college and fielding inquiries about establishing some sort of self-generated education program. Among the earliest and most productive discussions were those involving members of the Student Union for Peace Action, a nuclear disarmament group seeking to increase its participation in community issues. Also joining the talks was Rev. Ian MacKenzie, an Anglican minister who was to become president of Rochdale's governing council in 1969.

MacKenzie, a civil rights activist, had come to Toronto from New York and, as a resident of Campus Co-op and lecturer at the U of T's Trinity College, he was naturally drawn into seminal discussions about Rochdale in 1965. "A small committee of eight to ten people met almost every week," he says. "And out of those meetings came the idea of Rochdale as an educational institution—as distinct from a residence.

"We went through a very, very intensive process. Usually we'd start meeting at nine o'clock at night and end around three in the morning, hotly debating all sorts of issues in the context of Canadian society and the world situation and areas of social reform and so on. Out of that came the idea of making Rochdale a college and applying for a licence for Rochdale as a charitable and educational institution. The idea was to make Rochdale into a place where people could determine the form and content of their own education. And, as members of a co-operative, they would also be responsible for their own residential environment."

Since the matter clearly deserved further study, Rochdale Council agreed to proceed with its research and was aided by a grant from the Company of Young Canadians, a federal social service agency. The person apppointed to explore the issue was University of Toronto graduate student Dennis Lee.

Lee, who is today an award-winning author and poet, is often praised (and criticized) by those who assume that he alone masterminded Rochdale's education program. He was, in fact, one of many who helped bring the college to life. Nevertheless, Lee has attained the stature of figurehead, because he emerged as one of the most prolific and articulate writers on the subject of Rochdale's role as a ground-breaking experiment in radical education.

Born in a Toronto suburb, Lee received his BA in English literature from the University of Toronto's Victoria College in 1962 and continued with post-graduate studies. By the following year, at the age of twenty-three, Lee realized that "what they were saying in that seminar was without meaning for me, that doing graduate work had not become real, and that my entire undergraduate and high school education had been mainly a sham." Although he went on to finish his MA with high A's and taught English at Vic for three more years, Lee could not shake the feeling that "the surface of education, the inessentials of education, the travesty of education was what the university was about.

"You had to jump up and run to another overcrowded class and turn in another superficial paper and make a few more scrappy noises about something or other to satisfy some new requirement. The piecemeal life of the mind that resulted, where you're encouraged to get into things just far enough to know that you hadn't gotten into them at all, seemed to me to be a betrayal of classical university ideals.

"I felt like a heretic saying these things, because more senior people than I at the university had come through the University of Toronto or other universities earlier than me, and they'd never felt any of that. And there was no language to articulate the dissent I felt—well, there was language, but there was no body of shared experience. Ten years later, it was old hat to say that kind of thing. But it was a generational thing. More and more people were just beginning to discover the same sense of being at university, but feeling cheated by the whole experience."

Lee's report to Rochdale Council—a call for alternative forms of education more closely geared to the needs of the individual student—held great promise. And so, in the last days of 1966, just as construction was beginning, the council decided to refine the idea by mounting a sort of dress rehearsal. This dry run came to be known as the Rochdale Houses, half a dozen of Campus Co-op's rented homes in the university area. Nearly two hundred people attempted to forge a satisfying, new means of exchanging information, knowledge and wisdom. Watching the proceedings with a tremor of uncertainty was Campus Co-op. Here was the education program, once regarded as merely an intriguing and somewhat useful appendage, gradually gaining the strength and confidence to challenge the main body.

Campus Co-op was also dismayed by bylaw changes, passed by Rochdale Council in February, 1967, that extended membership in the college to non-students and non-residents. "Naturally," Jack Dimond recalls, "the students in charge of Campus Co-op became increasingly nervous. On the one hand, they could see that, in theory, it might make sense to have a real educational focus to the Bloor St. building. But, on the other hand, they weren't sure that the co-op should run it. The result was an internal debate and, finally, a general meeting in Hart House [in March, 1967], with an official vote to let Rochdale separate."

The practical, short-term result was to bring Rochdale even closer to reality. In a larger sense, it meant the loss of much-needed guardianship by the co-op, which was an experienced and business-minded supervisory body. Given the magnitude and expense of a project that was now under the care of administrative novices, Rochdale had, in some ways, come to resemble a toddler wandering blithely into traffic.

Creation of the Houses got a further boost in July, 1967, when the Ontario government formally issued a charter to Rochdale College. Included in the document were pledges by Rochdale's officers to advance learning, establish and maintain a library, conduct seminars and lectures, publish scholarly material and, perhaps most important, "establish an education-residential institution in which participants determine the form and content of their own education and the direction and intensity of their involvement." Two months later, when Rochdale Houses opened, Dennis Lee (who had left Victoria College the previous spring) and Ian MacKenzie were hired as full-time organizers.

"In some ways," says Lee, "we had a lot in common with groups that were meeting across North America and probably many parts of Europe, as this sort of dissatisfaction with multiversities began to surface. And it could have taken the direction of the standard model of the time for a 'free university,' which simply meant a few score people who would get together and create courses that they couldn't study at the local university. But the hope was that it would not be just a counter-institution, but that it would have its own dynamics and its own reason for being."

Rick Waern, who was to become registrar of the Rochdale Houses, says the education program had practical value, "because you couldn't increase your population in a situation like a co-operative without educating people about what a co-operative was about, so that people would be able to get along. It was a non-authoritarian situation in Campus Co-op. The students looked to one another to create their own structures and run their own affairs. People had to put in a certain number of hours a week and serve in various ways in running the community. And when you're going from houses, where there's maybe twenty or twenty-five people living together, to a building that you've tried to structure along the lines of the houses, there's a huge amount of education involved just to get those people to co-operate. It's not education in the sense of mathematics, but it is education in the sense of how people live together in a community."

Waern was another of the founders who had come to Rochdale by way of the Student Union for Peace Action and Campus Co-op, which he managed in 1965. Like Lee, he had strong links to the academic community and felt increasing dissatisfaction with traditional education at the U of T. "But," he adds, "I think it's important to make the point that it's not solely Dennis Lee's view of excellence that we're talking about when we talk about education. Dennis had a very particular view of what education was supposed to be. His view, unlike the Campus Co-op view or, for that matter, the Student Union for Peace Action view, was not concerned with social applications or social issues as much as it was concerned with turning out excellent scholars. The kind of study you do can be characterized, in his words, by excellence. It's not as if Rochdale occurred in a vacuum, expecting to do better than the university does in educating good students. That's the myth that comes out of Dennis's involvement, but it wasn't an approach that was shared universally."

Even so, the Rochdale Houses held great promise for people like Paul Evitts who quickly signed on as one of the college's first full-time students. A social activist, Evitts had attended Toronto's Jarvis Collegiate where he was strongly criticized for his role in the ban-the-bomb movement and other causes. Disgusted by the hostility directed toward him, he left school after Grade 12 and spent two years drifting through Yorkville. Finally, in 1967, at the age of eighteen, he began to serve as a volunteer for *This Magazine Is About Schools*.

"One day, Dennis Lee showed up in the office. I was not too impressed with Dennis, who was an older guy—he must have been twenty-five or something. He reeked of the whole academic thing, and I was trying to be as obnoxious as possible. I hit him with the question, 'How is Rochdale gonna handle drugs?' When he said, 'That's up to the college to decide,' I just fell—hook, line and sinker.

"As far as I know, I was one of Rochdale's first two students. This would have been the fall of 1967, when we had a couple of downstairs rooms in one of the co-op buildings that we used for meetings and marginal education things. We conducted seminars and God knows what else, and I organized the newsletter in true anarchic fashion. One month, it even consisted of a green garbage bag with all the pages littered inside.

"As a student, I also got a grant, which was kind of interesting, because this was before anybody in the government had really figured out what was going on. So I spent a year living on that grant, which was nice because I'd been living on pogey for a year and the money was running out. Sometimes I organized courses, sometimes I attended courses, sometimes I sat around with other people and talked about planning courses, and sometimes we just discussed things in a more philosophical way, in general terms. We also went out to high schools to proselytize to students and push the whole idea of alternate education."

Perhaps because of their idealistic preoccupations, few of Rochdale's academic leaders were fully aware that much of Campus Co-op's enthusiasm for education had stemmed from its vision of the program as a sort of tax dodge. Howard Adelman, while entirely sympathetic toward Rochdale's nobler aspirations, says he encouraged the scheme as a means of avoiding payment of municipal property taxes—a concession commonly granted by the government to educational institutions. "The property taxes came to something like $175,000," recalls Adelman, "so I said, 'Look, if we can run an education program for $75,000, we'll come out $100,000 ahead.' "

Dennis Lee says that if a plan of this kind " was primary in the thinking of people like Howard who were involved in the planning, they did a good job of keeping their cards fairly close to their chest. It was not something that was being passed around generally, and I'm sure it would have made other people completely furious to hear it at the time."

Early in the spring of 1968, Adelman severed his ties with Rochdale and devoted himself to student co-ops elsewhere. He saw Rochdale as mired in a classic no-win dilemma—unable to launch an education program for lack of funds, but unlikely to be granted relief from property taxes without a functioning education program.

At a council debate in the basement of one of the Rochdale Houses on Huron Street, Adelman restated his opinion that Rochdale should not have to pay the taxes, but disagreed with the board's assumption that Rochdale was certain to get eventual relief from the tax burden. He argued that, since taxes might have to be paid, large sums should not be hastily committed to the education program. "But because they were convinced that no money would have to be spent on taxes, they suggested we begin funding the education program. I said I didn't think it was right, because whatever else I am, I also believe in balancing the books.

"I was torn between a business sense of how you do things and a commitment to education at Rochdale. But the board's principle was wrong and I spoke against it. Finally, I was totally outvoted and I left. So they began to build a debt against the building and they set a precedent of fiscal irresponsibility."

Rick Waern insists that Adelman was not blameless in this episode. "Yes, we were pretty light-headed about the possibility of raising funds for educational activities," he says, "but if getting a tax rebate was a fantasy, it was a fantasy that Howard also participated in. And if your fund-raising efforts don't work, you don't quit and then turn around later and blame people for over-extending themselves financially. You stick around and say, 'We're over-extended, so we'd better retrench.'"

"In a sense, I was irresponsible at the time," Adelman now admits. "I think back how stupid I was for not fighting and arguing that it was fundamentally wrong. But, you see, the argument against my position was also very strong. If you didn't start the educational thing and invest in it, how could you then claim to get out of taxes? That was the argument against me, and I didn't have an answer to that."

Adelman's low-key resignation left Rochdale organizers feeling more confident than ever about their strategy and objectives. The call went out in the spring of 1968 for college members and residents to fill about eight hundred vacancies in the Bloor Street building in time for the 1968–69 academic year. Suddenly, the stream of inquiries became a flood, with nearly three thousand applications from across Canada and the United States.

The screening process, says Jack Dimond, was handled by residents of the Rochdale Houses "who were mainly connected with the university—young graduate students or faculty. Naturally, they selected a group of applicants who were very much like themselves—people who, by and large, were going to be associated with the university. Some would be full-time students at Rochdale, but that would be a small number. With that in mind the internal organization and the rules and procedures were deliberately not very finely developed. It was felt that, since this small, responsible group in the Rochdale Houses was able to develop rules as needed, then the larger group, being very similar temperamentally, could develop rules, too."

Rochdale still had to clear one final hurdle—a construction strike that brought work to a halt for three months in mid-1967 and left the project badly behind schedule. By the projected opening date of June, 1968, only three floors were approaching completion. When the academic year began in September, Rochdale was just ten storeys high. A few residents began to occupy some of the finished floors, but the building would not be truly habitable until the end of 1968.

"You can't over-emphasize the effects of that strike," sighs Dimond. "Rochdale Council had to decide whether to accept the building as it became available during the 1968–69 academic year, or to simply pass on the whole thing and take it over in the summer of 1969.

"The decision made was to take the building as it became available through the fall of 1968. The reasoning was that the educational experience of the previous year had proved sufficiently valuable that we didn't want to stop it in its tracks. We thought it had momentum, and people were coming to live in this new building specifically with the idea of participating in an educational experience.

"Many of the people we'd pre-selected to live in the building had university commitments and they couldn't wait for a room to become available in the middle of November. Naturally, they were forced to find accommodations somewhere else. So we started to make the building available to people who had not been screened in the same way that the original group had been screened. We essentially started to make rooms available to people who walked in right off the street.

"A very different kind of person came in. We of the Rochdale Houses were mostly very straight people, and those of us who were interested in the educational experience were much more like Dennis Lee. We thought that reform meant a rediscovery of liberal education—not simply passing along pieces of information or technical expertise, but giving students and faculty the opportunities to challenge assumptions about their own lives and to question how institutions were organized. But many of the people who came in from Yorkville and from other parts of the city or the country weren't interested in rediscovering values. They were interested in checking out of most kinds of restraints, discovering themselves and learning from experience—whatever that meant. It was a very anti-intellectual type of life.

"And we simply did not have the wit to see that, by this single action, we were radically changing the type of person who would be entering the building, from the moment we opened. We were sealing the fate of the Rochdale that most of us had wanted to experiment with. And since there were very few rules about how the place would be run, we were in effect handing the building over to people very unlike ourselves.

"After we opened, the key financial problem was to generate enough revenue to pay the mortgage, which kicked in during the spring of 1969. But the proper revenue flow wasn't there because many of the new residents contributed to the chaos of the first few months. They helped transform Rochdale from a place that was supposed to have steady, rent-paying inhabitants to a place that was much more governed by whim and the laws of the jungle.

"In hindsight, it would have been much wiser to wait until the summer of 1969 to accept the building. Delaying the opening would have caused much less damage to the educational component than opening when we did. By the spring of 1969, I had officially bowed out, Dennis Lee was increasingly disillusioned and some residents were actually questioning why resource people were being paid to hang around Rochdale. And by the summer of 1969, I think most of the people who were in the original Rochdale education group were either gone or incredibly disillusioned. Then a whole new generation of Rochdale people took over."

In the fall of 1968, these critical errors were eclipsed by the organizers' pride and elation in seeing a towering, physical form taking the place of what was once just a wild idea. One of North America's most unusual, most audacious and, for a while, most celebrated experiments in counter-cultural education and day-to-day living was about to open its doors.

C H A P T E R 3

The
House of
the Rising Sun

Rochdale's organizers were relieved when the first of the college's new population started moving in on September 15 even though only ten of the eighteen floors were ready to be occupied. It would be eight weeks before the entire building, which was systematically being filled from the bottom up, would be occupied. As the Rochdalians moved into their high-rise home with their packing crates full of books, suitcases and optimistic ambitions for the future, the number one pop song in North America belonged to Long Island's Rascals. The band's ode to the loss of Martin Luther King and Robert Kennedy, "People Got to be Free," caught the spirit of the time. It was a perfect anthem for the mixture of turbulence, chaos and hopeful idealism that was the year 1968.

1968 was a watershed year—an annus mirabilis. Writer John Hersey called it "a year of shocks." Shocks? It was more like a year of dancing in the mine field; wherever you turned you were rocked by another explosion: Martin Luther King gunned down in Memphis, Robert Kennedy shot dead in Los Angeles. The explosions kept coming all year long: North Korea seized the USS Pueblo; the Viet Cong launched the Tet offensive; Alexander Dubcek's hope for a liberalized Czechoslovakia (his "Prague Spring") was crushed under the weight of Soviet tanks.

To the older generation it must have seemed as if the entire youth culture went crazy. The campuses of the world ignited one after another: Mark Rudd led the SDS in a six-day occupation of Columbia; Danny the Red led a Parisian student revolt over dormitories that flared into a major confrontation that almost toppled De Gaulle's government; there were barricades and body counts in Mexico City and Tokyo and Berkeley and Cairo and Karachi.

It all came to a boil from August 26 to 29 in Chicago—as if ten years of pent-up frustration on both sides had suddenly come to a bloodstained, rhetoric-soaked head. Mayor Daley's police force battered the Yippies who had gathered at the Democratic Party Convention to protest the war in Vietnam and the failure of the government to respond to the changing times.

Nineteen sixty-eight, for all of its dramatic upheaval and turmoil, also saw the world of arts and entertainment enter a new, vibrant period, based in part on the absorption of the counter-culture's artistic impulses and approach; '68 was the year that "hip" entered the mainstream.

It was the year that psychedelic rock came into its own. Groups with names like the Doors, Cream, Steppenwolf, Grateful Dead, Jefferson Airplane and the Jimi Hendrix Experience expanded the horizons of pop music, and in the process became best-selling pop stars.

Even the idiot box, despite having its usual fare of Middle American hits like "Gomer Pyle," "The Lucy Show" and "Mission Impossible" absorbed some of the colourful energy of the times. "Laugh-In," a rapid-fire (200 jokes a show) joke machine, was a welcome relief from the steady stream of assassinations, political turbulence and war footage that dominated the small screen.

At the movies, Mike Nicols's portrait of the alienated youth of the late sixties—*The Graduate*—was the year's top money-maker. The Beatles premiered *Yellow Submarine*, ushering in a new age of cinematic animation (we can see how far matters had progressed by noting that the reviewer for the *New York Times* suggested it might be beneficial to "toke up" before seeing the picture).

On stage the major story was *Hair*. America's tribal-love-rock-musical arrived on Broadway on April 29. Depending on which side of the Dow Chemical fence you stood, the show was either a "theatrical landmark" or an "anti-American cry for anarchy."

On the bookshelves there were the usual bestsellers like Arthur Hailey's *Airport* and John Updike's *Couples*, but you also had Black Panther and Peace and Freedom presidential candidate Elridge Cleaver's prison-penned *Soul on Ice*. The "new America," as publisher Jann Wenner called it, had its own voice with the emergence of *Rolling Stone* magazine.

In Canada, Pierre Elliott Trudeau succeeded Lester Pearson as prime minister and then was elected PM on June 25. The founding convention of the Parti Quebecois suggested Canada was entering a period of its own political confusion and unrest. There was a new moral climate as the government relaxed laws on everything from Sunday horse racing to divorce, abortion and homosexuality.

Above all else, 1968 was the year of YOUTH. It was nothing less than a worldwide cultural revolution—a new belief system took a front-row position on the world stage.

Drug use of all kinds escalated—the FBI and RCMP reported dramatic increases in drug use and arrests. It was an alphabet soup out there—THC, LSD, STP, MDA, DMT.

Nineteen sixty-eight was the year that the Flower Power Revolution seeped into the mainstream. The avant-garde of the hippie movement had already checked out. "Hippie" had been "buried" in San Francisco's Haight-Ashbury back in October of '67. "The CBS Evening News" carried the symbolic funeral. The vanguard had retreated back to the land and, in the wake of Chicago, abandoned the dream of changing the world. They dropped out, in Voltaire's phrase, to "cultivate their own gardens." Those who didn't "tune in, turn on and drop out" hit the road looking for answers and a good time.

Rochdale resident Major Domo (not his real name) was typical of many who eventually found their way to Rochdale.

"I grew up in a small Ontario town and came down to go to the University of Toronto. I had an incredibly traumatic time in the first year, and everybody seemed normal except me. I was mainly interested in the sciences, and I decided at the end of the first year that all of my dreams and goals had been lost. I thought that I had failed and things like that. That was in '67–'68. It was a big shock, so I threw caution to the wind and hitch-hiked across Canada. And 1968 turned out to be an incredible year. There was a lot of people on the move. So the summer of '68 was, in my opinion, the year that I basically started my life. I hitch-hiked out to Vancouver and then I lived with some people farming sugar beets on the Prairies. I also had a real interesting time in New York City, but I returned to Toronto at the end of the summer. I needed a place to live and I saw the Rochdale posters. It looked interesting and since a friend of mine was already in there, I signed up as his roommate."

Here's how Pamela Berton, daughter of noted Canadian author Pierre Berton and an original Rochdale resident, recalls the opening: "I was supposed to live on the fifteenth floor, which wasn't finished. So I lived for a while with a friend of my parents and commuted to university. And I'd go by Rochdale and wade through the construction mess every day and say, 'Is my room ready yet?' And then one of my friends who was on the eleventh floor got in and her roommate was a friend of my roommate, so we traded. So I ended up on the eleventh floor and moved in October, 1968. The building was in a state of chaos, or it seemed like it at the time—there was no tile on the floors, because the floors hadn't been finished. There was a lot of plaster dust in the air—cement dust was everywhere. And, of course, the elevators didn't work because of the cement dust in them."

The expected opening date of June, 1968, must have seemed like a cruel joke to the new residents. John Jordan, one of the founders of the building, acting coordinator and part-time resource person, told *The Toronto Star* in late September, "Since we started moving into this place, we've had a new generation of people every week. They all seem to go through the same cycle of confusion and readjustment to whatever Rochdale is."

Resident and writer Sarah Spinks found the new experimental college "a jungle of concrete and window frames. When the first ten floors of the building opened, the window glass wasn't installed. You could get out of the bath to find a construction man putting the finishing touches to the baseboard in the hall. Psychologically and financially it gave the building a bad start." No windows? In Toronto? In the autumn?

Rev. Edgar Bull, the sympathetic rector of St. Thomas Anglican Church, a neighbour of Rochdale's, recalls lunching at the building. "I remember going in and having lunch in their cafeteria with no glass in the windows on a very cold day. It was remarkable—no glass, with the wind whipping through, but everyone seemed to adjust to the situation. There was a definite spirit to the place. They were beginning to move in almost ahead of time and people were being drawn from all over the place, all sorts of people. There were professors from the university who were teaching there free of charge. There were philosophers and a Hindu bookbinder and a Jesuit priest doing his own thing—a lot of creative stuff. There were writers and adventurers with stars in their eyes. And literally permeating the air was the drug culture, which got bigger and bigger. I see Rochdale as a kind of concentration of what was happening with young people back then. I was caught up in this, as many people were, with its idealism."

Symbolically foreshadowing its future life as an outlaw force outside the rules and regulations of conventional society, Rochdale began life in contravention of more than a few building and housing ordinances.

Any new apartment building is entitled to a shakedown period, a short period of adjustment to work out the kinks and straighten out any minor problems. With Rochdale the list of what went wrong from the outset is staggering: no hot water, floods and constant plumbing and heating problems, laundry and postal service screw-ups. Even the free phones in the Ashrams made a hasty exit, either through vandalism or ultimately when the college received the first bill. The *Daily*—Rochdale's in-house newspaper—licked its chops and published details on how to rip off the imperialist, multi-national "telephone" monster.

Trying to get insurance in Rochdale was often a short phone call. "Yes, I'd like to get some information about your home-owner's/apartment dweller's insurance." "Where do you presently reside?" "341 Bloor Street—Rochdale College." CLICK!

Once inside the doors of Rochdale the residents immediately changed their sterile high-rise environment of concrete and steel. The tusk white walls had to go, and in their place came psychedelic swirls and day-glo visions, graffiti, anything to bring the building to life. To some it was defacing, to others it was humanizing.

Even a utopian experiment in education and living has its share of thieves, although in those early days it was more pilfering than outright "shotgun-in-the-face-this-is-a-ripoff" thievery. How could someone resist a plea like the following one published in the *Daily*:

> Would the person or persons hitting the Rochdale laundry room please lay off—and please return Lindsay's bells to her in 805. It is her only pair of pants and she needs them very badly.
>
> Spock

Just how disorganized and ill-prepared the service aspect of the new college was is best illustrated by the cafeteria. Television broadcaster Alan Edmonds, covering the Rochdale story for *Maclean's* magazine, wrote:

> The first tenants moved in before the kitchens were finished. For two months, the college provided about 600 TV dinners a day. A total of almost 41,000 TV dinners was consumed before the kitchens and cafeterias opened. When they did open freeloaders caused chaos. Rents are inclusive, so residents don't pay. Neither did the gate-crashers. The manager finally appointed a crasher as cafeteria custodian. A woman of about 65, she sat at the door, asking for proof of residence. As payment, she ate free. She was the most efficient

screener the cafeteria ever had, but residents objected on the grounds that it was a contradiction of the freedom on which the college is based.

They took a consensus and fired the old girl. She stuck around freeloading for a week, then vanished. No one ever knew her name.

One controversial problem was general sanitation, the construction workers had left a major mess. The *Daily* announced on behalf of the residents that "we are sick and tired of carrying out rubbish left by the subtrades." The basement, or Hades as *Daily* contributor Orpheus dubbed it, "was littered with garbage, sand, lumber, heating pipe insulation, bottles, cardboard boxes and an amazingly wide assortment of other crap."

The central garbage chute for the building wasn't operational, meaning that garbage tended to pile up in the storage rooms on the individual floors. It seems that the residents couldn't be bothered to make the trip out to the back of the building where the administration had installed a large garbage bin.

Finally, the co-op attitude of pitching in and doing your required stint on cleanup and maintenance was almost entirely absent. In a piece on the college, Sarah Spinks wrote, "The cleaning crew was suffering from the same disorganization. They started by discovering that the storage space for equipment was grossly inadequate and that the budget for cleaning was half of what it should have been. There also developed a rather unsuccessful work arrangement where residents would do a job in return for a meal ticket. If the fellow who was cleaning the 14th floor happened to catch lunch with a friend, the cleaning crew was minus one worker."

According to senior Toronto health inspector Jim Flaherty, who made regular official visits to Rochdale beginning in the fall of '68, "We had a lot of problems there with garbage, vermin, cockroaches and mice, mainly due to the lackadaisical attitude of the residents. They had their own garbage people, and once you broke down the barrier with these people and got accepted, things got better. But every weekend everybody got stoned out of their minds and everything broke down. By Wednesday they generally had it cleaned up again. There tended to be a laissez-faire attitude. Toilets used to get blocked up, and as long as they didn't overflow, nobody got too excited until we came along. Even the smell didn't seem to bother people."

Of all the opening problems, two stand out as having a significant effect on the way Rochdale would develop: the elevators and the intercom. Rochdale was the equivalent of a small town and the building's four elevators were the "main street," the vertical avenue connecting the decentralized floors. The elevators were so central to the Rochdale myth that, as Paul Thompson tells us, when the people at Theatre Passe Muraille sat down to create a play about Rochdale, the dominant image that kept coming back was the elevators. They were a kind of meeting place. Often people took the elevators, not because they were going somewhere, but because they wanted to meet."

Elevator breakdown was a daily occurrence at The Rock. Contributing to their poor performance was overuse (they simply weren't designed for the kind of use they were getting at Rochdale, since it wasn't two rush-hour peaks, it was a twenty-four-hour boogie); the concrete dust in the mechanism; and most of all the thick-headed vandalism.

The Rochdale elevator experience meant different things to different people. Even members of the same family had totally different reactions. Pamela Berton says, "One of the things I liked about Rochdale to begin with was it was a small community with an outrageous mix of people. And you'd meet these people in the elevators. The elevators were overused but they were the main communication channel at Rochdale. My grandmother and mother quite liked being at Rochdale because nobody looked at them weird when they talked to people in the elevators. They're the kind of people who talk to others in elevators, which isn't really socially acceptable."

For Pamela's younger sister, Patsy, a high school art student at nearby Central Technical High School, the elevators were intimidating. "The first project we had to do was an illustration. For some reason, the subject matter I picked was a crowd of people in an elevator. And I realize only now that it had to do with Rochdale. There were all kinds of different people in the elevator, with bare feet and long hair and bellbottoms. And there's this little girl in the picture in this huge crowd of tall people. That little girl was obviously me, because that's how I felt in those elevators— 'Let me get up to the ninth floor and let me get into my room!' There was a lot of heaviness around those elevators that was scary for me."

The elevator, even as early as the fall of '68, could be a place with the potential for violence. Resident Nelson Adams recalls, "One day I was waiting in the lobby for an elevator, which was a stupid thing to do because it hardly ever came. But anyway, the door finally opened and there was a big pile of mattresses in the elevator, and a guy pointing a shotgun right between my eyes. He didn't say anything. He just stayed there motionless until the door closed and the elevator went away."

One could look at the elevator debacle as an inconvenience. However, the intercom situation posed a more serious threat to the building's stability. Resident and future college president Bob Nasmith puts it succinctly: "There were certain people who regarded the intercom as an invasion of privacy. And those who were more than a little paranoid saw it as an instrument for eavesdropping. So they were disposed of early on."

Resident Nelson Adams elaborates, "You've got these intercom buttons downstairs and there's the speakers in the rooms. And people thought, 'The cops have them wired up. Smash them.' So those were all smashed, because people were paranoid and thought there were microphones in there. Those were really paranoid times."

The intercoms were destroyed soon after the building opened. It was a seemingly innocent development but it had huge consequences. "The problem with destroying the intercom system," relates Major Domo, "was security. That's what caused our security problems. If we'd had a valid intercom system, then you could have someone simply stand outside the door and press the intercom. And if you let someone in, he's in. And if you don't, he's not in. Suddenly, because the intercom was broken, we had to have open access."

Initial opinions on Rochdale were sharply divided. University of Toronto President Claude Bissell offered his moral support; Students' Administrative Council President Stephen Langdon saw it as an important part of humanizing the educational process at the U of T; the press treated the project with approval. But there were dissenting voices. The reaction of the majority of the U of T student body is captured by an unnamed student's capsule comment on The Rock: "A posh, eighteen-storey haven for hairy dropouts, acidheads, filthy hippies and smart alecs who like to drop eggs on the heads of passersby." The jury was out on Rochdale.

Within the Rochdale community itself there was a feeling of inevitable, impending doom. Jack Dimond "felt depressed and exhausted when the building finally opened. I'm not exaggerating because the minute the building was opened, it was doomed. It was a mistake to have thought an organization that was deliberately understructured could alter the character of the people who were moving in and could have any focus."

For the enthused, committed members of the Rochdale tribe, the building itself took on the status and symbolic value of the "New Jerusalem"–the hipster's promised land. For one enthusiast, writing in the *Daily*, Rochdale was "the sun building, pyramid of parallel sides concrete and whole stretching its ridge-pole face to the sky."

Whatever growing pains Rochdale was experiencing, it was still able to have a good time. The attitude to sex was easygoing and casual as we can see from the following *Daily* ad: "THE WET BOD FIRST OFFICIAL CO-ED BATHING SOCIETY meets at Ken and Jude's place . . . come pre-paired . . . one of the Harrad Experiment Seminar activities." Music of all styles filled the building. Even the scams were fun-loving and lighthearted– "David Hallan and Ian Morrison plus a bevy of young and talented ladies will awaken you any morning. 20 cents for one morning, $1 for one week. Anytime of the day or night. Any method you desire will be used to awaken."

Despite the problems associated with the building's late opening, Rochdale still had an incredibly buoyant "up" mood. There was an intangible sense of unfettered freedom, a sense of exhilaration about the place. Toronto musician Michael Waite was a teen member of a Unitarian youth organization–the LRY (Liberal Religious Youth). The LRY had one of its conventions in Toronto in the early fall of 1968 and, as Waite recalls, Rochdale was a part of that experience.

"The LRY was just basically a collective organization of freaks throughout North America. The kids got together for these convention weekends–in Chicago, Montreal, wherever. These weekends were totally unsupervised. You'd have these sixteen- to eighteen-year-old kids freaking out for the weekend, there'd be tons of workshops, consciousness-raising, mind-expanding experience without drugs. Outside the actual workshops it was 'peace, love and groovy' with people doing the regular stuff: trying to get laid, getting high, that sort of thing.

"We'd be billeted at the local Unitarian Church or people's homes. At around that same time somebody discovered Rochdale. There was always the problem of finding everyone a place to stay–there'd be upwards of 700 kids at these conventions. So a bunch of us went down to Rochdale and crashed there.

"There was probably only half a dozen people living there at the time. There were no windows in yet, not even in the big windows at the front. The elevators still had pads in them. We just went in. We were squatters–about thirty of us. We owned the building for two days. We rode up and down the elevators and screamed Hendrix songs at the top of our lungs. We stayed up all night. We didn't do drugs, just tripping on the lack of sleep, imagining all sorts of shit. We went through most of the building, it was wide open. It was great. Then we heard about the concept of the place while we were there and it was right on in terms of the LRY—a free-learning institution where you could experiment with all the things that were illegal in a regular societal structure: school, home environment. We were right into it."

Bryn Waern, sister of Rochdale registrar Rick Waern, was a resident in psychiatry at the Clarke Institute of Psychiatry during her stay on Rochdale's eighteenth floor. For her Rochdale was a refuge from the storm.

"Rochdale was like magic, like a dream, in terms of the community that was there. I felt stressed during that first year, but I don't think it was the building so much as my residence in psychiatry. It was a caring and nurturing community. For me, it was a place where, when people saw what my need was, they'd step right up and give it to me. It was the only place where I've ever been where I've been stressed out, and somebody comes up and puts a bowl of fruit in my hand and says, 'Eat.' That literally happened.

"There have been comments about the elevator, but the whole elevator thing, from what I remember, was a wonderful thing. And when you walked up and down the hall, there was contact and you knew your neighbours. Where in Toronto are you in an apartment setup where you know your neighbours and have interaction? You may be very different, but there's still that family feeling."

For some, like resident Valerie Frith, Rochdale was a source of national pride: "I remember when the building was going up my friends and I kept a close watch on its progress. We kept hearing rumours about what it was going to be like. Then it didn't open on time and I was off travelling. Earlier the feeling about Rochdale was very positive, very optimistic. It was to be part of the Revolution that was going to happen right here in Toronto. Everything that was sensational about the counter-culture was primarily American or English. There didn't seem to be anything indigenously Canadian about what was happening. But Rochdale—that was going to be Canada's contribution to the counter-culture, the Movement."

For others, like classical scholar Nelson Adams, Rochdale was the journey's end—the hip Mecca.

"I came through Rochdale in the summer of '68. The week of

the Chicago convention, I remember watching the convention on TV in the airport. I was travelling from Fredericton, N.B., where I was a post-graduate bum. I have a degree from UNB in Greek lyric poetry. I was going to be a professor of Greek literature.

"And I just made it through the undergraduate stuff when I started smoking dope in '66. My roommate in New Brunswick brought marijuana back from Berkeley. Ta-da! Holy grail! You know, Mecca! Berkeley! The next day, I stopped shaving and I bought some beads. I went and bought some ladies' beads, because they didn't have beads for men. I didn't even ask for beads for men. I just asked for necklaces. And I haven't shaved since.

"In Fredericton I had been a student leader, so I knew many people who were involved in Rochdale because they were always travelling around and inciting to riot. So I knew I'd be coming here. But the real reason was that Dennis Lee and [House of] Anansi published a book called *The University Game*. And the only article I remember from it was one by Dennis Lee called "Getting to Rochdale." It was about what he hoped it would be like once it got going. Ha, ha—poor guy. I got to know him after we arrived. Anyway, I read that thing by Dennis Lee and I said, 'Yes, this is right, this is true, I'm gonna go.' So I applied and they said, 'Sure,' so I ran.

"The day I arrived I did the two-hour bus tour of Toronto to get oriented and then went to Rochdale. It was a big construction site, so I found the office on Huron Street. And I thought it didn't seem any less disorganized than any other frosh day or orientation day that I'd been through. I got somebody to take me over there and show me my temporary rooms. So we walked up Huron Street, and right behind some stairs was this garbage bin and these two guys shovelling dirt and stuff into this garbage bin. They had long hair, headbands and shovels. And we walked past them and heard them talking about Aristotle's politics. 'Wow,' I thought. 'This is it! This is the place! I'm here!' "

Certain floors, in particular the eighteenth, were showing signs of domestic stability. It was a supportive community within a community, what Rochdale as a residence was ideally striving for. True, the eighteenth floor was located in the stable west wing and was populated by older professionals, but the fact remains the eighteenth floor worked. Bryn Waern lived there. "The eighteenth floor, especially when Jack Dimond was there, was nicknamed the Teacup Society because most of us were professionals. We had jobs and didn't take part in all the craziness with the crashers. We had six apartments on the top floor and there was just the laundry room on the other side. So we had these six apartments and they were like one big home where everybody had his or her own unit. And, in fact, when Rochdale was on its way out, a bunch of us set up a community in the country—Toad Hall—and it was based on the experience at Rochdale. It involved a lot of privacy—a huge house with six units, each with its own bedroom, living room, plus a big common kitchen/dining room. To me that's a real statement of how warm it was and what a good way of living it was."

Rochdale's Ashrams were ideally suited for communal living. Throughout the opening months, like-minded residents tended to group together and pool their resources, ideas and visions. Understanding communes and the communal spirit is absolutely vital to understanding Rochdale as a whole. Some feel the commune was Rochdale's crowning social achievement. It was a radical experiment in urban living where, as resident Frank Cox puts it, "people were living together rather than apart. This was a new order where people would live differently, people would take responsibility for their own environment and lives. You could call it a political statement, it was used as a political statement at times, but it was more of a social choice. It was an extension of the nuclear family. We lived like a family, it was a family-type environment."

Nicky Morrison, co-founder of the fourteenth-floor commune, describes her floor's organization. "We met once a week to discuss problems, we cooked together and we had rules and expectations that everybody would participate. If you didn't agree to participate, you just didn't live there. That was basic.

"We had twenty-five to thirty people and it was like a large rooming house with meals. So, obviously, we had to be organized. For instance, shopping was a big thing. We bought a van and people took turns driving it to Kensington Market or Knob Hill Farms to buy bushels of potatoes or what-have-you.

"We also had quite the age range in our commune, from young people all the way to someone who was sixty or sixty-five, with the average around twenty-four."

Rochdale, as an educational institute, learned early on about disappointments and frustration. The cloud hanging over Rochdale's educational ambitions was a decision rendered by the Metro Assessment Commission in September, 1968. After evaluating 341 Bloor Street, the commission ruled that Rochdale was not "a seminary of learning." Rochdale was nothing more than a student residence and as such was not entitled to an exemption from paying municipal property taxes.

The commission's decision meant that Rochdale had to pay out $134,000. Unfortunately, Rochdale's original planners had already earmarked the money they so confidently thought they would save in the anticipated tax break for the educational side of things (the actual figure allotted for education for the first year was $190,000–$90,000 of that total figure was to have come from the tax break).

To make matters even worse, the college lost out on a building material rebate from the Department of National Revenue, another $200,000 that was anticipated and never realized. Rochdale's independence, its desire to be under no one's influence and control, meant that it would have to fend for itself via fund raising, rent collection or fees and memberships.

The educational side of Rochdale always struggled for financial and moral support. There would be ongoing discussions and debates on the value and use of educational space throughout the life of the building. More than one Rochdalian felt caught in a tug of war between educational ideals and financial realities. Even in the preliminary meetings, where the Rochdale council was deciding on the shape and direction of the college, education seemed to take a back seat. The council leaned in the direction of financial expediency and felt that the college would be hard pressed if the second floor area was used for seminar space. Even as late as May, 1967, with construction of the site about to commence, the use of the second floor's eleven suites hadn't been finalized.

Just what was the educational vision of Rochdale? Here's how *Newsweek* saw Rochdale College in its November 25, 1969, edition:

The philosophical question of what is worth knowing is left to the students themselves. Anyone interested in taking—or teaching—a particular course simply tacks a notice on a bulletin board. Some current courses: Gestalt Therapy, Intellectual Origins of the Black Revolt, Conversational Hebrew, Computers and Communication. Most Rochdale students say they are interested in learning for its own sake; few profess to be goal-oriented. Bob McArthur, a tall, mop-haired twenty-one-year-old who dropped out of the University of Toronto in his senior year says, "I have no intention of getting a degree. A degree is nothing more than a certificate to function in society." "It's great to walk around the halls and not feel that ominous pressure to be somewhere, to be doing something that you always feel at a university," says Linda Bomphrey, twenty-two, a blonde who has a psychology degree from the University of Saskatchewan.

One aspect of life at Rochdale would prove to be extremely "educational"—in that life-embracing "everything we experience is an education" attitude—the government and administration of the building and college. Rochdale was a self-governing institution whose charter stipulated that a governing council be elected annually by the membership. While the pre-building council dealt with the overall planning and general questions, they left much of the nuts and bolts work to the council that would represent the residents. The first Gov Con (as the General Governing Council came to be known) was elected at the college's first general meeting, in November, 1968. *The Globe and Mail* described the general meeting as an "exercise in Yippie-style anarchy. The chairman, who volunteered to be chairman, said he could not be a chairman in the conventional sense, that the council could not be called a council, that it could not (even though elected representatively) make decisions binding upon all members of the college."

At the time Dennis Lee admonished that "council takes months to come to non-decision in matters that demand decisions in weeks, administering purity tests to niggling details while the college falls to pieces around them. This council is capable of the Great Debate, and now of the Great Gesture, but when it comes to calm assessment of where we are and trudging, unglamourous man-hours of work to get somewhere else, it is a non-starter."

James Newell, who would go on to be college treasurer and president, gives us the background on Rochdale's Governing Council. "The Governing Council was the ultimate body. It had a board of directors with twelve directors; like any co-op corporation, the board was elected by the membership. The council was responsible for giving the building a direction, some kind of leadership. It was like being a politician in a small town. Then you had the administration, which handled rentals, accounting, maintenance, security. That was the structure, which in some ways was a front of interfacing with the outside world. They represented Rochdale to the community outside. A lot of it was irrelevant to the general population—like the small-town politician and clerk are irrelevant until paths crossed or swords crossed with an issue that concerned you personally. It was that way at Rochdale. You could get away without knowing anything about politics and the administration. You had your own circle of friends and your own little world unto yourselves."

"The council itself was a marvel," Jim Garrard proudly recalls. "Anybody who wanted to could come. And the decisions that were made there were more or less binding. There was some kind of quorum procedure, but it was a terrific form of government. I always think that what I learned at Rochdale was primarily political science. We evolved through so many forms of government so quickly that it was like a microcosm of the social and political development of mankind. I think that after four or five years of turmoil and rapid evolutionary development along social and political lines, those four years were like forty years in a village or 4,000 years in a society. We went from 'let's have no lock on our front door because we don't need it' to 'we not only need a lock on the door, but we need a bunch of heavy-duty guys down there making sure that if you don't live here, you don't get in.' We behaved like the society that we felt was not serving our needs in the first place. But I don't think that that was proof of our naivete. It was just too tender a shoot on very rocky ground. And it needed a bit more patience from society and a bit more support from it."

The college administration (an eight-person operation headed by a twenty-six-year-old fugitive from Bay Street, general manager Bernie Bomers) struggled with the accruing chaos, but it was ill-prepared for the scenario unfolding before its eyes. Resident Sarah Spinks had a tough time requesting even basic information: "Even as you wandered into the building on a cool September day, it was difficult to find the office where you could rent a room. For those first months there was no central office or information wicket."

The bureaucratic mess was made worse by a record-keeping system that appeared to many to be "filed" in the memory of the secretarial and bookkeeping staff. Rent collection started to take on nightmarish overtones as the difficulty of clearly establishing who lived where surfaced.

However the books were kept, the figures told the same story. After its opening, Rochdale had a surplus of $1,165. By the end of the first four months the accountants were jotting down their figures in red ink. Rochdale was beginning its slow descent into financial hell: $46,000 behind in rent collection, $40,000 lost due to vacancies, $17,000 lost by the food operation. The silver lining in that cloud was an earlier agreement with CMHC that no mortgage payments would be due in the first year if the college was in the red.

Rochdale registrar Rick Waern says the college felt the "financial pinch immediately. The building wasn't finished in time, so the people that we had so carefully selected to move into the college—these handpicked people—had to find somewhere else to live. We had vacancies, and all the people whom we'd selected and had a way to pay their bills were not there. So when the hordes from Yorkville started climbing in through the windows, there were spaces for them to climb into. And that meant that no one could take their place. If the people we'd selected had moved in and the building had been ready, it would have had much more momentum towards the kind of mixture of education and social goals that we tried to define. As it was, a large part of it became bogged down with caring for street kids and dealing with the drug situation."

The original screening process had sought out committed, like-minded individuals in pursuit of "wisdom" and "excellence." The post-opening screening process was more casual, to say the least. Barry Zwicker wrote, "Programs for screening applicants come and go. One scheme was to have one person, by more or less common consent, do all the interviewing and use his judgement. The day I talked with him about his criteria, in an off-campus attic with an eighteenth-century atmosphere, his first words were 'Have some dope,' as he offered me a smouldering corncob pipe. Five or six others, relaxed around a heavy rectangular table, were bathed in a near-silence. One, wearing heavy boots, absently and expertly drew a haunted, muted melody out of a beaten-up guitar. I settled as unobtrusively as possible into a deep chair and tried not to disturb the luxuriousness of the situation. 'I just use my judgement like anyone else would,' the admission officer said before taking another long drag from the pipe. Had he turned anyone down? 'Yes, three.' Why? 'Because they would have been complete disasters.' A girl offered a more particular explanation: 'If someone comes in waving a gun, you turn him down.' "

Rochdale needed rent-paying bodies. Most of those "bodies" were beginning to make the three-block trek from Yorkville.

Yorkville—"Haight-Ashbury North"—was cousin to any number of similar hippie scenes that mushroomed around the continent in the mid-sixties: the Haight, the East Village, Coconut Grove, Carré St. Louis in Montreal and Gastown in Vancouver.

Yorkville started out in the late 1950s as a haven for Toronto's "beat" crowd. The beatniks, writers, painters and assorted other artists and students frequented the coffee houses and folk music clubs. It was all very low-key and intellectual.

With the influx of the hippies in 1966 and 1967 came a new style and large crowds of interested onlookers, gawking tourists and the mandatory bus tour of the "hippie street." "The Village" was a riot of new colours, sounds, smells and attitudes. Everywhere you looked this street was alive with the vibration of a new generation—the Love Generation. As the ranks of the Yorkville youth swelled, the city fathers, pressured by the Yorkville businessmen, decided to lean on the hippies and drive them out. Controller Alan Lamport demanded that all hippies be banished from Yorkville for a year. From the Establishment point of view, the hippies and their type had to go. They were blocking the street, lowering property values and starting to cause real trouble, especially with their notion that "their" street should be closed to traffic.

On July 13, 1968, the Yorkville cauldron came to a boil when 6,000 anti-war demonstrators jammed the area, climaxing a week of sit-ins, demonstrations and arrests. Two days later the Toronto Board of Control agreed to a suggestion by Yorkville merchants that the hippie contingent should be encouraged to get out of Yorkville.

Once the hippies were out of Yorkville, where would they go? Word started circulating that there was a hip, new—FREE—college at 341 Bloor Street. It was worth checking out.

The connection between Yorkville and Rochdale, as *The Globe and Mail*'s editorial page put it, "cannot be avoided. Has Yorkville gone highrise? Yorkville is not so much a district in Toronto as a word in Toronto's argot. It has only to be uttered. It requires no adjectives, no expanded narration to conjure all sorts of repugnant images in the public mind."

"It was a very liberal thing to do," states Matt Cohen, "in terms of the political atmosphere of the Sixties, which believed everything could be integrated into the mainstream if you just opened enough doors. But I was very sceptical, because having worked with these people to a certain extent, I just couldn't see them fitting into a place like Rochdale. There's no reason why they should. From their point of view, Rochdale had nothing to offer besides shelter and food, and that's ultimately what they took from Rochdale. And then when they did that, people complained that Rochdale was failing, when in fact it was succeeding in a perverse sort of way."

Watching the events at Rochdale were Metro's finest. Former Metro police chief Harold Adamson, who was then deputy chief of operations, states that "it was a concern because prior to that we'd had Yorkville with all its inherent problems, the drug situation was starting to spread and we had runaway kids from all over there, they were streaming into the place from everywhere in North America. And as far as we were concerned, Rochdale just added to that problem because many of the kids who had been problems in Yorkville became problems in Rochdale. And I think that some of them graduated from causing problems or getting involved in drug problems from Yorkville to becoming actual dealers in Rochdale."

College registrar Jack Dimond is convinced that the "Yorkville invasion" forever changed the nature of Rochdale College. "We essentially started to make rooms available to people who walked in right off the street. And we simply did not have the wit to see that, by this single action, we were radically changing, from the moment we opened the doors, the type of person who would be entering the building. We were sealing the fate of the Rochdale that most of us had wanted to experiment with. Since there were very few rules about how the place would be run, we were in effect handing the building over to people very unlike ourselves."

C H A P T E R   4

Crown
of
Creation

Perhaps the saddest tragedy surrounding Rochdale is that many of its redeeming qualities are today overshadowed by the unsavoury incidents that aroused such strong public censure.

And yet, for the first years of its existence, Rochdale realized many of the goals it had set for itself. In some cases, institutions and businesses were created that are now numbered among the finest of their kind in Canada. Even when no visible or long-lasting results were achieved, Rochdale was fulfilling the vision of its founders as a community that enshrined the greatest privilege of all—the freedom to fail fearlessly and, in so doing, to learn from experience. In an atmosphere dedicated to exploration and experimentation, no venture was deemed truly unsuccessful or valueless if it taught its participants worthwhile lessons that could be applied to future situations.

In fact, day-to-day life during Rochdale's early years was much more peaceful, innovative, challenging and invigorating than is generally acknowledged. In the unnewsworthy but highly productive intervals between suicides, drug arrests and mortgage crises, Rochdale thrived as an artistic and intellectual hothouse. It became a protected environment where knowledge and experience were allowed to fuse in new and intriguing patterns to produce a bewildering—and sometimes comical—array of hybrids. Its residents were constantly eager to gauge the strengths and weaknesses of society's time-tested values, while indulging in frequent excursions to uncharted realms of the mind, the body, the social and political fringe and the artistic frontier. Not content to be merely a passive element in the highly publicized counter-culture, Rochdale took a leading role in what it regarded as a budding *encounter*-culture.

Although in a very real sense nothing happened at Rochdale

that was not educational, the early years saw substantial activity in what might be considered education in a vaguely traditional setting–seminars, discussion groups and forums. (Of course, prescribed texts, examinations and any sort of marking system remained anathema.) This was a direct result of the influence of academics who were searching for alternatives to the rigidity, aridity and formality of the standard university curriculum.

As early as the winter of 1968–69, Rochdalians could join a myriad of groups or partake in literally dozens of makeshift courses lasting anywhere from a few sessions to many months. On the menu, for example, were the Utopian Research Foundation ("a structured, systematic, physical, chemical, biological, cosmological and technological investigation laboratory"), the Barry Luger Institute for Silent Studies (BLISS) dedicated to non-verbal pursuits, and a cornucopia of seminars on such topics as magic, primitive religion, yoga, ceramics, Confucius, sculpture, revolution, chess, cooking, Jungian psychology, flying saucers, the history of Atlantis, social journalism, and the history of folk, jazz and pop songwriting.

The college's 1968 calendar suggested that education ought to be "directed towards the re-opening of fundamental questions: What is important to know? What is the best way of learning? How does academic knowledge relate to other kinds of knowing? How can the search for knowledge be humanely and fruitfully carried on within an institution?" Guides in this quest were the resource people–"anyone whose experience, views or talents are deemed by the members of Rochdale to be valuable to the College. Some have other traditional academic backgrounds and recognized ability as creative teachers in a Socratic context. Others may be community organizers who, in their work, bring together theoretical analysis and neighbourhood action. Other concrete possibilities are those with experience and recognized talent as film-makers or artists. The resource person has no definite duties to the College."

Such a system, coupled with the tremendous burden of managing and maintaining the building, was not without its problems. Part of the solution, the handbook advised, was to be found in the psychology of language. "The secret of dealing with the confusion and uncertainty of Rochdale is to use 'We' in place of 'They' when referring to the operations of the college. For example, say 'What are we going to do with the seventeenth-floor terrace?' rather than 'What are they going to do ... etc.' This simple trick clarifies many otherwise ambiguous problems and helps eliminate bureaucratic flatulence."

By 1972, the educational impulse was still evident, but it concerned itself less with theory and to a greater extent with crafts and practical applications. Most prominent were groups dedicated to photography, video, radio, paper-making, carpentry, weaving, silk-screening, batik, candles and day care. In large part, this transformation was due to the gradual disaffection and disappearance of the academics who had envisioned Rochdale primarily as a community of non-conformist scholars. Nevertheless, for more than half of Rochdale's seven-year life, the quest for enlightenment remained a potent element of the residents' psychological make-up.

"The whole point, especially in the early days, was that there were no formal courses," says Theatre Passe Muraille's founder, Jim Garrard. "An initial item of debate among the people on the educational committee was whether there should be courses or not. But that subject was abandoned and disposed of in ten minutes.

"Of course, anybody could say, 'I'm gonna give a course on sculpture. And even though I'm gonna find money out there to support myself, I'm attached to Rochdale because I live in Rochdale. So what I do can be part of the Rochdale educational environment.' To that extent, there would be a course. But I don't think anybody went much further than that, except for the odd sharpie. It's also true that the courses that were important didn't appear in any syllabus."

Paul Evitts, who had been one of the original students during the days of the Rochdale Houses, plunged right into the educational program and immersed himself in five or six courses during 1968–69. "One of them was with Dennis Lee, analyzing King Lear from a variety of different viewpoints. And what I found so amazing was that Dennis was convinced that the quality of what was coming out of that course was significantly better than what he was used to at Victoria College. So he was really turned on by it, and so was I."

"I did a weekly—or it may have been a bi-weekly—seminar on the serial poem," recalls poet Victor Coleman, who had grown up in Montreal and Toronto, dropped out of high school, worked for a British Columbia publisher and returned to Toronto to become involved in Rochdale's Coach House Press. "It was essentially like a literary workshop and I thought it was quite successful. It only went on for a while, but at least it put me in touch with other literary types in the building.

"We tried to make it as open a community as possible. I remember a friend of mine, a poet from Vancouver, coming to town and staying with me at Rochdale. One of the first things he did was post signs in the elevator saying, 'This elevator is a magazine,' with suggestions asking people to tack up their poetry and Xerox art and various other stuff—fast, easily displayed material. The idea was that the material would keep on changing as time passed. And that's exactly what did happen for a few weeks. It was quite exciting and I can't imagine that kind of thing happening anywhere else.

"So to me, the educational process that was going on at Rochdale seemed quite good. But it was the intellectual range that was really amazing. I mean, you had everything from groups like Praxis, which was publishing post-structuralist stuff, to streetwriters who were semi-literate. And because of that range, it was a spawning ground for a lot of activity."

Michael Waite, a frequent visitor to Rochdale in its early days, remembers wandering through the building and being astounded by the scope and variety of subjects under discussion. "In one room they'd be discussing Nietzsche, in the next room they'd be talking about UFOs, in the next the war in Vietnam, and over in the next room they'd be rappin' about changing the drug laws—just all these alternate ideas.

"There'd be a selection of people, too. Some would be U of T students, some were bikers and, of course, a few were morons who just came down to pick up chicks and contribute dumb comments or break up the conversation wherever possible. But it was always interesting. You could always go down to Rochdale and get some interesting conversation and meet some neat people, or just hang out in this totally weird environment."

Before long, Rochdale was playing host to a steady stream of writers, musicians, artists and thinkers, many of them with the highest—and most controversial—international credentials. Timothy Leary, the high priest of LSD, dropped in and tripped out at Rochdale. Although he now admits he can't remember specifics about his visit, he does recall being generally "impressed with the atmosphere and the experimental way of life."

Beat poet Allen Ginsberg also accepted an invitation to visit Rochdale in September, 1970, and was so impressed that he scrapped plans for a brief stop-over and stayed overnight to explore the building. Today Ginsberg remembers Rochdale with mixed emotions, especially "the general sense of both confusion and attentiveness" on the part of its residents. "It was kind of bewildering, because it was modernistic and yet everybody was trying to live in a primitive way. Some of the rooms were quite messy. It seemed to be organized, but I couldn't figure out the organization—mostly some sort of anarchist, communal thing. There was also some indecision about what kind of education was going on there, but the people were quite familiar with my work. They were very much up on that."

"Rochdale was important," says movie exhibitor Reg Hartt, "because it was the only place where the ideas of the sixties and seventies—from people like Baba Ram Das, Timothy Leary and Abbie Hoffman—were actually tried and applied. And what was found was that, in almost every situation where those ideas were tried and applied, they were simply valueless.

"When people lectured at Rochdale, they expressed the same ideas as they expressed at, for instance, Cal Tech or Columbia. But somebody in our audience could get up and say to someone like Timothy Leary, 'Timothy, I'm sorry. It won't work.' And his response was, 'How do you know?' And our response would be, 'Because we tried it.' Everywhere else in North America, it was all ideas, with no actual attempt to work with those ideas. At Rochdale, we worked with those ideas and we found that not a single one of them was valid."

Although enlightenment remained a constant goal, Rochdale's ultra-liberal approach did tend to weaken the structure and organization of some programs. Dennis Lee recalls that during the fall of 1968, he was involved in "a course that was looking into phenomenology and existential thinkers. It was actually very interesting, and there were such bright, passionate, talented people around in those early years. There were about half a dozen people in this particular group, although it fluctuated somewhat.

"There was also no leader, but people hadn't read much in the area, so it wasn't a bad approach to take. None of us knew more about the subject than others, so we rather blindly mapped out a reading course for ourselves. But when we hit Heidegger, we just ran up against a brick wall, because nobody's mind worked that way. We were stuck on an essay about nothingness or something, and I remember my brain just locking. So we all showed up and said, 'What the fuck was that about?'

"Simultaneously, we were getting tangled up in the process issues of how decisions were going to be made, and what happened if nobody bothered to show up, and what kind of commitments were implicit in starting a course like this. It was a serious undertaking that probably ran until Christmas and then petered out. I remember feeling sad and puzzled about not being able to keep things going and not knowing for myself what my role or responsibility should be—whether it would be uppity to be more directive."

Resident students felt the effects, as well. "What I found," said Major Domo, "was that an unstructured course basically meant that the person with the biggest mouth got to sound off all the time and bore all the people. From an educational point of view, that taught me a lot, because I never again got involved in anything that advertised itself as unstructured. Some people might like to listen to one guy sound off, but not me."

As with any new enterprise, there arose philosophical disagreements among those who were in positions of nominal authority. Victor Coleman remembers Judith Merril and Dennis Lee "having meetings and putting together grandiose plans for a literary magazine that would be like the *Paris Review* or something like that. I would go to the meetings and laugh at them, make fun of them and say things like, *Paris Review*—gimme a break, what are you talkin' about? Let's get real, really real. Let's continue to put our imagination and energy into a newspaper like the *Daily Planet* or our own little publications and internal stuff. Let's communicate with each other before we start thinking of ourselves as world-class."

One such attempt at communication was creation of a headquarters for the Institute for Indian Studies—an effort to extend Rochdale's idealistic vision into the native community. The concept was embraced by many mainstream residents, because Indian culture meshed neatly with the counter-cultural interest in non-traditional spiritualism, folk arts and the recreational use of exotic new drugs such as peyote. However, for a sizable core group, the institute was seen purely as a means of preserving and celebrating the Indian way of life. Rev. Ian MacKenzie, who, along with Wilf Pelletier, helped develop the program, proudly calls it "the first Indian educational institution in Canada. We actually started it in 1967, and then moved in as soon as the seventeenth floor was completed. We had half of the seventeenth floor, which we used for apartments and our offices.

"Initially it was the Rochdale College Institute for Indian Studies, and later it became the Nishnawbe Institute. It was mostly native people who lived there. And while everybody else on the other floors was freaking out and going nuts, the native people were the only ones who seemed able to keep their heads together. It's not that they didn't share in the use of a variety of drugs. They just didn't get freaked out.

"We used to do cross-cultural workshops and one of them was held in Rochdale in the spring of 1969. About twenty probation officers from across Ontario attended. And in their evaluation to the province of Ontario, they recommended that all future workshops of this kind should take place at Rochdale."

In addition to their positions as president and secretary-treasurer of the institute, Pelletier and MacKenzie remained on the Rochdale payroll as resource people. With success came expansion and higher costs. Dissatisfaction on the part of Rochdale's leaders was compounded by the institute's special privileges, including a contract that entitled two workers to six months' severance pay. Finally, in early 1970, after a short but productive affiliation, the Indian Institute severed its ties with Rochdale and departed, leaving frayed tempers and bad blood in its wake.

Rochdale's tolerance for a wide array of interests and political causes went hand-in-hand with an acceptance of a sometimes bewildering collection of religious groups. The quest for spirituality—and, in some cases, a disgust with the excesses of hippiedom—led to a rediscovery of Christianity and the born-again movement. Even among the Christians, there was a decidedly unorthodox outlook on life, which was heavily influenced by the liberal lifestyle that Rochdale espoused.

"The only real religious commune we had was the Jesus Forever group on the third floor," recalls resident Martin Burns, a chartered accountant and father of ten, who gave up suburban life in Scarborough for the high times of Rochdale. "It was led by an ex-theological student who had a mouth full of rotten teeth, played guitar badly and sang much worse. But he was the actual charisma that held it all together.

"He'd been a dope dealer. And at one point, the cops nabbed

him but forgot to search him. So he did all this acid—eighteen hits—in the back of a police car. When the cops realized what had happened, they got pissed off and threw him out of the car in the middle of the night in High Park. He told me that he just walked around High Park for two days and two nights because he couldn't find his way out. He just kept walking in circles. And since he was on acid the whole time, Jesus kept popping out from behind the trees and pointing to him. So he took that as a sign and he became born again."

A familiar sight on the streets of Toronto during those years were the chanting, saffron-robed members of the Hare Krishna organization. For a brief period, Rochdale became their base of operations, as attempts were made to recruit impressionable and open-minded residents of the high-rise hippie community. Among them was Bill Charnell, originally from Winnipeg, who had joined the Hare Krishna movement in Vancouver in 1969 and moved to Toronto in 1970.

"I came out of university in 1967 and was involved in the hip revolution," says Charnell (known as Rocana in Krishna circles), a Winnipeg businessman who still adheres to many Hare Krishna tenets but assumes no active role in the organization. "At the time, Hare Krishna was practically at the vanguard of the spiritual side of the hip movement, because people were looking for a bona fide alternative to the materialistic lifestyle. There was a lot of hope that the Hare Krishna movement would be an integral part of that.

"But the hip movement became more and more contaminated with drugs and low-life. And people in the hip movement realized how strict the Hare Krishna philosophy was about things that they considered sacred—drugs and sex, for instance. So after a while, people started to pick up on the fact that we weren't so hip. And people, especially in the big-city hip scene, weren't able to identify with us.

"We were based in Cabbagetown in an old house that we renovated on Gerrard Street. We were fairly active in those days and quite evangelical, with a lot of street chanting. We also had a program of spending one evening a week at Rochdale in the corridors, sitting around and chanting and passing out spiritual food. That went on for about a year.

"We decided that because many of the married couples had to live outside the temple and needed apartments, it would be a good idea to rent rooms in Rochdale. We actually spent quite a bit of money renovating, because the place was really gross. About four or five couples moved in—one couple to a room. There was also a common area where we'd have an altar and do some chanting and invite people to join in.

"Sometimes some of us would stay overnight and have a morning program similar to the temple. Other times, we'd walk all the way from Rochdale to Gerrard at 3:30 in the morning to get there in time to participate in that program. We were trying to feel out Rochdale to see how receptive it would be.

"There was some receptivity, but a lot of people were almost hostile toward our program. There wasn't exactly any violence directed toward us, but there were some verbally offensive exchanges and mild threats. We were always hoping to save somebody and try to help someone to escape the dead-end scene that was going on. But we finally decided it wasn't fertile enough to set up a permanent temple. So we tip-toed out of there before it went down the tubes."

Often the attitude toward exotic groups such as the Hare Krishna movement was one of openness and curiosity. American expatriate Lorraine Darling remembers "talking to the Krishna girls all the time, especially out in the park where we took the kids. I'd ask them about their ways—for example, getting married and only going to bed in order to have children. But I always thought they were good for the building. Whenever we had parties—like the solstice parties, which were sort of the building's festivals—the Krishna people would get involved by bringing their food and participating."

It was not unusual for the Hare Krishnas to be the butt of derision and prejudice, sometimes because of rituals that bothered other residents. "People by and large didn't like the Krishnas," says Rochdale security guard T.J., "because they would chant in the middle of the night. They took over an Ashram on the seventh or eighth floor and they'd chant at these weird hours—in the middle of the night or 6:00 a.m. It didn't take long for people above and below them to start complaining."

Attend a Canadian play, pick up a book of home-grown poetry, spend a few hours in a downtown Toronto library, listen to music by Canadian composers, catch a feature film—and you may be enjoying an aspect of Rochdale's rich artistic legacy. Rochdale's impact remains most apparent in the continuing work of writers, actors, artists and musicians who were drawn into the building's sphere of influence, especially during the early years of heady experimentation.

This spirit of innovation survives most noticeably in the work of Theatre Passe Muraille—whose name, loosely translated from the fractured French, means "theatre beyond walls." Like other pace-setting Toronto theatres, Passe Muraille actively searches out and develops original Canadian scripts. For more than twenty years, it has remained at the forefront in its use of unusual and sometimes utterly bizarre stage techniques. On occasion, this has resulted in financial crises that date back to Rochdale, but, backed by a more conscientious administration, Passe Muraille has persevered. In so doing, it has allowed playwrights, performers and directors to develop their craft by granting them one of Rochdale's most precious freedoms—the freedom to fail with honour on the road to success.

Theatre Passe Muraille was founded in the fall of 1968 by Jim Garrard, who had spent three years as an elementary school principal in the early Sixties, followed by three years of study at Queen's University and two years at the London Academy of Music and Dramatic Arts. "By that time, I felt ready to start a theatre in Toronto along the lines of the interesting European companies I'd seen. So I went to the Ontario Arts Council. And at that time, there was a woman there named Charlotte Holmes who, in her early career, was very interested in new forms of theatre. There were a couple of other people there in the educational arm who were very interested in the type of theatre I envisioned. They also happened to be very interested in Rochdale and talked to people like Dennis Lee. So Charlotte said, 'I think Rochdale'—which I hadn't really heard of, because I was just back from two years away from Canada—'might suit what you want to do.' And she sent me to see Dennis.

"So I talked to Dennis in the spring of '68 and he sent me to see Paul Evitts, who was one of the most interesting people I ever met at Rochdale and one of the most imaginative guys. He was interested in this idea and he gave me a few tips about Rochdale—where the bulletin boards were, how Campus Co-op worked, where the money came from and so on. Jack Dimond, the original registrar of Rochdale, was also there and he was very sympathetic to the idea. It was May of '68 when I ran into these people, and the building opened in September. I moved in when my floor was ready in November of '68.

"They provided us with a house on Admiral Road where we gave modern improvisational workshops and all that kind of stuff. And we drew a lot of kids who were associated with Rochdale, who were intending to move in or who were excited about the educational promises that were emanating from Rochdale. It was quite a big group—forty people, I guess—and not all of them were trained in theatre. But they were interested in dance and improvisation and the kinds of things that were so easy to do in the Sixties.

"I brought the idea and the name of Passe Muraille with me from Europe. And I started to do a project based on *Tom Paine*, written by Tom O'Horgan, in the basement of Rochdale. In doing that, I met a draft dodger from the States named Frank Mossey—a brilliant designer—and his wife Judith who was an actress, and a peculiar fellow named Ron Terrill who was the first administrator of Passe Muraille. And the four of us claimed to be the professional arm of Theatre Passe Muraille in its absolute infancy.

"The workshops that I'd already been doing were the in-house, educational arm of Theatre Passe Muraille. But we also wanted to have a community front, so we did a lot of workshops in high-rises and YMCAs and schools. They could be in improv or mask-making or whatever. We even did a production of *Oedipus Rex* with students at Northern Collegiate.

For legal reasons, the show could not be staged and to make up for the loss of *Tom Paine*, Garrard added a show to the 1968–69 season—the notorious *Futz*, a stinging social satire about a farmer who falls in love with his prize pig. "*Futz* was written by Rochelle Owens, a kind of intellectual woman, a New Yorker, a university mind. I'd actually seen a production done by the La Mama Company in New York, directed by Tom O'Horgan. And when I was in England, they did it at the Hampstead Theatre Club. I was really excited by it, because I thought it was an awfully nice approach."

Quite by chance, *Futz* became part of a season's theatre package assembled by Bill Marshall (who was later instrumental in starting the Festival of Festivals) for general theatre-goers interested in a variety of works. This allowed the Passe Muraille company to move into the somewhat more convenient Central Library Theatre at St. George and College streets. And, above all, it meant publicity.

The advance feature by Marci McDonald, published in *The*

Toronto Star on March 5, 1969, promised the following in that night's premiere: "In one scene, a twenty-two-year-old American actress who calls herself Temperance Loyd unhooks her dress to the waist and bares her bosom to both the audience and fellow actor Ashleigh Moorehouse, who plays her son.

"In another, actress Sylvia Tucker remains fully if scantily clad, but graphically pantomimes every conceivable physical possibility in a scene where she rolls in the mud with two fellow actors. . . .

"Ticket-holders will be led to their seats over a labyrinth of actors lying stretched, arms and legs akimbo, in the aisles. Then for the next hour, the audience will hear a poet and his girl read obscene poetry on a record, while the rear end of a pig is projected on a screen onstage and the actors cavort in the aisles, playing games, interviewing audience members on their attitudes toward love, bestiality and pigs and presenting what the group calls a poetry reading, but which is essentially a dramatically staged collection of suggestive songs and dirty rhymes."

The article also included an interview with Garrard (twenty-nine years old at the time) who explained that *Futz* was meant to wipe away the boredom that afflicted other theatre productions. "People today are very insulated by urban living and by the speed of events. This play is full of taboos, so we ask the audience what do they think of them. Of bestiality? Of pigs? Of love? What makes taboos?"

The answer came the next day in Don Rubin's review in the *Star*. *Futz*, he said is "an emotionally innocuous and intellectually fatuous theatrical experience." After slamming the play at length as unchallenging, self-indulgent, dreary, artificial and a total failure, Rubin concluded: "Theatre Passe Muraille, it seems, does deserve praise for at least trying to reach beyond the common ground of theatrical experience to give Toronto a glimpse of one direction in which the contemporary theatre is heading. For that reason alone, this company deserves encouragement. Perhaps its next production will reach some greater level of fulfillment."

The police were not prepared to be quite so charitable. After attending the second-night performance, three morality squad officers charged Garrard and all twelve of *Futz*'s actors and actresses with staging an immoral performance. "Summonses were issued to absolutely everybody associated with the play," says Garrard today. "And the police came back every single night with more summonses until a reasonable number had been issued—five thousand or something—and then they stopped. But they still came back and sat there and watched this stuff. And later, everybody had to go to court.

"In the end, I guess *Futz* ran about six weeks. I think it was actually held over, because it was originally scheduled to run only three weeks. By that point, the lawyers—a couple of the partners who backed the show were lawyers—were worried about getting disbarred. So they decided against continuing it. And then they defended it in court for a year at very great cost to themselves in money, effort and anxiety.

"Eventually, they dropped the charges against everybody except—after a long time, after screwing up everybody's plans—the three producers. And they put us up against a seventy-seven-year-old judge who said, 'I can have philosophical conversations all day with you, Mr. Garrard, but I don't think it has anything to do with this trial.'

"But we appealed, and a year later the charges were dismissed. The original trial was in September of '69 and the appeal was in the late spring of 1970. As part of the defense, we even took the judge down to see *Hair* and actually had the court assembled there—I think it was some official session of the court. And when he threw the charges out, he criticized the morality squad and said the case should never have been brought to court in the first place.

"Also we got very little support from the artistic community. I think that if even the most lowly theatre practitioner got in trouble today over the new obscenity code or something like that, there would be a tremendous rallying. But there was no rallying for *Futz*, and I never could figure out why. Finally, the dance community came out and did stuff and there were various benefits, but you really had to drag people out of the woodwork."

Despite these early problems, Theatre Passe Muraille was far from finished and, in early 1969, it began renting workshop and rehearsal space at the Trinity Square Anglican Church (on land now partly occupied by the Eaton Centre). "That rent was paid by Rochdale College out of its educational funds," says Garrard, "so Rochdale was actually the prime supporter of the professional arm of Passe Muraille. But we still continued to do workshops in the building in a Zeus suite. To raise money for the rest of the theatre, we'd hire ourselves out to the community. So we had that lovely space in Trinity Square for quite a few years afterward.

"Then I went off fund-raising and Martin Kinch tried to design a season, with Paul Thompson showing up from Montreal or somewhere as the tech director—quite a good tech director, I think, although I didn't have too much to do with him. Because I was fund-raising and Martin was apprenticing or assistant directing at Stratford, we formed a triumvirate to run the theatre. I think Martin was called the artistic director, I was called the managing director and I think Paul was the heart of that triumvirate."

Thompson had studied at the University of Toronto in 1964–65, trained in France as a theatre director and worked as assistant director at Stratford for two seasons, but Rochdale and Passe Muraille proved to be unlike anything he had encountered until then.

"I think the theatre would have disappeared without a trace, if not for Thompson," says Garrard. "He inherited very little in the way of resources—a bit of Rochdale support, a nice theatre, a tax number and a few good reviews. And he picked it up from there and really hoisted it up into something totally on his own. The Passe Muraille I knew and was responsible for, I think, would have died without Paul's attentions."

Another operation that continues to thrive is Coach House Press, a small and staunchly independent company that has published notable works by such authors as Margaret Atwood, Michael Ondaatje and b.p. nichol. Coach House pre-dates Rochdale by several years, having been founded in 1965 when Stan Bevington began operating out of a tiny, tumble-down coach house near Bathurst and Dundas streets. Nearly three years later, the area was slated for slum clearance and Bevington was forced to move. After word of his plight circulated in the literary community, Dennis Lee came to the rescue by finding the publisher a new home in yet another ramshackle coach house on Huron Street, around the corner from Rochdale. Although considerably modernized and renovated, those quarters retain much of their old homeyness and still serve today as Coach House's base.

"We moved from the Bathurst site in April, 1968," says Bevington, "but Rochdale wasn't complete yet. So we moved into this building on Huron instead. The plan was to camp out here temporarily and then move into the other place, because I'd had it with old coach houses and old buildings with heating problems. But we never did move into the main building because of all the instability over there. We all lived there—I lived on the eighteenth floor for three years—but I didn't want to risk doing business there. It was too crazy. Besides, the basement, which was the only space that suited us, was very, very dirty and dusty because of the cars going in and out. Security was also spotty and I couldn't put machinery there, what with people bashing around and the danger of drug busts and shit like that.

"Even so, we all thought that building Rochdale together as a publishing centre would be a great thing. By having space near the Bloor building to invite authors and publishers and editors, it could also be a great community resource. So we became part of the cultural and educational rationale for anything that Rochdale did. The suggestion was that we would be print manufacturers for the college. House of Anansi Press got some books printed here, and we provided educational courses and workshops and stuff like that. We stayed an independent business, but the spirit of Rochdale was a twenty-four-hour-a-day part of our lifestyle."

Nelson Adams, who still works at Coach House as a typesetter and jack-of-all-trades, began by sweeping floors in 1969—"except that in the beginning, there were hardly any floors, no heat, no insulation, no electricity, no water—just a shell. I think practically everybody in '68–'69 and '69–'70—for those two winters and summers—who was around here at Coach House was living at Rochdale. If they were visiting Coach House from out of town, they were probably crashing at Rochdale. It was pretty close. The press printed stuff for Rochdale and occasionally we even got paid for it. I even remember that the first thing I ever collated was a Rochdale calendar."

Poet Victor Coleman, another Coach House associate, recalls an article about Rochdale written by Sarah Spinks in *This Magazine Is About Schools*. "In it, she said that Rochdale was a failure, it was falling apart, it wasn't working, and so on. But what she did point out was that Coach House Press was the embodiment of all the various ideals that went into the creation of Rochdale and how Coach House was actually seeing these ideals through successfully."

Another highly successful survivor of Rochdale is the Spaced Out Library, founded in 1970 by science fiction author and anthologist Judith Merril. As a division of the Toronto Public Library system, it's believed to be the world's largest publicly accessible collection of science fiction and related materials, many of which can be borrowed with a simple library card. Based on

Merril's own extensive collection, the Spaced Out Library now
contains approximately 16,000 novels (including many first
editions), 14,000 periodicals, 2,500 books on science and
pseudo-science (including flying saucers, futurology, the Loch
Ness monster and similar topics), 1,200 fanzines, and a wide array
of pulp magazines, critical works, artwork, posters, records, tapes
and newspaper clippings. It's all housed at 40 St. George Street,
just a few steps north of the former Central Library where *Futz*
was performed in 1969.

   Merril, who had left the United States in disgust at the age of
forty-four after witnessing the violence of the 1968 Democratic
Convention in Chicago, arrived at Rochdale "with this really
rag-tag collection of science fiction. I had never been a collector
type, but it was all the stuff that I happened to accumulate while I
was writing fiction, doing book reviews and editing anthologies.
I kept comparing it to an eighteen-year-old dog—you can't leave
it behind, and you don't really want to take it with you. But with
a library you don't have the alternative of sending it to a
veterinarian and having it put away. So I brought it with me.

   "At Rochdale, a lot of people were into science fiction. So I
thought, 'Why don't I set up a common library space and get
someone to tend the shop?' And that's what happened. Most of
the stuff that was in there initially was mine. A couple of other
people did put in smaller amounts, so it ended up being about half
science fiction. And that's where the name Spaced Out Library
started. It was an honour-system library, so we lost a lot of books.
But you knew that would happen when you put them in. You
weren't donating your books—just making them available. But
you knew you were going to lose them."

   The library formally opened at Rochdale in July, 1969, to
coincide with a festival organized by Merril to celebrate Neil
Armstrong's first step on the moon. Although Merril's original
collection contained approximately 10,000 items, about half that
number stayed in Merril's hands or had been stolen during her
first few months in Toronto. That left a still sizable 5,000 items for
the Spaced Out Library. In fact, it was so impressive that when
Harry Campbell, chief librarian for the Toronto Public Library,
learned of the project, he offered Rochdale display cases and
technical assistance to ensure the collection was properly
administered.

   "After that," says Merril, "the library was sometimes open and
sometimes closed. It depended on whether there was any money

to provide meals as compensation for someone to work there. But it continued until I left in late 1969, or shortly afterwards. Within a year at most after I left, there simply was no more education money for anything–for maintenance or for a person to sit in the library. Stuff was just getting ripped off. So I took back the basic science fiction library.

"Then Harry Campbell came back to me in 1970 and said, 'I hear you're thinking of disposing of your library. Why don't you give it to the Toronto Public Library system and then you'll still have access to it. We'll take care of the books and you'll use them. And we'll establish this special branch exclusively for science fiction and fantasy.' Harry also wrote into the agreement that I was to be given office space in the same building with the Spaced Out Library."

Because of her experience as a writer, Merril was also keen on developing an in-house publishing centre. But this project was not quite as successful as the Spaced Out Library. "At first, I did try to form a seminar, but anytime the seminar was not scheduled, I would have sixteen kids in my apartment wanting to talk. Whenever it was time for a seminar, nobody was there.

"Finally, I arranged to get a room on the second floor, which was called the publishing centre. We equipped it with four or five scrounged typewriters and a mimeograph machine and later we got a Xerox and various other equipment. I also advised people in the building that I was going to open this room and be there for a substantial amount of time each day. And anyone else who had experience in writing or publishing and wanted to come in as a resource person should do so. Similarly, anyone who wanted to write something or publish something or get it disseminated through the building or outside the building was also welcome to come and use the equipment and get whatever advice or criticism they wanted. I don't remember people using it all that much, but they sure liked coming in there and thinking about using it."

Unlike the theatrical and literary projects, the musical ventures were never particularly sophisticated or structured. But music was an integral part of Rochdale's artistic atmosphere, just as all forms of rock, folk, blues and jazz were perceived as near-revolutionary forces in society at large.

As Rochdale general manager Bill King noted in a 1975 letter to one of the Toronto daily newspapers, "Music has always been a large part of the Rochdale experience and about half of the city's working rock bands have a link of some sort with our community. They either have members who have lived here or they made records here or they met each other here. Rochdale-connected major groups include Downchild, Syrinx, Perth County Conspiracy, Dollars, Knights of the Mystic Sea, Horn-Mateski, Heavy Duty and Rhythm Rockets."

There was, at one point, sufficient organization to arrange for construction of a rudimentary studio in a corner of the building's underground parking garage. Built, ironically enough, by members of an anarchistic commune at Rochdale in 1971, the studio bore the evocative name Sound Horn—a reference to neither music nor brass instruments. Someone had noticed a sign in the garage, "Sound horn before turning corner," and somehow decided that the first two words would suit the studio. It was here that some of Canada's most notable musicians made their first recordings or honed their considerable skills.

Among them was Geddy Lee, composer and bassist for the internationally renowned rock band Rush, whose stumbling but promising early efforts were first taped at Sound Horn. Engineer for the session was Billy Bryans, drummer and co-founder of Toronto's socially aware rock group Parachute Club. Neither musician lived in the building, but like so may people in the music scene in the late sixties and early seventies, they gravitated to Rochdale because that's where the action was.

"I remember we did the sessions in this tiny studio downstairs," says Lee. "We did four tracks, although I'm not sure what we recorded. It may have been some Led Zeppelin songs. Thankfully, those tracks have disappeared from the face of the earth and from memory. There was only one copy and no one can find it.

"For us, it was just a place to do some recording—eager, young, high school kids that we were. We didn't actually have anything to do with the building or the Rochdale scene because the folks seemed a trifle weird to us. We just went in and did the session and split. But it was fun, I guess, just being part of the history of the infamous Rochdale College."

Bryans had recently arrived from Montreal and, in checking out the Toronto music scene, happened to catch a performance by Downchild—then, as now, one of Canada's premier blues bands. "I'd never seen anything like them in my life. People in the audience were standing on chairs and tables, just wailing away. There was a really healthy, developing blues scene in Toronto at that point. So the Downchild people—including Dick Flohill, their manager—arranged for the band to record its first album at Sound Horn."

Flohill says, "Sound Horn was a tiny place, with a studio of only twenty square feet for the musicians. Then, behind it and separated by a panel of translucent glass brick, was a minuscule cupboard masquerading as a control room, with this two-track Revox equipment set-up. We put the band, evenly distributed, in the twenty square feet, leaving absolutely no room to move between the drum kit, the amps and the six musicians. Technically, there was no mixing, there was no overdubbing, there was no nothing. We could only mix right channel and left channel. I remember we did it at night—a fairly good party time, but it was never out of control at all, because the band was very cognizant of having to get it right.

"Over three nights, we recorded every single song in the book—twice. And at the end of it, I think we'd got something like thirty-five or forty songs down, with two versions of each. Then we weeded and wound up with the nine cuts that are on the *Bootleg* album. We calculated the total cost of that record at about $500—done, finished, copies in our hands. Afterwards, we sold about two thousand copies almost instantly to friends and fans.

"Three weeks after we put out the record, we'd more than made our money back. And then along came RCA and offered us $2,000 for the rights to distribute it. Now, an offer of $2,000 at that time was like—unbelievable! Jackpot! We'd already made our money and this was a bonus. And that record stayed in the catalogue until about 1986 when RCA finally pulled it."

"The beauty of it was that the whole building had access to the studio," adds Billy Bryans. "All the residents had to do was come up with the cost of tape and then book the time. I remember many an all-night hash jam in the studio and rehearsal space when we got to some very weird musical spaces. We'd have all kinds of musicians renting the studio after that—from folkies to Rush.

"There was a happening music scene at Rochdale. You had people like Luke Gibson, Nancy Simmons, Michael Hasek, Murray McLauchlan—folkies, rockers, jazz. Even the late jazz great Lenny Breau played there. And there was the band Horn, the musical wing of the Horn-Mateski commune that set up the studio. It was a politically active band that would go out to the various demonstrations and political rallies and play in support of the cause. It was part of the emerging New Left, but it was also a fun organization that deflated the pretentiousness and pseudo-seriousness of the political radicals."

Hanging out became a favourite pastime for musicians at Rochdale. Names were dropped, contacts were made and, on rare occasions, idols were glimpsed. Among the occasional visitors was rocker Alice Cooper, whose outrageous, blood-spurting theatrics and bone-crunching music acquired a loyal following in Toronto. Since Cooper also recorded several albums in Toronto with producer Bob Ezrin in the early seventies, it was only natural for him to drop into Rochdale and add to its aura of perversity and lawlessness. "I really started to get into the city," Cooper recalls. "I'd be walking around with all my leathers on and people would stop and say, 'Hi.' They were real friendly. This is such a great city.

"I remember going there for a party after we played a festival at Lamport Stadium in 1970 or '71. Another time, we headed back to Rochdale after one of our gigs at a place called the Fillmore North. We came back to Rochdale with some of the security people who were working the gig. It was pretty happening, that Rochdale—a good party. I remember thinking at the time about how tough it would be to get a place like that going down in the States. There was such a different relationship between young people and the authorities in the States. But Rochdale, yeah, it was definitely a party."

Michael Waite, a Toronto-based musician and record store owner who has produced albums for Nash the Slash and FM, still has vivid memories of an impromptu performance by bassist Denny Gerrard, formerly of the Toronto band the Paupers, the only Canadian group to play the legendary Monterey Pop Festival. "I remember sitting in the Rochdale common room one night rappin', havin' a good time. This guy comes in and he's unrecognizable as Denny Gerrard, because he looks like a truck driver with his bass and a twelve-pack of beer. He sits right in the middle of this group and just starts playin', wailin'—but everybody's talking around him like he's not there. And after he lays down twenty-four bars of this amazing bass playing, I'm in awe. But he didn't say a word. He just kept playing and drinking until he polished off his twelve beers and split. It was the best hour and a half of bass-playing I've ever heard. At the end I asked somebody, 'Who was that guy?' And they said, 'Oh, he's Denny Gerrard.' "

Spontaneity of this sort was not out of the ordinary in a climate that thrived on the unusual. Resident Howard Brenner recalls one woman—"a real space case"—who seemed unable to function in regular society, but wandered aimlessly around the building. However, when she sat down to the piano, this psychedelic idiot savant was able to play the most complex, melodious classical music imagineable. Then she would get up from the piano and resume her wanderings.

Another fellow, Brenner recalls, used to give impromptu concerts in the stairwell by plucking Liszt compositions on the banjo. "Can you imagine fuckin' Liszt on the banjo? And you could hear it in the whole building because of the way the sound carried in those concrete stairwells."

One of Canada's top blues musicians, a U.S. draft dodger and former teacher who wishes to be identified only as "Red" Rebel, also lived in Rochdale from the fall of 1971 through the spring of 1973. For the first eight months, he occupied not an apartment or even a room, but a closet. "It was one of these big, walk-in closets—big enough to put a mattress in. I rented it for twelve bucks a month, plus I got living-room privileges. I put a lock on the door and kept my clothes in a knapsack. And from morning 'til night I played music. I basically slept, played music and jellyrolled in that closet. There was no ventilation in there and, man, the sweat would be pouring off the walls—I ain't lying.

"So I was in the closet, working on my chops. And I started playing around the building. In fact, that's how I turned professional. I'd play in front of some of the free-enterprise establishments in the building—sandwich shops, boozecans, whatever. I'd be outside the apartment and I'd sing in a talkin' blues style or straight-up blues about how good the sandwiches were or how cold the beers were. And I'd make some pocket money.

"The music scene—that was the best part of Rochdale to me. There was always a jam happening somewhere. Something was always going on musically in The Rock. It was great. I met a lot of great players there. I met David Wilcox there—he didn't live there, but musicians were always hanging around. I played everywhere—in the lobby, outside the building. I played for nickels and dimes. There was all kinds of music happening at Rochdale—blues, country, great rock and roll."

In 1969, Rochdale became Greg MacDonald's ticket into the Toronto cast of *Hair*. The ground-breaking rock musical had already opened to rave reviews at the Royal Alexandra Theatre and, appropriately enough, a cast party was organized by the Rochdalians and held at the University of Toronto's Convocation Hall.

"Afterwards, they were all invited back to Rochdale," recalled MacDonald, who lived in the building. "And along with the cast were [writers/lyricists] Gerry Ragni and James Rado. At that time, my hair was really long and I looked like the kind of person they were writing about. My jeans were all covered with patches and I had a psychedelic, tie-dyed T-shirt. So I was walking by when Rado grabs me and says, 'I want that guy! Jerry, Jerry! I want him!' And he says to me, 'Can you sing? Can you dance?' And I say, 'Sure! I can do all that stuff.' So they both came up to my apartment and we sat around and had a couple of joints and talked about the thing.

"I did the parts of the moms and dads, I did the principal roles, I did all the dance routines and I did a lot of the acrobatic stuff.

"And, of course, I did the nude scene just about every night. But the thing was, you took all your clothes off and stood up there, but you were completely still. It was symbolic of people blossoming and flowers opening up to the sun, but there was no touching. The way the law was back then, we could get closed down if we weren't like statues.

"I remember one night Anne Murray was in the audience. It was the part of the show where you're walking in slow motion through the audience, and I'm walking along and—bingo! There's Anne Murray, right in front of me. So I bend down and say, 'How's it going, Anne?' And she says, 'Oh, Hi.' Well, she's like me—originally from Springhill, Nova Scotia. So I point to my picture and bio in the program and say, 'Here, on the page. That's me, right there. See that? Springhill. Remember me?' So she looks again and says, 'Oh, yeah. How are your brothers Wayne and Bruce?' And I say, 'They're doing great, thanks.' And then I walked back on stage.

"People at Rochdale thought it was great that I was in *Hair*. They said, 'It's about time they got a real hippie down there.' We did four shows on weekends and a show most other nights. And the pay was dynamite! I made $260 a week, plus another $50 or $60 for extras. I went to Europe and lived there for six months on that money after the show closed."

After music, cinema was the art form that most intrigued the younger generation. True to form, Rochdale provided an environment where the craft could be learned in a hands-on situation or the movies themselves screened as simple entertainment. While the rest of society lapped up the latest pap that Hollywood cranked out, Rochdale's curious residents indulged in a feast of silent films, classic animation and just about any visually arresting item that acquired new meaning through a haze of marijuana or LSD.

Among those who were drawn into Rochdale's sphere was Michael Hirsh, an award-winning film-maker and co-founder of Toronto's Nelvana studio (producer of such movies as *Rock And Rule* and *The Care Bears Movie*, and the TV series "The Edison Twins"). In early 1968, Hirsh was producing the low-budget, avant-garde film *Assassination Generation* with fellow York University student Jack Christie. The search for financing led them to York professor and Rochdale founder Howard Adelman who offered to help in fund-raising.

"We continued making *Assassination Generation* and held film-making seminars. *Assassination Generation* did get finished, but it had its title changed, was seen at a few festivals, and that was that. But in the process of this and other film work, Rochdale helped give birth to organizations like the Canadian Film Makers' Distribution Centre and the film-maker's co-op.

"One of the things we also did was start a little cinema called De Fat Daddy Cinema. We rented films from the various distributors around town and we showed sixteen-millimetre prints of things like *Alice in Wonderland*, *The Ten Commandments* and Martin and Lewis double-bills. We were into nostalgic fifties pictures—that was what we specialized in. Our little cinema was doing great, but we were terrible at business. Then Reg Hartt started his cinema and suddenly we were splitting business."

As Hirsh grew more interested in movie-making, it fell to eighteen-year-old Reg Hartt to become Rochdale's prime exhibitor. As early as 1968, Hartt had dabbled in movies by taking over the Queen Victoria Cinema at Asquith Avenue and Yonge Street (present site of the Metro Toronto Central Reference Library) and renamed it the Public Enemy. "Unfortunately, it was not a healthy choice of names for a film theatre, even though I was taking it from the James Cagney film. Most people didn't know what the heck the Cagney film was, and those were pre-punk days when you didn't use names like that. So it was kind of the death blow to the theatre.

"The first time I got involved with Rochdale was just after the building opened in the fall. I was still showing films at the Public

Enemy, but also using the theatre for seances. And somebody mentioned that Judy Merril had come to Rochdale and she was an authority on this stuff. So I went over there dressed in basic black—and several years later, she told me that I'd scared the tar out of her. Anyhow, I had a talk with Judy, who was then a resource person, and through her I met [Rochdale president] Peter Turner, who was engaged to her daughter, Ann Pohl."

Although the Rochdale connection had been established, Hartt was determined to remain a free agent. After spending a year showing movies at Ottawa's popular Le Hibou coffeehouse, he returned to Toronto, held a few film screenings at Rochdale and promptly hit the road again, only to return several months later.

"Back in Toronto, I ran into Peter Turner and he asked me what I was doing. I said I wasn't doing anything, so he said, 'Why don't you come to Rochdale and run the film program?' That was in the spring of 1970 and they gave me the second-floor cafeteria as a theatre. And even though there was no budget, I had complete freedom. I was answerable only to myself.

"It started with eight-millimetre films from my own collection—*The Cabinet Of Doctor Caligari* and things like that. Then, once the audience was built up and my own natural curiosity was going full gear, I made an arrangement with Universal Pictures for access to the complete library of their own films and the pre-1948 Paramount film library. I used that as the basis for my program for a long time.

"Pretty soon, posters were going up all over town, but I was asked to remove the Rochdale name. It seems the city was complaining about the posters being up around town, and Rochdale didn't want to deal with letters of complaint from the city. So I had to change it from Rochdale's name to my own name. But then people got angry and asked, 'What are you trying to do—trick people into coming to Rochdale?' You couldn't win.

"The audience, you'd think, would be young. Well, it was a spectrum—all ages. On one occasion, I was showing Marlene Dietrich in *Blonde Venus*, and the audience was partly from inside the building and partly from outside the building. And somebody starts passing a joint back and forth, back and forth. There's a bald-headed man sitting with his wife in the second-last row. And I'm watching that joint moving and wondering what's going to happen when it gets to him. Well, he takes it and tokes one long, long toke and passes it to the back row. You see, younger people in the building resented the intrusion of older people because they thought they were straight. But what I found in my own experience was that the older people tended to be a lot more hip."

While Rochdale's artistic experiments resulted in the creation of several long-lasting organizations, only one endeavour can be called a monument in the true sense of the word. That project was the Unknown Student, a massive statue that still sits on the spacious, concrete plaza at Bloor and Huron, in front of the building that was once known as Rochdale College. It remains the largest and most obvious example of the teamwork and craftsmanship that flourished during Rochdale's early years of promise.

The Unknown Student is a hulking, humanoid object that towers roughly ten feet from the ground at its highest point. Smooth, naked, beefy and bald, it depicts a faceless individual (its sex is open to debate) sitting cross-legged and hunched over, with its arms wrapped around its knees and its navel-gazing head tucked down to its crotch. Although coloured to resemble weathered bronze, the sculpture is actually made of highly durable plastic.

The idea of building some sort of statue was suggested in October, 1968, by Ed Apt, the resource person who headed Rochdale's six-member sculpture workshop. After considering several proposals and voting by secret ballot, the group chose the design by Derek Heinzerling, a twenty-two-year-old draft resister from Fort William, Indiana. "I'm still surprised every time I see the sculpture out there on the street," Heinzerling told *The Toronto Star* when the statue was unveiled in April, 1969. "People go up and pat it and get happy. When I designed it, I was unhappy and discouraged. I could never do anything like that any more, because I'm not so discouraged now.

"The way the sculpture got its name was really beautiful. We were sitting in the Rochdale cafeteria and we showed the drawing to this guy—he was pretty unhappy. I think he just got out of the hospital. He said it looked like the unknown student. The sculpture suddenly became meaningful to me."

Apt's group spent long hours in a Rochdale workshop on nearby Dupont Street, where they built a clay figure that served as the basis for a plaster mold. Strapped for funds, they even coaxed a number of industrial firms to donate $2,000 worth of materials to the project. After four months of intensive labour, the

Unknown Student was proudly lowered onto a concrete pedestal in front of Rochdale. It was a symbol not only of the practical results that idealists could achieve, but of the ability of artistic visionaries to co-operate with the outside community.

In another nod to symbolism, the sculpture was positioned in such a way that its back faced Bloor Steet. This conveyed to startled passersby the none-too-subtle message that Rochdale was contemptuously baring its buttocks to the rest of straight society. More than likely, the statue was placed so that residents on the north side of the building could enjoy the sight of the figure's placid, contemplative head. Still, the pose seemed sufficiently haughty and offensive that when Metropolitan Toronto later bought and renovated the building, the Unknown Student was turned to face the street.

C H A P T E R 5

Stoned
Soul
Picnic

No matter what bizarre turns the mind took at Rochdale, the body still had to be fuelled—and that meant availability of a wide variety of foods and food services. Indeed, this cornucopia was a major factor in creating an aura of self-sufficiency, and it greatly enhanced Rochdale's image as a fully independent community. After all, why trouble oneself with the hassles of a cold, unfeeling city if spiritual and physical sustenance could both be found under a single roof?

For the first two years, the second-floor cafeteria supplied many of the residents' nutritional needs through a fee structure that linked rent with food. In some cases, the cafeteria was also opened to resource people whose services as educators or instructors were exchanged for food and lodging. Greg MacDonald, who began in 1969 as one of the workers and eventually became co-ordinator of the cafeteria, remembers being "scrutinized every day by the health department because they wondered how these long-haired people could possibly have a clean operation. You know, if you had long hair and sandals, you were supposedly a dirty, filthy hippie. That was the stereotype. And precisely because of that, the place was kept spotless. Otherwise, they would have shut us down.

"I grew up in Springhill, Nova Scotia. Anne Murray's father delivered me. My family moved around constantly, to the point where it was a joke after a while.

"Finally we ended up in Boston. I had two older brothers who both went into the military. And when they got out on leave, they said, 'This ain't no John Wayne movie. It sucks. You don't know who's who, who's what, who's bad. It's a fucking joke.' So I remember seeing an article in a magazine that showed a bunch of hippies hanging out in Yorkville. It said 'Toronto, Canada' and I forget what the caption was. So I said, 'Wow, man. I'm Canadian! I would really like Toronto.'

"And this was also the time when everybody was coming to Canada to avoid the draft. But I never really could be classified as a draft dodger, so I went in 1968. I bought a plane ticket and was stopped at the border. They took me into a little room and started hassling me and I went through the whole third degree. They opened up my baggage, and all I had in there was albums, a couple of pairs of socks and some underwear—mostly albums. So they took it for granted I was a draft dodger. I said, 'Wait a minute! I'm here to visit my cousin. Look, I'm a Canadian coming back home.' And three guys look at each other and go, 'He's Canadian! Didn't anybody ask what the hell he was?' So they let me go.

"The first thing I did was hop in a cab and look for a hotel. So this driver gave me the around-the-world tour, and we ended up at the Spadina Hotel. So I go in and spent one night in there. You could hear the ladies of the night working over their clients in the next room. And I thought, 'Oh, God! What am I into now?'

"So the next day, there was a concert happening at the Rock Pile at Yonge and Davenport. I went there and bingo! Hippies everywhere—getting high, having fun. Frank Zappa and the Mothers of Invention were playing and I had a great time. And I met all kinds of people, so I asked, 'Where's a great place to hang out?' And a guy says, 'Rochdale, man. Rochdale's where it's at.' So I went to Rochdale.

"I get to Rochdale in October of 1968 and I'm there for three days and nights and I completely lost all track of time. I partied all the time I was there and met all kinds of people. They had lounges and Ashrams where you could hang out, and it was a twenty-four hour city anyway. At the end of it there, it was like 'What day is it?' But nobody wore watches and it didn't really matter what day it was. One day kind of ran into the other and I never saw the sun because I never left the building.

"So on the third day, I said to myself, 'This is weird, man. I gotta just go outside for a little while. I gotta touch reality here.' So I walked out, saw the sunshine and then walked right back in.

"I had to find housing, so I went to the University of Toronto and looked up the housing lists. I ended up living at 76 Admiral Road in a fully furnished basement apartment for $15 a week. But because I was visiting Rochdale all the time, eventually I moved into Rochdale in November of 1968 on the sixth floor. I started working in the cafeteria and I eventually ran the cafeteria. I became the cafeteria co-ordinator.

"Our cook was a guy named Wu and his food was excellent.

You had your choice of meat or vegetarian meals–part of the natural style that spread throughout the whole building. Eventually, the cafeteria became a sort of focal spot, but not like the council meetings where people were always arguing. In the cafeteria we usually enjoyed the lighter side of life, the fun side.

"Wu himself was quite a striking person in a physical sense, because he was tall and lean and very intense. He served thirty-two different kinds of teas and sixty-four different kinds of jam. And he was very much of a Zen type of person–a great guy to work for."

"Rochdale actually changed the burger experience," says resident Carol Shevlin. "You couldn't walk in and just order a hamburger. They'd say, 'Okay, we have whole wheat buns, pumpernickel buns, bran buns, seven-grain buns'–no white buns, of course. And for God's sake, don't order the tea or you'd never make a decision."

Still, not everyone held the cafeteria in high esteem. Even now, Judith Merril pales at the thought of Wu, "who was a complete and absolute vegetarian, and cooked some of the most disgusting vegetarian food I have ever seen. He did have to compromise, though, and put in hamburgers fairly early in one corner. And then they redesigned the cafeteria with a downstairs and an upstairs. The upstairs was the insiders' vegetarian thing, and the downstairs was for anyone to come in and have hamburgers and popcorn and chips and all those things."

Since the cafeteria was generally reserved for residents, it was only natural that an open-to-everyone restaurant should emerge as part of Rochdale's self-contained community. Housed in a street-level space opening onto Bloor, it originally went by the name of the Same Twenty-Four-Hour Restaurant and eventually evolved into Etherea Natural Foods.

Stan Bevington, founder of Coach House Press, preferred the earlier version, if only for its striking appearance. "Ken Dahl, who was a graphic designer at Coach House, did the design for the restaurant and he did a fabulous high-tech thing, years before anyone knew about high-tech. It was incredible! Out of key clamps–that's steel pipes–he made monkey-bar shapes that were classic restaurant booths, with perforated steel seats, glass table tops and metallized mylar forming rough booths. It was a great construction. The menu was printed with all the ingredients in the kitchen and it listed what each one cost in portions that were realistic to make.

"Unfortunately, the environment was so strange that it was unfairly blamed for many of the problems in the restaurant. So when Etherea came in later, they cleaned it up and tried to make it look and feel organic. They threw out all that high-tech stuff and replaced it with wood—a real backwards move. If that restaurant were there now, it would be a real trend-setter."

More often than not, the restaurant's problems revolved around cleanliness. "Sanitation wasn't one of their high priorities," says Toronto health inspector Jim Flaherty, "but that's not to say anything against the preparation of the food or that they were using dirty dishes. The problem was that they stored a lot of grains and they weren't too high on keeping away weevils and things like that. And you couldn't put the arm on anyone, because you'd never see the same person twice. I'd ask, 'Who owns this place?' And they'd say, 'We all own it.' So I'd say, 'Who's the president?' And they'd say, 'Aw, we don't have that stuff, man.' "

Rochdale was also home to several illegal, unlicensed operations that, in the spirit of free enterprise, catered to a market whose needs were not otherwise being met. One of the most successful and profitable was the weekend pizza business based in Walt Houston's apartment from about 1969 to 1971. "The Pizza Pizza across the street hadn't been built yet," recalls Houston, "so there was no close pizza delivery in the area—certainly nothing within several blocks. But Rochdale people had a very strong tendency to not want to go out of the building, and they usually had the munchies. So we set up shop right there.

"It was a lot of work making pizza from scratch—making the sauce and the crusts and slicing all the vegetables fresh. But it was worth it, because it helped support me and pay my way in the building. We were doing deliveries by hand in the building and we just had the business going on Friday, Saturday and Sunday nights. We usually sold fifty to seventy-five pizzas a night.

"Some time in the winter of 1970–71, the New York Times had a reporter wander through the building and he noticed several of the more unusual things that were going on, including the pizza operation. So he wrote an article about us. And about a day or so later, the board of health and a bunch of other people descended on the building looking for these businesses that were listed. And, of course, it was absolutely impossible to find them because they broke down and turned into ordinary apartments and kitchenette areas when we were done. There was absolutely no trace of them."

Keeping the body fed was child's play, compared with keeping it healthy—especially in an environment that condoned or encouraged a permissive attitude toward sex and drugs. But within months of the building's opening, the Rochdale Free Clinic had already swung into operation. Its founder was eighteen-year-old Ann Pohl, the daughter of American science-fiction writers Frederik Pohl and Judith Merril. Although raised in the U.S., she attended school in England until 1967, followed by six months' employment in a German hospital.

"I returned to the States in January or February of 1968 and went to live in New York and got active in an integrated, community-based theatre company.

"I eventually became second-in-command of the art department for New York State for Eugene McCarthy. And since we were so well organized, we were asked to do his art for the Chicago Democratic Convention. We turned out two thousand posters—of which about five hundred were hand-lettered—and they were supposed to go in the convention hall or be used outside. But when we got there, we discovered the people in charge wouldn't permit any of our posters in the hall. Mayor Daley, who was the chairman, had made a ruling that nobody could bring in posters on sticks because there was too much danger of the delegates and the alternates hitting each other over the head. In the end, we printed 'Stop the War' on pieces of fabric and distributed them. And they were very effectively used on the floor of the convention hall.

"I was actually there for the police riot, but luckily, I wasn't injured. When we got out to the street, most of the bloody part of the thing was over. I got gassed a couple of times, but they weren't beating people up any more by the time we managed to surface from the hotel and get out there to see what was going on.

"I moved from New York back to Millford, Pennsylvania, the small town I'd once lived in. I didn't have any family there and I had hardly any friends because I'd been in Europe for so many years. I worked in a diner for two or three weeks—until one morning, I woke up and just couldn't go to work. I had this long argument with myself about whether I should join the Weather underground resistance or not. I very clearly remember coming to the conclusion that I was too young to decide that that was the way to change society. And that gave me no alternative but to leave the country.

"So I took the first bus I could get and I came to Toronto in

December of 1968, because my mother was already living here in Rochdale.

"I wasn't planning to stay at Rochdale for very long, because I had always thought I might go to nursing school. When I was in New York, I supported myself by working as a nurse's aide. And in England I completed the entrance requirements and was actually accepted to nursing school. But that fell by the wayside, because I got involved trying to set up the free clinic at Rochdale.

"I started the clinic because a lot of young people were coming to Rochdale and nobody was prepared to help them deal with their drug problems or the problems of sexual disease. There was already a group called the Trailer operating in Yorkville at the time, and some of their people lived in Rochdale. They had an office where they answered medical questions, but it was hardly ever open. It was run like a regular office and they had visiting hours on maybe two days a week.

"First I started as a volunteer for them and then realized that the way they were running the place really wasn't suited to Rochdale. So eventually, I identified an alternative type of service that suited Rochdale and I took the proposal to the council. There was a big argument because the Trailer people thought they were doing what needed to be done and that I was supplanting them unnecessarily. But council decided it was more interested in my idea of a clinic and gave me a letter offering employment—just what I needed to leave the United States. I went back to the States and packed up my stuff and immigrated in March of 1969."

Armed with a $1,000 council grant, Pohl (newly nicknamed Aunty Flo in reference to Florence Nightingale) opened her clinic (also dubbed Aunty Flo's Parlour) that very March. Additional support was later provided by the federal Opportunities For Youth program—resulting in 6,000 visits to the clinic (5,000 of them by non-residents) during the first year.

"We had a room of our own and council gave us the money for medical supplies. The day I opened, this guy showed up—Michael Bilger, who had been a deserter and trained as a medic. He and I lived in the clinic and operated it, taking turns working there on a twenty-four-hour-a-day basis, seven days a week.

"There wasn't much work to it. It was quite easy, really. We treated everything, but mostly drug problems and sexually transmitted diseases of one kind or another. The public health department also used to come by and give us a list of names of people they couldn't track down in the building. So we'd put up the list in the elevator and ask people to come to the clinic to be treated for the sexually transmitted diseases.

"As far as drugs went, it was either speed—which you couldn't do much about, except to tell people not to do it—or a lot of psychological problems that resulted from taking LSD or mescaline or one of the other hallucinogenics. I spent a lot of time talking people down off drugs, but there were never any values attached to the work that we were doing. It was just—'Okay, you've got this problem, so let's deal with it.' "

Most often, it was drug cases that came to the attention of clinic workers, who took a firm but sensitive approach, even in the most difficult circumstances. "There was this dance teacher named Waldo," remembers resident Horst. "One time, he did too much acid and he went down to the clinic for the millionth time to get some valium. But the clinic people said, 'Look, Waldo, we've told you again and again, no valium.' Waldo says, 'Nope, I'm not leaving this chair 'til I get some valium.'

"So a couple of the clinic workers picked up the chair and put him out in the stairwell facing the wall. A while later, I went by and there was Waldo muttering and complaining about the filth in the stairwell and how it was so close to a medical facility. So he took out a matchbook and began to scrape the dirt off the floor. After several hours, he managed to clear about a three-square-foot area. And he spent the entire night in that stairwell, just scraping away."

Aberrant behaviour was most familiar to Dr. Bryn Waern, who lived at Rochdale from late 1968 until early 1971 and returned to work there in 1973 and 1974. Her brother, Rick Waern, had helped to get Rochdale going in 1968 and it seemed obvious to him that Bryn's skills could be put to good use in the new community. She had already graduated from the University of Toronto medical school and was beginning a residency at the Clarke Institute of Psychiatry in the fall of 1968. The timing seemed perfect and Waern accepted her brother's invitation.

"Since I was available for emergency work, I'd get called in the middle of the night and go down to find police standing in front of somebody's apartment. But instead of going in, they'd ask me to check on the person—do an assessment and come out and tell them if everything was okay. So I'd go in, tell the police whatever it was I saw, and they'd usually go away.

"I mostly encountered the human and emotional garbage—the overdosing and the despair—and I committed about a dozen

Rochdale people in the first two-and-a-half years I was there. I had an arrangement with the Queen Street Mental Health Centre that if I committed somebody, they would take the person in and not give us any flak over it. But committing people was not something I did lightly, especially in a tolerant place like Rochdale. By the time we as a community couldn't tolerate certain people, that was about as extreme a situation as you could get. So I never had any problems or opposition from people at Rochdale about committing someone. By that point, it was just way beyond what could be tolerated.

"But on the whole, Rochdale was a very caring community—much more so than in regular society. For instance, one of my neighbours in Rochdale had been hospitalized a couple of times with schizophrenic episodes, and when he got sick, people at Rochdale would take care of him. We would literally set up a therapeutic community. And there would be a list, where different people would take care of him at different times of the day. This person is now a businessman—a really successful, thriving person—because he got our help and was finally able to leave all that stuff behind.

"And that was not an isolated thing. That happened continually. There were people in Rochdale who went through a lot of identity crises of one sort or another. Many of them were refugees from the Vietnam war, and the anguish that they were going through required a lot of healing. So Rochdale was a real therapeutic community in that sense. It's not that it was a loony-bin as such, but it allowed people to go through the healing process without locking them away or institutionalizing them."

For Dr. Ty Turner, the eye-opener was Rochdale's revolutionary methods in treating victims of drug overdoses. He had already graduated from Queen's University in Kingston and was just beginning his internship at St. Michael's Hospital in 1971, when the notion of volunteering at Rochdale occurred to him.

"I was a fairly idealistic young physician wanting not just to help individual patients but to have some effect on the greater system of things. I was looking for something else to do besides being an intern and working hard in hospitals in a relatively orthodox way. And because we were in an institutional setting at St. Mike's, we tended not to get to know our patients very well. What also bothered me was that the patients were on our turf—not us on theirs. So I volunteered for duty and showed up about once every two weeks for about six months from late 1971 to early 1972.

"The first thing that struck me about the clinic was how relaxed it was. Remember that I'd been doing emergency work at a hospital, so it seemed incredibly relaxed. First of all, there was nobody at the front entrance asking for your OHIP number and your address and your next of kin—the kind of stuff that tends to get you all keyed up. Second, the lights were low. Third, there was attention to colour, texture and tone. It had the effect of tranquillizing. People spoke in smooth, modulated, laid-back ways. It was my first experience with this kind of thing in a health care setting, having been used to a pretty fast-paced, tense cadence.

"There was also a lot of staff for the number of patients who came through. The staff were generally untrained volunteers, and they were sympathetic, empathetic people who had an orientation towards healing. And there was a keen sense of egalitarianism. Just because I was a doctor with an MD or just because a nurse had an RN, that didn't set us above the other staff. However, it was recognized there were certain things only we could do, such as prescribe medication, order tests or refer to specialists.

"The kind of treatment I remember most vividly was treating people with bad reactions to drugs. By bad reactions I mean agitation, panic, paranoia and depression. And I recall seeing some pretty seriously disturbed people. The drugs were acid, some speed, some peyote and mescaline, and always alcohol and marijuana. I don't recall ever running into heroin or cocaine. It was mainly hallucinogenics, marijuana and alcohol.

"The people who came in were generally not residents. I think they were coming to Rochdale for recreation. They'd be escorted to the clinic by two or three other people, often with their arms around them. And there would be almost no processing to enable billing, identification or getting the old chart. And there was also relatively little of the clinical processing like the history and physical examination. Basically, the non-medical staff would look at the patient, ask a few questions, take a history from the person and the escorts, and they would make the diagnosis. My role as a physician was relatively minimal because the emphasis was not on giving medication. It was on bringing the person down, and they had some innovative ways of doing that that didn't need medication.

"The person was taken into another room that was quiet and the lights were low. I remember it had a lot of browns and grays. It didn't have a lot of pictures in it, because if you're hallucinating, you don't want bright, vivid pictures. And I recall that people would sit on the floor on a lot of cushions. There was also a stereo with music playing. And there was holding—the person was held and hugged when it seemed appropriate. And the part that I liked the most was the use of small, furry animals—live animals, particularly cats. It astounded me to see somebody who had been brought in with a panic reaction a few minutes before sitting in a corner in this room on a cushion with a pussycat in his or her lap, stroking it for maybe an hour or so. The healing emphasis was on reducing stimulation to the person's overwrought nervous system. And I remember only on rare occasions having to prescribe medication.

"This was a startling contrast to what happens in a hospital's emergency department—a lit room with lots of noise, people coming in and slapping stethoscopes on and tightening blood-pressure cuffs around the arm and putting thermometers in body cavities. Then the doctor comes along and asks a lot of rote questions and once again applies the cold stethoscope to the patient's skin. The emphasis in an emergency department is on dispatch and alacrity—getting things going and giving an injection. It was certainly nowhere near as esthetic an approach as the one used at Rochdale College."

By all accounts, there were very few beyond Rochdale's walls who felt that warmth or made the effort to understand the motives of its founders and inhabitants. And so, much to the residents' dismay, a key element of day-to-day life at Rochdale became the attempt to convey a more presentable image of the building to relatives, friends, neighbours, professional colleagues, politicians and police.

In a few instances, Rochdale won the unexpected but welcome allegiance of respected celebrities such as Pierre Berton. "I thought the police were very hard on the Rochdale kids," says the writer and broadcaster whose daughters Pamela and Patsy spent time in Rochdale. "It simply became a political football. People like that opportunist Tony O'Donohue were using it for no particular reason.

"I defended Rochdale in print on one particular occasion, because the police came in without a 'by your leave' and smashed stuff up and took kids into jail without any real reason for it. I just thought the police were using Rochdale to cover themselves for a lot of things that were happening which weren't the fault of Rochdale at all. There was a lot of drug dealing going on elsewhere, but Rochdale was the easiest target."

Opinions such as these earned Berton the enmity of many police officers who, to this day, roll their eyes and curse vehemently at the mention of his name. O'Donohue, too, still believes Berton caused untold damage in painting an unrealistically benign picture of Rochdale. "He was the most depressing one of all," says O'Donohue. "I remember being sucked into the CBC once to discuss Rochdale. And lo and behold, Pierre Berton was sitting there. Anyway, in the course of defending the place, he says to me, 'I have a daughter in Rochdale.' And I say to him, 'Mr. Berton, I don't think I would let my son go into Rochdale.' And he says, 'If your son were in Rochdale, I'd take my daughter out.'"

Not only did Berton defend his daughter's way of life, but it was he who originally planted the idea in Pamela's mind. "I was at school in Switzerland in 1968," she says, " and I was going through university brochures. I think my father sent me the application forms for Rochdale and I liked them because they weren't boring, while all the other application forms were seriously bureaucratic. This was really fun, and it was the application form, more than anything else, that made me think this might be an interesting thing to do."

"No, I had no misgivings," Berton says firmly. "I encouraged Pamela to move in because the University of Toronto is a great big place and I thought she'd be lost. I would never go to a university that big, and I thought it would be much better for her if she went to a small college. And that one interested her. I had no reticence and I still don't because she got something out of it.

"I may not have been typical of many parents, but she wasn't typical either. I think she was the only member of Rochdale College who wore a print dress and kept her hair combed all the time. I remember she told me once that she was in the elevator in December and she told someone she was going home for Christmas. And they said, 'To your family?' She said, 'Yeah.' And they said, 'My God, why would you go home to your family?' That was the attitude.

"I didn't worry about my kids, because they had a good background and a good upbringing and we never had any problems with any of them. We had no generation gap. If they wanted to go to Rochdale, fine! It turned out Patsy didn't even like Rochdale. It wasn't her bag. But Pamela was on the student council for a while, and I thought they were doing some pretty interesting things. I don't think it had any effect—bad or good—on Pamela. She just breezed through it as if it were a regular school. And of all our kids, she's probably the least off-the-wall."

Justine Darling was among the chosen few—the young children who lived in Rochdale with their parents. So, in her case, the kid-glove treatment was reserved for grandparents. "My grand mother told me a few years ago about the time she came in to visit us from New York. She was coming in from the airport by cab and the driver was going on about this place in Toronto where everybody was jumping out the windows and smoking and hanging out. And when she tells him where she's going, he says, 'Lady, that's the place I was talking about.' "

"My parents were coming up to visit," continues Justine's mother, Lorraine, "and I had made arrangements for them to stay in the empty apartment next door that belonged to people who had gone away for Christmas. And I told them, 'Listen, if the fire alarm goes off, don't be afraid. It's not a fire. It's only a police raid. So don't be scared.' They looked at me kinda funny and just said, 'Oh.' You see, I was trying to keep it from them that there was all this smokin' going on. But people kept pouring into the apartment and sitting in the kitchen and pulling out some joints. But the folks took that pretty well.

"That night, my mother came over to our apartment to use the washroom. I said, 'Mom, there's a washroom in the apartment where you're staying.' And she said, 'But I don't want to disturb the men who are sleeping there.' And I said, 'What men?' So I went over there and the tenants had come back and were actually sitting there and planning a dope run, with my parents in the apartment. I said, 'Geez, guys. I thought you were gone.' It did look pretty funny—my mother so humble, shuffling over to my apartment to use the washroom because she didn't want to disturb these characters who were planning a dope run."

Reaction to Rochdale was sometimes so hostile that just the suggestion that someone had visited the building carried a degree of notoriety. While still living with her parents in the Toronto suburb of Don Mills, Sandra Littler paid an occasional visit to Rochdale—a lark that even her classmates found questionable. "Everyone in my classes knew about Rochdale, but not very many actually went down there—a small percentage, a very small percentage. Everybody in Toronto knew about it, all the young people. It's just that a lot of people thought it was a scary place.

"So people at school completely ostracized me. Well, that's not completely true, because I'd just started to meet a small bunch of people at school who were really different—all ages and degrees of mental stability. But a lot of people in the suburbs were carrying on and going to university and this and that, and I was just tripping out.

On the other hand, Rochdale's relations with its immediate neighbours usually proved comparatively benign. Around the corner and a few steps away on Huron Street sat St. Thomas's Anglican Church, where Rev. Edgar Bull made a special effort to open the lines of communication and co-operation. "Much to the consternation of the Church authorities," he recalls, "I allowed a Rochdale meditation group to come in and use our lower-level chapel, which was carpeted but had no chairs in it. That often meant that our choir people would come in for their practice and find a lot of strangely dressed people lying on their backs by candlelight going, 'Ommmmm.'

"But everybody was searching for a faith or a religion or a meaning for life in that crazy, mixed-up world. And I thought that St. Thomas might be one of the places to do that. It was and is a High Church with a lot of ceremonial ritual and so on, but I felt the young people should be there because they were searching for something.

"I guess I was fairly liberal-minded about that. One could have said, 'Hey, let's see your membership and are you an orthodox Christian, and an Anglican to boot?' But I didn't ask that. If these people were searching for some kind of spiritual centre for their lives and were exploring the whole realm of transcendental meditation, I thought it was fine to give them a space to keep exploring."

Not surprisingly, Rochdale became a lightning rod for newspaper reporters and broadcasters. This high-rise community was a writer's dream, since its activities could be used to support or refute any conceivable argument about sex, drugs, music, protest or any aspect of the younger generation. The inevitable result was a good deal of misinformation and false or misleading impressions.

"Shortly after the building opened," remembers Judith Merril, "we agreed to let a camera crew from CTV come in to film Rochdale. But there was one condition—it had to be done naturally, with no fake set-ups or moving people around or unnatural lighting or anything like that. CTV agreed, but that's not what actually happened. The crew moved in and started putting us in all sorts of posed shots, and we resented it. So we fought back. We quickly made these signs that we held up in spots that they were shooting. The signs said something like, 'Motherfucking TV men, go away! This is my home!'

"In that same period, our council passed a resolution that no further publicity would be allowed unless Rochdale was paid. If people wanted to come in there and do things for their newspapers and magazines and TV stations, they had to pay a fee. About two days after this resolution was passed, while we were all still hot and happy about it, a man came in from *Time* magazine and said he wanted to do a story. He said he thought it could even be a cover story. So we said, 'How much are you willing to pay?' This guy jumped up and said, 'We don't have to pay the president of the United States! Why should we have to pay you? I don't need your permission! I can go and talk to anybody here!' And we said, 'That's right. You can go and talk to anybody who'll talk to you. And you'll always be wondering how accurate the information is.' "

"Rochdale at its worst point was thoroughly a media creation," grumbles Peter Turner, a former Berkeley student and Eugene McCarthy activist, who left the United States in dismay after witnessing the 1968 police riot at the Chicago Democratic Convention. "Certainly, Rochdale itself existed, but the media helped it to exist because they focused on problems when they were very small. And in that focusing, they created an image for us—that is, that we were a major haven for drug dealers. By the time they were finished, we were exactly that, because people were attracted to the image they created."

"Rochdale was not, in people's eyes, controlled by anything that was familiar to them," believes former mayor David Crombie. "One of the great themes of Toronto politics always has been order. I don't mean law and order only, but there has to be a sense of appropriateness, a sense that it's okay for something to happen, even if you don't like it. There's an amazing amount of tolerance that comes with that. But in Rochdale's case, it was beyond the pale of Torontonians' understanding. I think it was the fear of a new generation not marching to familiar tunes."

"I suppose it's in what you perceive," adds health inspector Wayne Pollock. "If you were a clean-freak and you saw a paper tissue on the street, that would be a pile of rubbish. In the same way, older people weren't used to seeing so many young people together, with beads and bandannas and walking around with sloppy jeans dragging along on the ground and dirty bare feet. These would be rather bizarre people to them."

Sometimes, says Paul Evitts, a direct but peaceful confrontation with the community at large yielded unexpected results—especially the debate with the Toronto Board of Trade. "The Board of Trade set it up, and they got some of what they believed to be hotshots from the Junior Board of Trade to come out—their best speakers—to debate various issues with us in 1969. I think the intention was basically to just wipe us all out. We had Jim Garrard and Jack Jones, who had been a senior vice-president at an ad agency and knew how to deal with things in public. And there was John Bradford, who was Jesuit-trained, and an Indian chief, as well. So we had our side covered off fairly well.

"Halfway through, the debate was obviously not going favourably for the Junior Board of Trade guys. I happened to be in the can, and the guy who, I guess, was the president of the real Board of Trade came in. We both stood next to each other at urinals. And finally he said, 'You guys are killing us. You're fantastic. If you want to come and join the Board of Trade, just give me a call.' He was serious!

"And that sort of summarized Rochdale for me. Despite the bullshit and the chaos and so on, we managed to bring together a lot of bright, sensitive, creative people who tried a lot of things. A lot of it fucked up, but there were a lot of opportunities for individuals to grow. And I think a lot of things came out of that, which are just starting to have some impact today."

C H A P T E R 6

Love
the One
You're With

Rochdale's planners attempted to establish a harmonious balance between the various elements that would comprise the total entity. Full-time Rochdale students, resource people, students attending other schools, committed people from the outside community, all had their place in the theoretical scheme of things.

Historically, the seniority position belonged to the "old Rochdalians." The term comes to us from Kent Gooderham, a forty-two-year-old scholar who moved his family of seven into a Zeus (two bedroom) in September, 1969, in order to conduct an anthropological study of The Rock, entitled *Come Live With Us*. Gooderham wrote, "The politics and the economics of the building were controlled by a small group of people who had lived in the building since it was first built. Many of them were former University of Toronto students who had conceived of the idea of a free university a year or more before the building was started. I name them the 'old Rochdalians.' For them the idea of the college came before the building and their prime motivation was for the welfare of Rochdale the college. It was the old Rochdalians who controlled the council. They ran the projects (Theatre Passe Muraille, the Indian Institute), which received financial support in the way of salaries and grants. They walked through the halls with a proprietary air. After all, it was their idea. And it was a good idea until successive waves of 'heads' moved into the building and succeeded in fucking up the whole deal. The political hassles involving the selling or retaining of the building were of deep concern to the old Rochdalians. It was not a matter of moment for the other residents. There was a real difference between the 'oldtimers' and the 'newcomers.' There was a real nucleus of avid council meeting attenders but for the vast majority of the people living in Rochdale, the council and its activities were of little or no interest."

Counted in with the old Rochdalians like Jack Dimond, Rick Waern and Ian MacKenzie were the college's "resource people." Committed to the educational ideal of the college were teachers like Australian-born Philip McKenna, a thirty-four-year-old Dominican priest who held seminars on religious languages, Hegel, Violence and Institutions, and Theology; and Brewster Kneen, a theologian and freelance producer who preached the "gospel of involvement." The resource people came to Rochdale via the educational route, a route that according to Sarah Spinks involved "the concept of mastering certain books and philosophies, which was alien to the new Rochdale residents. Their orientation was toward the sensual, bodily kinds of activities. The projects that gathered and kept them were the creative arts—batiking, photography. It was reflective, unfrenzied work, but it did not require some experience in the world. The older people involved in the project shared this need to be reflective, but the gap of some ten years between them and the kids had meant that they had experienced and reacted to a non-reflective society in a different way. They hated their high schools and universities, too, with their fragmentation of knowledge, six subjects/six exams. They hated the image of the tough, competent businessman or lawyer that they were expected to emulate, but they were unlike the Yorkville and Rochdale kids, in a twilight zone between their parents (who remembered the Depression so vividly) and the teenagers (who were hitch-hiking to pop festivals all across the country). Instead of joining a business or smoking grass, these people devoted themselves to a pursuit of truth and they chased it with the same rigorous competence that businessmen twenty years ago had built their businesses. Unspoken but clear messages transmitted themselves to the stoned kids around them—most resource people expected intellectual rigor and competence."

Connected to the old Rochdalians and resource people through their belief in the Rochdale alternative way of life and radical overthrow of conventional thought and lifestyle were the "hippies," the social activists and street radicals like Paul Evitts. Most of the activists who played a vital role in helping establish Rochdale College came from the streets of Toronto. Some, like Nelson Adams, travelled from other parts of Canada.

The majority of Rochdale's population came from the ranks of the "regular students," post-secondary students attending degree-granting institutions in Toronto (University of Toronto, Ryerson Polytechnical Institute, the Ontario College of Art). In this segment of Rochdale's population there were two basic approaches and responses to the Rochdale experience. Students like Pamela Berton embraced the multi-faceted, albeit chaotic, lifestyle and education experiment. They participated in some classes and in general took an active part in the college's political, economic and social life.

At the polar opposite were the college's equivalent of Richard Nixon's "Silent Majority." These students didn't really belong to Rochdale College. They were involved in Rochdale the student residence. They didn't subscribe to any of the ideals of the college or the Revolution. Their primary interest was in adequate accommodation close to classes. They, by and large, hated Rochdale's noise, filth, drugs and fire alarms going off at all hours. As a residence, Rochdale got a resounding "E" from these students.

John Dalton (not his real name), an engineering student at the nearby University of Toronto, recalls his stay at Rochdale: "This one incident I'll always remember. To me it symbolizes what was wrong with that nuthouse, although through the years I've grown to hate it less than I did at the time. Trying to be a regular student in that place was just about impossible.

"Anyway, this one fall morning I had gotten up to do some studying early, getting ready for a big test or something. I was sitting by my desk looking out of the window. Rochdale really did have a great location and view of the city. Below me was this scene right out of a postcard—city ablaze in autumnal colours, that sort of thing. It must have been around seven in the morning.

"Suddenly, shattering this moment of silence, I hear these incredible whoops and yells—it sounded like a herd of fuckin' banshees. I rushed to the door, looked out, and there, banging on pots and whistling and carrying on, is this group of people—about three or four guys and a couple of girls. They're painted like Indians (that Indian motif was really big back then). They were definitely blotto on some sort of mind drug.

"I didn't do much about it—something like a general, 'Hey keep it down.' I just gritted my teeth and took it. Maybe that was my problem. But you see what I mean—seven in the morning and there's a goddam LSD party going on while you're trying to study.

"I really didn't feel like uprooting myself and moving. If it had gotten any worse I would have. So I hung in through until the end of the school year. But I tell ya that I didn't feel any guilt at all when I skipped out on my last couple months' rent. Why should I?

The place, when you add it all up, was a rip-off. Always screwing up the food—you should have seen the days of the TV dinners. I haven't touched one since my Rochdale days. Laundry, phone, elevators, you name it, there was a screwup. So me and a bunch of other guys from the U of T just split without paying the last couple of months. I mean what were they going to do? Report us to the university? They didn't care, Rochdale wasn't even a part of the university."

"There was a group of students," says Peter Turner, "who were just that—students. Ordinary students who moved in because they were simply looking for a place to live. They weren't part of the co-op or the free university. They didn't participate, they were essentially 'filler.' This new part of the population didn't have any of the previous history of Rochdale, they had not experienced it, nor really cared about it for that matter."

In the winter of 1968–69, Paul Evitts removed the front door lock. It was a symbolic act of defiance that would have long-lasting consequences for the fledgling college.

"I always thought one of the key early things that happened at Rochdale," says Jim Garrard, "was in 1968 when Paul Evitts wanted to take the lock off the front door. That meant that there wasn't any way of saying, 'There's enough people in here now, so let's close the doors,' or 'You can't come in unless you have a key.' Anyone could come in and there were thousands and thousands of people who wanted to pay a visit to Rochdale."

Paul Evitts replies, "I was a member of the governing council at that point. The first stage was actually a kind of battle between the forces that put the building up and those of us who got involved with the idea itself and tried to carry it through. I was a practicing anarchist, and the idea that we were going to have a lock on the front door struck me as beyond consideration, which now sounds very naive. So I single-handedly went downstairs when the building was up to about twelve or fourteen floors. There was a regular apartment lock on the front door. And the problem with this lock was it cut off access to the second floor, which was where all the educational and communal stuff was supposed to happen. And the lock stayed off the door for six months."

Once the lock was off, it was literally open house at 341 Bloor Street West. Anyone was free to come in off the street and wander about. This open-door policy immediately led to roving bands of drunken fraternity boys out on a Friday or Saturday night hoot, looking for "hippie action," and maybe punch out a long-hair or two, put them in their place. As annoying as that was, it would be nothing compared with the effects the Yorkville crashers would have. They descended like locusts, eating whatever they could pilfer, sleeping in closets, hallways, Ashram lounges, elevators.

Peter Turner, speaking to *Change* magazine in late 1969, described the effect the crashers were having on the Rochdale community by using the example of the thirteenth floor: "Thirteen had a 'community.' At the beginning of last year there were all these extremely enthusiastic people on thirteen. It was totally idealistic. There weren't really any hassles to be resolved. A few people had pets and they got adopted by everybody. And if a couple of people did things, others would come along and pitch in. And everybody would sit up until all hours.

"And then there started to be a lot of people crashing. It started in the middle of October. To the end of October, idealism prevailed to the extent that everybody agreed that the kitchen shouldn't be locked. Then it was decided that crashers couldn't take food from the kitchen. One group felt crashers were a group that had been rejected by society and must be helped. 'Society has failed. These are children; be friendly to them.' It was part of the raison d'être of Rochdale. Another group didn't want crashers because they thought they'd be detrimental to Rochdale. Crashers disrupted the whole community. You came in to eat breakfast in the morning and there were these ten bodies all stretched out on chesterfields.

"It was then decided that crashers would have to find places to sleep in people's rooms if they wanted to stay for the night. This was decided in the second week of November. But a lot of the crashers were 'speed freaks' who would just sit around for hours—just sitting—not making any attempt to involve themselves with the residents. So it was decided that crashers who were people's guests would be allowed, but people who just sat there would be kicked out. Then people started locking doors. . . ."

The crasher situation was not easily resolved. It wasn't a simple matter of evicting the intruders by sheer force. That's what the Establishment was all about, not Rochdale. Rochdale wrestled with a moral dilemma that would plague it, in one form or another, for all of its life.

Judith Merril maintains, "There were a number of things about the group ethos that were different from the outside world. One of them led to the biggest problem Rochdale had in that year, which was that you couldn't refuse a crasher who came looking for a place. You couldn't turn away someone who needed a place to stay in 1968–69. Of course, it was the year of the great youth migration across Canada. It was long-hair time–you could tell who your friends were by the length of their hair. Every long-haired kid who hit Toronto at the outskirts would wait until he saw another long-haired person, and he'd say, 'Where can I crash?' And that person would say, 'Rochdale.'

"By February of 1969, in a building that was designed for 850 rent-paying people, we had about 700 paying rent and a total of 1,500 people living there. So all the big news stories about maintenance problems, about trash and garbage and plumbing not working and the great myth that grew up about the elevators–about how we were working the elevators so they'd never work when the police came–well, nothing worked. And it was because everything was so vastly overused.

"It wasn't just people who needed a place to stay. It was pilgrims. All over North America, people were hearing about Rochdale, and those people you couldn't really turn away at all. These were people who wanted to come and stay for a while and then go back to Iowa or California or Vancouver or whatever and make it happen there. It was more likely, if I put someone up, to be someone from the States who was fairly political or who really had come to try to study what was happening at Rochdale. Everyone, though, was under thirty, mostly early twenties, some teens."

Matt Cohen jokes about being the college writer-in-residence, but he says, "I did do one official duty while I was there, which was to conduct the crasher survey.

"It turned out that I thought I knew more about them than I really did. The level of literacy was much, much lower than I had thought. I knew that most of these people were from Yorkville and I knew that they weren't just students or middle-class people looking for a break–which was the official Rochdale conception of all people. I knew these people were much different from that, but I didn't realize just how completely different they were. And that's because I'd always talked to them and never communicated with them in writing. I never realized just how bad their writing skills were. I think about half of them were functionally illiterate.

"It was also my opinion that 70 per cent of the crashers were addicted to one form or another of amphetamines. And certainly, ninety per cent were using some sort of drug heavily. So they were in a state of heavy fantasy, plus they were living in an institution which was, in itself, such a complete fantasy that it really encouraged people."

"Some of the crashers are good people," building General Manager Bernie Bomers told *Maclean's* magazine. "We've taken in about fifty and some of them work for their bed, like cleaning up. One has even started a crasher's industry: they make paper flowers in the second floor lounge. But at weekends we have had maybe 200, including kids from the suburbs in for kicks or to get dope or who think they can come here and get a quick lay. They have taken over at times, and then everyone you see in the public places is probably a crasher, some of them lying on the floor, dumping filth, dealing in dope, cranking up (injecting themselves with speed or methedrine) in washrooms, walking around making a noise, pulling fire alarms, just generally imposing."

This is how things looked from the crasher's point of view. Val R. was one of the hordes that tramped over to The Rock for shelter and a good time:

"I grew up in the west end of Toronto. Did the usual school thing until I was about seventeen, when I finally got booted out of school. It was the usual mid-Sixties scene—long hair (I had this really great pageboy cut). I came from your typical west-end immigrant family—the folks, they didn't understand shit about what was going down with me. Can't blame them but there was nothing happening there communication-wise. I took off for the bright lights of Yorkville.

"Once in the Village, I fell in with a bunch of LSD-eaters. They had this place downtown and we did a lot of doping over there. Just the regular village hang-out scene—goofing on the tourists and straights. I wasn't into any of that political bullshit—David Depoe, he was okay, so was this guy Blues—The Diggers, they tried to get things going, get the coppers off our back, but, hey, to tell you the truth, I didn't give a fuck about that political shit, you know what I mean? I was into my own thing—chicks and dope. Although I did get involved in the summer riots, mostly to get some shots in on the cops. Didn't get busted although some pals went down—they got something like ten dollars or two days.

"I don't remember my first time at The Rock—I must have been fucked up or something. But once I got in there, I was a regular. I fell in with this bunch—I forget the room—I think it was nine something. That was our base—sometimes there'd be a dozen freaks in there, piled on top of each other. The setup at The Rock was perfect for crashers—those lounges by the elevators—perfect, man, just perfect.

"There were all these real serious hippie types around. They'd give you a hard time—'This is private property and you are disruptive.' Generally we told them to fuck right off. Sometimes there'd be scuffles. They might throw us out—or ask us to leave is more like it—but we would just double back and come back a few hours later. We couldn't stay away.

"I hung out at The Rock till I guess it was February-March of '69—I don't know, time is a little vague. I knew if I stayed I would die or just totally fuck up my life."

The new Rochdalians came from the ranks of the working youth. Unlike the crashers, they at least carried their weight rent-wise. However, as Barry Zwicker points out, these new residents also changed the complexion of Rochdale. "The replacements for those who have left have been mostly young working men, typically high school drop-outs with $55-a-week jobs driving bakery trucks. The average age and level of education thus is dropping, as is the proportion of women students. The turnover has vitiated Rochdale in two ways, by downgrading its population and by robbing it of an effective collective memory, thereby lowering the level of intellectual exchange that does occur and stretching out the period Rochdalers arrive at a consensus on major problems."

The magnitude and the severity of the crashing problem comes into focus when you consider some of the numbers involved. Peter Turner estimates that during the year 1969, 100,000 people came through the doors of the college; of that figure he estimates 4,000 stayed for at least a month. One of Rochdale's sworn enemies, Alderman Tony O'Donohue, figured by his own count that on a normal weekend about 3,500 visitors streamed into 341 Bloor Street West. All this in a building designed to house 850 residents. Not surprisingly, the Rochdalians were not pleased.

Resident Joel Kerbel voiced his opinion in the February 5, 1969, edition of the *Daily*. "What can be done? I for one am not prepared to pay my rent and then turn the building over to crashers and freaks, needle and spoon users, greasers, bike gangs and suburbanites who come down like they were visiting a zoo. During a 4 a.m. tour of the building we found a total of six crashers in various storage closets, equipped with dishes, cutlery and food, courtesy of Rochdale. Some of them were very upset that anyone should 'dare' to hassle them. It was their right, they thought, to break the locks or doors and take whatever they wanted and crash here, forever."

Rochdale officially reacted to the crashers by holding an emergency general meeting in January, 1969, when the council barred crashers unless they were guests of a resident. The crashers, except those who didn't get involved in anything outside of their own drug habits, tried to assimilate themselves into Rochdale. They established a Crasher Co-op, whereby they were given Rochdale membership status and free meals in exchange for work hours. A Crasher's Workshop was held on February 9 on the second floor. The crashers, even as outsiders, felt they had a rightful place in Rochdale. Some of them even carried 'bona fide Crasher Cards' that read:

"I hereby declare myself to be a bona fide crasher. As crashers, we expect to seek community and seek participation with other Rochdale residents. I declare on one hand to beat any system Rochdale sets up for or over us, which we as crashers consider unfair, and on the other hand I recognize and respect Rochdale's imminent need to reduce crasher cost to nothing. I further agree not to make a mess for others to clean up, not to con people, and not to exploit people in any way. I declare my intent to respect Rochdale's need for economic survival and agree not to exploit others in any way or to be servile."

The strangest bedfellows of the Sixties had to be the hippies and the motorcycle gangs. The two groups certainly shared the solidarity that comes with being outcasts from mainstream society. From the hippies' point of view, a truly non-hypocritical society should embrace all, especially brother outlaws. Rochdale, like the Rolling Stones and the organizers of the Altamont Speedway concert where the Hell's Angels went on a violent killing spree in the name of security, would learn there was a price to pay for this association.

For the first two years of its existence, Rochdale was visited by local gangs like the Vagabonds, Satan's Choice, the Black Diamond Riders and the Para-Dice Riders, as well as out of town gangs from across Canada and the United States. In fact, the Detroit Renegades caused a commotion when they tried to recover some misplaced drugs in the building—residents ended up calling the police for help.

Like the street hippies, the bikers were squeezed out of York-ville where they controlled the drug trade. Dean Audley was part of the force that pressured the bike gangs out of Yorkville.

"We had confrontations with the bikers. I guess it was the Black Diamond Riders at the time. They had kind of taken over the coffee houses in Yorkville and we had to get fairly heavy-handed with them. They also used to have people known as 'strikers,' and they used to send these strikers out to find young, impressionable girls and take them back to their motorcycle houses for gang-bangs and drugs and that sort of thing. So we came down fairly hard on them, and over a period of years, we gradually forced them out of the Yorkville area."

Once out of Yorkville, it was but a short hop over to Rochdale, and for the bikers it was business as usual. Their world was an alien one to the old Rochdalians like the scholarly Jack Dimond.

"While I was still working at Rochdale, there was a Sunday afternoon when I saw some bikers there. I remember going up to them and telling them to hit the road. That was foolish, because I got slugged and had my glasses broken. That distressed me immensely, because it was the seamy side of life that many of us hadn't had much experience with. And we hated to think we'd spawned a project which would give shelter to this type of person."

Larry Simmons was the president of the Satan's Choice motorcycle gang for seven years. As the gang's leader, he spent considerable time in Rochdale although he was never a resident.

"I'm from west-end Toronto, Weston Road and Lawrence. When I grew up in that area you couldn't even get a drink there—it was dry. You couldn't even wear jeans to high school. One night I went for cigarettes when I was eighteen or nineteen. I never came back for eight years. Never seen my mother, father, brother, sister, nobody. The gang was a twenty-four-hour-a-day thing. When I left all I took with me was one suit—a double-breasted brown pinstripe mohair. The first place I went was 79 Madison—within the first half hour someone stole the suit. I haven't owned one since. I got hooked up with Bobby Lattice, Duke Bernard and I never looked back.

"I did finish Grade 13 and I took two years of psychology after. When I went to the pen they said, 'What the fuck are you doing here?' I scored in the top 0.001% of all the people who took the test there.

"I consider myself different from a big percentage of guys in the clubs. I was in, I fit (in fact, I more than fit) but I took it one step further, but I was still a thinking individual. I'm not stupid. I weighed 155 pounds, although the average guy in the Choice ran about 200, and I was president for seven years and that wasn't from brawn. My mother's favourite saying in those days used to be, 'Oh, he's joined the navy.' If you picked up a newspaper in the '69–'72 era and there was a story about bikers, my name would be there. There was a lot going on during that period.

"You got to remember that at that time the Village was going real strong and between us and the Vagabonds we had it all locked up, so you knew that Rochdale would be next. Rochdale was just across the street, you could walk right in, and everybody was at Rochdale—they'd see a 'biker' and they'd up half their dope—that's just the way it was. The doors were wide open. We didn't fit in either place. We were there sitting on the street in the Village and any of the dope running through there—one of us was involved somewhere along the line. It was open house, the place to hang around.

"Our relationship with the Rochdale hippies worked like this—nobody would deny what anyone of us would ask for, you know what I'm sayin'? That's how it worked with the hippies (and I don't like that word because it has such a strange connotation—hippies were really an entirely different trip). We weren't that demanding, but anytime we asked for anything they upped it—sure there was peaceful co-existence. Sure, but step out of line. I can remember somebody would say something to someone's ol' lady and he'd be flat on his ass on the sidewalk. It was co-existence until you moved just a little from what was expected.

"I never threw my weight around, not in the Village, not in Rochdale. We were there all the time—seven days a week. We were just a presence there but there were no real confrontations. It was physical, but it was just pushing and shoving but not real physical—like with guns. It didn't mean shit. One concession we did make was we didn't wear our colours in there. We didn't wear colours. It was a matter of self-preservation because we were getting a lot of heat at the time. It was kind of stupid, like riding a bike with no colours, it didn't make a helluva lot of sense. But we did it because it wouldn't freak the straight people out. It wasn't obvious, the red and white Choice colours, it wouldn't be as obvious. But the people there, they'd cross the road before they'd walk on the same side of the street as us. It's not that there was that much violence, it was more the implied threat. Do you remember Darcy's? Well we totalled that place one night—cleared every nigger out of that place. Now that was violent.

"Bikers didn't have a 'role' at Rochdale, not the Choice anyway. We didn't take part except in the sense that we would walk through the building and we were there for two reasons and two reasons only: the dope and the broads. You'd walk through there and you could take your pick of anything that was going on. It wasn't a question of being there and saying, 'Hey we own Rochdale.' It was the same thing with the Village. We were a presence. It was strange to instill so much fear and have so much power.

"The cops—they were there. It was a joke where we were concerned. They were there and we were there. They would hassle us but nothing major. It's hard to describe. They'd bother everybody but us. I can't think of anyone in the club taking a pinch at Rochdale. Never. I can recall all kinds of incidents where they played the tough guy. I can recall beating the fuck out of someone and having the cops stand there with their backs turned to us. We're talking territorial here—property as in bikes and ol' ladies. If anyone messed with those it was instant 'Look out.' I've got friends—and I don't use that term loosely—who are narcs, sergeants, everything else. And the only difference between them and me—and they know it and I know it—is that they're on a different side of the fence. But they are in it primarily for the excitement, primarily for the rush. They know it and I know it. I sit down with these people, I smoke with them, I drink with them, we're identical except we chose different sides of the same fence, that's all there is to it."

Tales of the bikers' exploits—riding their bikes down the stairs, playing Russian roulette, cleaning their bikes in the hallways—litter Rochdale's folklore. The bikers were such a presence that the council had to hire a special liaison person to facilitate communication with the leather angels. The liaison person—a Californian named Chico—let the bikers use his fifteenth-floor Ashram double as a base camp. In return he tried to cool them out on the rip-off, burn, violence front. The April 17, 1969, *Daily* chronicles a council meeting where Chico is fired, thereby placing his life in jeopardy with the Vagabonds. "The whole meeting," reads the *Daily's* entry, "had turned itself inside out to please the bikers. 'Please love us,' we said, 'because we're so liberal-minded and we want so hard to understand you.' This feeling was expressed by our king in his 'seminar' speech, by Ann Pohl in her appeal, 'Talk to us,' and by many others. Each appeal was coolly and sardonically rejected by the bikers. Finally, they had to remind us of our only real common ground, the Man."

The bikers, like the speeders and some "uncool" dealers, were targeted for expulsion as the Rochdale community started cleaning up the environment during the course of 1969. Getting rid of the bikers was the combined effort of the council and the building's "cool" dealers.

"There were confrontations," admits Bob Nasmith, "actual fights where people took a licking. But they would come back the next day for more. Joel Kerbel was like that, very brave about it. But he did it just to make a point. The building ended up evicting the bikers. Through little deals that were made. Edgo was president of the Vags, a very sharp guy, he made a deal—in return for some presence in the building, he would keep his men from running roughshod through Rochdale. He'd guarantee that as long as he had a couple of people with access to the building. Billy Littler was an important liaison with the bikers, especially the Vags. He had a good reputation with them just as he did with us. Just a four-square solid guy. Tough as nails. A bit avaricious but very up front about it. The bikers just sort of trickled out because there was too much heat, too much sweat. They had bigger fish to fry."

Beneath the peace-love-groovy surface of Rochdale beat a primitive heart; in this subterranean world of dealers, informers and bikers, the gun was no stranger. Although the extent to which Rochdale was an "armed fortress" is debatable, there is little question that guns were in the building from the fall of 1968.

Metro Police Inspector Robert Crampton informs us that after the building had only been open for six months he had "the dubious distinction of being one of the first officers to execute a warrant in the building. It was for firearms. A man had been, we thought, supplying American carbines—M-1's—to the underworld. We didn't make any arrests, but we did recover several of these firearms. Our investigation led us directly to Rochdale. I was able to gain access to Rochdale without incident and into the apartment without incident where I recovered one fully loaded M-15 or M-16 rifle. At that particular time, it did not fall within the limitations of the Criminal Code, and what it was was a restricted, unregistered firearm. The man was out to make money, he didn't have a job and he'd come up from the States, and he found a ready market for his wares. We arrested him without incident. I understand the FBI and other agencies in the States eventually took custody of him because there had been warrants out for him in the United States."

The council reacted by outlawing unregistered weapons on February 22, 1969. Like so much of the legislation passed in

Rochdale, it was a take-it-or-leave-it proposition, but it did impress upon everyone the antipathy most felt for the way of the gun. Guns would continue to cast their shadows on Rochdale for the entire history of the building.

Rochdale was not backing down—it would stand and fight for its own turf. When the Vagabonds, enraged over a bad acid deal, threatened to return to the building, Rochdalians armed themselves with gasoline-filled bottles and stood prepared to repel the invasion by force if necessary. Another time when two bikers assaulted a pregnant woman, council put a money reward on their heads.

"That was a strange time," says resident Tony Zincker. "They used to come in the spring. I guess it started in '68–'69. The spring of '70 was the last time they tried to come in and basically take over the place. But we were organized—to the point when they tried to come in the alarm went off and we all came rushing down to the front door. We'd gather there. It was the only way to keep them out. In individual confrontation, it was just the community getting together and saying, 'We don't want you people here.' There were those kinds of numbers.

"There were no bikers on security. We had people that had affiliations with bikers, and one actual biker that worked security for a while. You hear about extortion and so on, but he wasn't into that. It was just a job for him. There were other people in the building that may have looked like bikers, but they weren't associated with bikers as such. They were just rubs. They sometimes ripped off people and stuff but that was before my time at the door.

"I mean when the bikers came in, they didn't even pay rent, let alone could you tell them what to do. But once they were stopped that was the end."

As Rochdale's reputation as a drug and party centre spread, the building naturally became a magnet for the runaways of southern Ontario and Canada—both female and male. Bobbie Malone (not her real name) was sixteen when she arrived at Rochdale.

"I grew up in a small town in southern Ontario. I just didn't get along with my folks. They had their own problems, I suppose, the mortgage—the ol' man was a boozer. So the scene at home was a drag. Fights about everything I did. I knew I was going to leave first chance I got. My girlfriend and I hitch-hiked to T.O.—and we ended up at the Village. We knew some people there from our hometown. That must have been in the spring of 1968. I was around fifteen and a half.

"Then in the fall a girlfriend of mine was standing out in front of one of the clubs—the Penny Farthing or the Upper Crust—and this big ugly biker comes up to her, puts his arm around her and says, 'Let's go to a party.' This girl was a bit of a space case. She should have known better but she goes along with him. Next day I see her wandering around the Village like a zombie. This creep took her back to the gang's house and they splashed her. It was sad. She was walking around, these bloodstains on her white bells. Just kind of spaced out, whimpering. We took her to the hospital.

"I made my mind up to split the Village that night. I headed over to Rochdale, which had been going for a few months. We had heard about it but didn't pay it much attention. It was a school after all. And who needed that shit? But I get there—I knew a guy who lived with somebody. I crashed there. He was into a little dealing and I helped him. I didn't really become his girlfriend but I did sleep with him. I wasn't a virgin when I got to The Rock but I did pick up a few tricks there. It was a wide-open place sexually, especially when the booze and drugs would flow.

"I ended up with this other dealer type. I ended up doing some dope runs for him—Bobbie the Mule. I guess I survived in Rochdale for almost a year.

"No matter what anybody says about that place, I'd have to say it was okay. They took me in and in a way took care of me. I mean, I didn't turn into an angel or anything, I was still wild, but at least I had a home and if I got into real trouble, I had somebody to help. Rochdale, yeah, it was all right!"

But Bobbie was one of the lucky ones. Just how grim and seedy the runaway experience could be at Rochdale is exemplified by this police report: "On May 27, 1969, a woman reported that her 13-year-old daughter was missing.

"Further investigation revealed that this girl and another young female had gone to Rochdale College on May 27. There they met two men, both of whom had criminal records. All four persons stayed on the thirteenth floor for four days, during which time, intercourse took place. One of the males injected himself with some type of drug. The other man injected some substance into her arm and gave her pills to take orally. Criminal action was instigated against the two males and the older female"

Alex Martin (pseudonym), a Rochdale runaway, gives us his experience from the male point of view.

"I was born in England, raised in Canada, then because my father was a soldier we went back to England. I came back to Canada for a summer holiday.

"A friend of mine lived in Rochdale. I went for a visit and I stayed. I eventually wound up working for Rosie, the dealer. I was sixteen but I was fairly big for my age. Especially with the long hair, I passed for much older. I had tripped prior to coming to Rochdale, I had done some hitch-hiking in Europe. I had some freedom away from my parents. And this friend of mine helped me get a place together at Rochdale. I lived on the ninth floor. The ninth floor was a clean floor—especially in comparison to something like the sixth floor where the people were parading in off the street. On the ninth floor you couldn't just walk in, you had to have some sort of business there or the residents would check you out. No one would help you or co-operate with you if they didn't know you.

"I decided that this was the life for me. I was young and impressionable. I came for a holiday and just decided not to go back—I guess you could say I was AWOL.

"The thing that I remember about Rochdale, and when I look back fondly at my days there, was that I never felt alone there. I always felt that I had friends that cared about me. I had enemies, too, I thought were friends—especially among the speed freaks. This one guy in particular—I trusted him and he kept ripping me off. But I was never in dire danger. Looking back now with three kids of my own, I think, 'God, if they ever did that to me,' but really there's no place like Rochdale now. It just couldn't happen again. Even the cops weren't that bad. I was only threatened once.

"People were always looking after you. I'm sure that I wasn't eating right—usually I ate in restaurants. I didn't have home cookin' or anything like that. But everyone kept an eye out for you, made sure you weren't getting into trouble.

"Some of the runaways were abused. I mean one fourteen-year-old girl having sex with different guys every night is a form of abuse. We had this one girl on our Ashram, she went from room to room, staying a few days in each one. When the guy got tired of her, he'd send her packing and she'd show up at the next guy's door—that's abuse. I didn't think so then but I do now. They slept around because they needed a place to stay. I saw it then as a fair exchange. The youngest runaway I saw was a fourteen-year-old. There was this one young French Canadian girl, her old man he wouldn't let her go, he just kept her drugged.

"After a while in Rochdale I started speeding, I also got into some heroin a few times. Those were the bad times because I wasn't in the real world, especially when I was speeding—I was living in a fantasy world. When I was high I'd be feeling great—life was great—I was going to do this and that, but when you came down it was stark reality—it was a cold Canadian winter. I was away from home. I didn't have much money."

As part of the community these kids needed help and guidance. Council member Bob Nasmith felt that Rochdale had an obligation to be socially responsible in dealing with the teen runaways. "I wouldn't say Rochdale was like Lady Liberty saying 'Give me your poor huddled masses of runaways,' but it was there. It was like a magnet and it was the place to be. And we, of course, had to respond to that. Because when you get juveniles, especially juvenile girls, the sharks will gobble them up and use them and we didn't want that. So we would direct them to various good people in the building to talk to to see what could be done for them.

"We even had the community service people—and they're cops after all—look after them. They were like a bridge—responding to needs. They were aware that some runaways were in over their heads, so they didn't pump them for information but they did try and keep them out of trouble. Obviously, there were forces within working to help them—reconciliation of families, that sort of thing."

On January 31, 1969, at 10 p.m., General Manager Bernie Bomers, joined by nine other residents including five council members, pulled the Communications Desk across the front door, in effect creating a barrier. It was an unauthorized act that plunged the college into the depths of its first moral-philosophical crisis—just how open was Rochdale going to be? Was it open to the pushers, bikers, speed freaks, crashers, runaways, as well as those who were seeking "excellence" and "wisdom?" How could Rochdale, which scorned authoritarian control and prided itself on its egalitarianism, adopt the same discriminatory screening procedures it initially rejected?

Another variation on that same theme was what to do with the political revolutionaries? Case in point: M4M. Named after May 4, 1970, that day of infamy when the National Guard gunned down four students on the campus of Ohio's Kent State University. This group of young radicals was the equivalent of the American SDS in that it believed that physical revolution was needed to establish the ideal revolutionary society. These were the kids making bombs in the basement and planning apocalyptic revolutions. M4M demanded and got to use Rochdale as a basis for what it termed its "revolutionary gains." After yet another lengthy debate, M4M was admitted. You could argue from dawn to dusk but in the end to deny the group entry was to deny the ideals of the movement. The radicals were not only given a free room for the summer, but also given access to the publications office. From that base M4M planned its first major attack on the system—a May 9 demonstration at the U.S. consulate on University Avenue. Five thousand anti-war demonstrators gathered in protest, and when the smoke cleared, ninety-one were arrested and the damage was in the hundreds of thousands, the result of the mob being herded onto Yonge Street, the main downtown street—where the demonstrators went on a window-smashing rampage.

Rochdale was part of the North American radical network. The Toronto Anti-Draft Program even published a pamphlet for draft evaders and armed forces deserters that made special mention of Rochdale as a supportive institution. According to author David Sharpe, when it opened, Rochdale had seventy-five Americans, twenty-five of whom were political exiles. The college also had an understanding with AMEX, the American Exile Support Group. Indeed, the college went beyond the call of duty, offering moral and financial support. A draft dodger could expect a free room at least for a period of time to adjust, counselling and some limited financial aid. The college actively raised funds for their cause and threw benefits—one early one in November of 1968 featured a mock election and satiric political theatre. Even if only $700 was raised, Rochdale was making a point that it was a safe, sympathetic harbour. Not surprisingly, the American presence in Rochdale would continue to grow both in statistical size and influence.

"Many of the Americans were uneducated people who, if they hadn't ended up in Rochdale, probably would have been doing some serious prison time by the age of nineteen," says a pessimistic Walt Houston. "There were no critical skills to speak of and no motivation other than self-aggrandizement and making a quick buck."

Moral judgements aside, the journey's end for Americans at Rochdale was, as Tripper recalls, an emotionally powerful moment. "I remember this van pulled up full of Americans. These guys jumped out and there to greet them was this other group of Americans who were already at Rochdale. It was like, 'Are you living here in Toronto? It's great to see a buddy from back home!'

There was incredible camaraderie, because these strangers in a strange land had found friends up here."

Luckily, for people like Buffalonian Tom Shevlin, the adjustment was relatively easy. "It was basically a case of moving a hundred miles and putting the whole war thing behind me in a very easy fashion.

"Toronto seemed very sane. When I emigrated, I got a short haircut and wound up getting heat from the local kids. Nobody got hassled for having long hair in Toronto—at least, not like they did in the States."

One way or another, the Americans made themselves at home. Some, as Bob Rowbotham remembers, even became business associates in the drug trade.

"We'd be sittin' there and havin' a toke, and some guy would say, 'I've got a friend, but I can't go down to the States.' So I said, 'Well, I can certainly go.' And we began planning how to arrange it, because the infrastructure in their own subculture back home was already set up. That did a lot for commerce across the border.

"Not only that, but the Americans taught us how to riot. They'd been shot at with real bullets at a time when only rubber bullets were being used in Canada. So we relied on their training. But don't forget, we only rioted in retribution for what the police did to us."

As part of the political network, Rochdale was the recipient of visits from "big name" revolutionaries. The visits could be well-publicized media events or clandestine back-door-at-midnight underground operations. One shining moment for the radical segment of The Rock was the visit of Yippie leader and "Chicago 8" defendant Jerry Rubin on February 28, 1969. Rubin was on the college lecture circuit, preaching the Yippie gospel and publicizing his future trial along with seven others in that piece of high drama/black comedy dubbed "The Chicago 8 Trial."

Newly elected Canadian Prime Minister Pierre Trudeau declared in November 1969 that Canada would retain its open-door immigration policy despite the fact the country was becoming a haven for draft dodgers and political dissenters and exiles. With that kind of attitude in the corridors of power, it was little wonder that Rochdale became an important stop on the Sixties' underground railroad.

Despite the mandatory "Black Studies" course, Rochdale had very little to do with the Black Power Movement of the period.

However, as Bob Nasmith tells us, Black Panther celebrity Bobby Seale did speak at the college.

"It was an event," recalls Nasmith. "I was there but I didn't spend much time around them. I didn't jump on that bandwagon. I thought, 'Well they've got a legitimate gripe and they are certainly doing it in a tough, flamboyant way,' but I realized, contrary to radical chic, these were a bunch of very tough dudes—they were going to kick ass, deal dope, rob banks anyway, regardless. Now that they had a real political cause to get into was wonderful. They just got smart, got the organization and publicity and said, 'Hey, here we are and this is what we stand for.' At any rate, there weren't very many black people in Rochdale."

Malcolm was one of the few regular black visitors to Rochdale and although he did "detect some ill feeling from the biker-types or the hard core elements," by and large "the hippie thing—the spirit of live and let live" permeated the racial relations.

Tony Phred claims that he participated in hiding American Carlton Armstrong who was on the run for a fatal bombing of a military building in the States.

Among the visitors to Rochdale was Marshall McLuhan, the University of Toronto professor who had gained a worldwide reputation for his revolutionary insights into communications and the mass media. In November, 1968, while Rochdale was only in its infancy, McLuhan told *Newsweek* magazine that the building had "all the makings of a utopian flop. They're all hurrying backward into the past as fast as they can go." A few months later, McLuhan visited Rochdale for a speaking engagement and, recalls Rev. Ian MacKenzie, he was "booed out of the building."

Not surprisingly, Rochdale soon acquired nationwide notoriety as a magnet and haven for intellectuals and student radicals—even those who had never been there. In one particularly troublesome incident early in 1969, it was widely believed that black militant Eldridge Cleaver had sought refuge in Rochdale after skipping bail in the United States. At the eye of the storm was Judith Merril, in whose apartment Cleaver was supposedly a guest.

"Part of the reason they were so sure it was me," says Merril, "was that, a week or two before, I'd had a visit from a black friend of mine from New York who happened to be extremely visible—a tall, handsome guy who's an actor and university professor. He had an enormous Afro. So as soon as word about Cleaver settled in, people figured that's what Judy's friend was doing there.

"I was getting phone calls from every newspaper in town, with reporters begging me, 'All I want is an interview with Cleaver. I won't let anyone know where he is. I won't let anyone know how I found out. I promise you I will reveal nothing to damage him. And I don't work for the CIA.' It was comical at first, and then after a while, it got less comical. When people start telling you in every third sentence that they don't work for the CIA, then you suspect that they might. And I kept saying to them, 'I wish I really knew where he was. I'd like to meet him myself. I'm sorry, but I don't have him. You may come to my apartment if you like, and look under the beds. He just isn't here.' "

Reg Hartt remembers, "Once when I was showing *Intolerance*, I went downstairs to see how things were going. And there was a huge man at the front door—he must have weighed three or four hundred pounds. And he was trying to get in to see *Intolerance*. And I said, 'What's the problem?' And the guy at the door said, 'Well he's a narc.' I said, 'He's not a narc.' And the guy said, 'How do you know?' And I said, 'Narcs don't dress like that. They come in, they look like you, they look like me, they don't look like that. I mean, how the heck's he going to infiltrate the building looking like that? Look, let me talk to him for a second.'

"And it turned out he was from the Deep South and he had been trying for over thirty years to see *Intolerance*, and he was damned if he was going to let anything stop him. So I said, 'Fine. Give me a couple of minutes and I'll get you in here.' So I took the security guy over and had a talk with him and said, 'Look, he's not a narc.' But he said, 'How do you know he's not a narc? We're not gonna let him in.' I said, 'You've gotta let him in. He's come to see the film and it's important to him. Now, if he makes a move during the film to go beyond the second floor into the rest of the building, then as far as I'm concerned, kill him.' And they understood that!

"So what you had was these two people who came in who were armed to the teeth but didn't look it. And they watched this man watching *Intolerance*. And he was in heaven because he was finally getting a chance to see this movie. It was like his life was in the balance but he didn't really know it."

Some Rochdalians saw the Americans as being important contributors to the texture and quality of life at The Rock.

"They never seemed to straggle in," observes Jim Garrard. "They always came in with great style. I thought they had brains and style, and they brought a lot of Yankee know-how. They were organized and skilled. They really know how to handle power tools and chain saws and stuff. They had a lot of training and knew how to do things.

"I think a lot of the great strengths of Rochdale came from all the Americans who came here to avoid the draft or who deserted. They were first-class people, and they came up here and weren't treated like criminals at Rochdale, although they weren't treated like heroes either. Nobody complained that they were Americans or that they were faster than we were or smarter than we were."

It would be foolish to try and create the impression of a prototypical American Rochdalian. Like any experience in Rochdale the American one was not homogenous; there were as many American perspectives as there were Americans. However, the exiled Americans all shared one thing: they were strangers in a new land "with no direction home."

In fact, in comparison with bloody events like the People's Park confrontation in Berkeley where a student, James Rector, was killed as the police, armed with shotguns, reclaimed the Park, Rochdale's revolutionary activities seem tame.

Tame or not, it was all part of the restless spirit of the times. The year 1969, like the year before, saw continued campus unrest and violence worldwide. Even the staid London School of Economics was forced to close for three weeks due to demonstrations and occupations. Students everywhere rallied around the Vietnam war cause. That conflict embodied all the evils that they were trying to purge from a misdirected world. "Moratorium" was the newest word in the counter-culture's vocabulary. John and Yoko held a bed-in for peace at the Queen Elizabeth Hotel in Montreal. Joined by luminaries like Timothy Leary and the Smothers Brothers, they recorded the anthemic "Give Peace a Chance" in their bed.

Canada did more than host a symbolic statement: Montreal's Sir George Williams University was the scene of an act of political violence that destroyed two million dollars' worth of computers. It brought home the fact that even quiet, conservative Canada was not immune from the fevered times. Still in shock over that, the Canadian calm was once again shattered as bombs were set off at the Montreal and Toronto stock exchanges—twenty-seven injuries resulted. Revolution wasn't knocking at the door, it was kicking it in.

C H A P T E R   7

Purple
Haze

With its starkly visible location, Rochdale gradually became a focal point for Metro Toronto's drug culture. It didn't matter that in those early days there were more drugs in any of Metro's suburbs than at Rochdale, The Rock was still singled out as a convenient target for the outraged authorities and citizenry. As writer Eric LeBourdais put it in *Toronto Life* magazine: "It's as if, during Prohibition, a high-rise with a concentration of young people known to drink bootleg booze had appeared in downtown Chicago. Our police have no choice but to single it out for special attention, especially since marijuana and LSD are illegal. So Rochdale is repeatedly raided."

On May 29, 1969, the federal government, alarmed at the growing number of young people being drawn into the drug culture, appointed Gerald Le Dain to head a federal commission into the non-medical use of drugs. The Le Dain Commission assumed almost mythical proportions for Canada's drug community—Canada appeared be the next Holland, with humane, reasonable drug laws. The first step toward an enlightened society had been taken. Or so the reasoning went.

Growing drug use was, of course, a widespread societal concern. It was also a concern for the Rochdale administrators, albeit in a different way than for the RCMP or the PTA. Rochdale could live with the soft drugs and the good chemicals but it couldn't live with speed. Toronto for some reason (probably relating to manufacturing) had become the methamphetamine capital of North America. While in New York City, San Francisco and other urban centres the problem for the hip communities was heroin, in Toronto it was speed, one of the ugly side effects of the Yorkville migration.

"Rochdale—the place was like a fuckin' shooting gallery," says Val R. "That's how we used it. Maybe it wasn't seedy and rundown like a Harlem shooting gallery, but it had the same function. And come to think of it, we were none too clean and considerate about our accommodations. Hell, we were filthy. That's the thing about speeders, they don't give a flying fuck about anything but spiking that stuff and getting off.

"It must have been quite the scene—a million of these goofs running around in lumber jackets (it didn't matter if it was summer or winter), teeth chattering, talking a million miles a minute, always talking about rip-offs, burns—seems we were always planning some kind of score.

"A lot of that time is hazy to me—I stayed on and off at The Rock for maybe eight or nine months. Time in The Rock was weird—you got in there and you lost track of time. Once you got into that whiz—look out—you could come out days or weeks later. Any food you might need, you just grabbed out of the Ashram kitchens, or you scrounged or ripped off the cafeteria (although they got hip to that early on).

"Rochdale, no matter what anybody tells you, was not a love-in! The reason I left, besides the fact that I got tired of sleeping on the run, in closets (have you ever slept in a fuckin' closet? Try it and you'll know what I mean)—I left because one night a fellow speeder pulled a knife on me. Stuck it right under my chin and ripped me off. I didn't have but a few bucks on me but I figured I should get out while I had a chance. The funny thing is I never went back, not even for a visit."

Rochdale may have been the first place in Canada to recognize the severity of the speed epidemic. In a letter dated April, 1975, resident and building general manager Bill King summarized the situation: "In the fall of '68 Rochdale opened and publicized that all would be free 'to do their own thing.' The people who made these statements were liberal academics who had no idea what a motorcycle gang's thing was. They soon found out.

"No one in Canada had any real idea of what a speed culture would be like, but at Rochdale they learned quickly when 400 freaks gathered in Rochdale that winter with an estimated 10,000 or more in the rest of Metro. In March, 1969, Paul Evitts proposed that all speed freaks be thrown out because they weren't paying rent, they were tearing the place up and growing emaciated before our eyes. It was a bummer.

"It took Paul two months to convince Rochdale to take the drastic measure of evicting people from Utopia. The people decided that no one was free to be a speed freak. On May 15, 1969, the entire twelve-person council went to the thirteenth floor with a shotgun and a lawyer to tell forty speed freaks they had to leave immediately. The people who were involved with these evictions regard it as one of the most frightening experiences of their lives. Three weeks later, a new council headed by John Bradford and Paul Evitts began the process of evicting all the speed freaks by the end of the summer.

"News of the speed freaks' evictions spread rapidly through the hitchhiking grapevine which spread youth culture from Vancouver to Halifax in the big travelling summer of 1969. Within six months Rochdale and the Trailer [Vic Swartzman, Barry Luger] shut down the best drug-crisis centre because the speed culture had subsided."

King went on to say that Rochdale helped stem the tide of speed use. "Kids wouldn't listen to the Establishment doctors and government studies, they would listen to The Rock—the best voice of youth culture." The government, according to King, got its $6 million worth from Rochdale on that front alone. He concluded by saying, "Listen to the lyrics of Steppenwolf's 'Goddam the Pusher.' "

From February (when the council first addressed the problem of speeders) until the end of the summer of 1969, the building was cleared of most of the needle-using speed freaks.

Nelson Adams was among those who actively evicted the speed freaks. "I personally was part of vigilante gangs that grabbed speed users and threw them out," relates Adams, "threw their baggage out the door and said, 'Don't come back.' LSD and marijuana—I'm not gonna blame those. But Rochdale was swamped by people coming here to look for drugs, too. And they were into a lot of macho bullshit with dogs and guns and so on."

Don Washburn (not his real name), who first came to Rochdale as a nineteen-year-old to join his biker brother on security, was part of the building's growing organized attempt to rid itself of the abusers who were bringing the project to its knees. "One of our functions was to evict known speed users and heroin addicts. We would go up to their apartment and start moving them and their stuff out into the hallway. We'd know if they were using by the usual signs—tracks on their arms, needles around the apartment, it was a dead giveaway. We were always kicking them out. They were always crashing in the building. They wouldn't have a place to live, no apartment or room number. They might have got in with a friend and then split on their own and were living in a car in the underground garage or something. Lots of times it got to be heavy, everyone on security had a gun pulled on them by some drug-crazed hippie. Having a .357 Magnum go off while you were evicting some speed freak is quite the experience."

Tripper was one of the abusers, although his choice of poison was heroin. Tripper was born into old Toronto WASP money. During the time he should have been learning the ropes of his father's business—like many other upper-middle-class youths—he was off on a chemical voyage of discovery. "I had come back from California with a habit," says Tripper. "As my habit grew, I managed to find people in Rochdale that sold junk. I was working at a head shop in Yorkville at the time. The rule at Rochdale was, of course, no needles or hard drugs allowed.

"I started going to Rochdale to middle some grass and hash deals, but I knew that if I made money on those deals I could turn around and get what I really needed and wanted. I used to cop it from this dealer on the ninth floor. He used to deal hash but I could also pick up some junk. When I moved in they put me on the same floor with him and there were these black junkies from Detroit. In fact, these characters threatened my life. They were bad. I wouldn't say there were a lot of junkies around The Rock then, but they were there, you had to know where to look.

"I moved into The Rock and lived on the ninth floor. I lasted for about two months before they caught me in a speed check. They walked into my room, which happened to be full of junkies in the middle of a Saturday or Sunday afternoon. It was just after Christmas. I had this shaving kit with my works and shit and in comes Ed Walsh and his brother—two of the heavies on Rochdale security.

"These guys on security were like Nazis—fuckin' Fascists. So these two come into the room. I managed to grab my junk out of the shaving kit while they were momentarily distracted by something else happening in the room. I was going to throw it out the window. They grabbed us and said, 'You have twenty-four hours to get out of the building.' It took us until about six that night to get out. I heard the cops were there by midnight. They cleaned out a bunch of other junkies and speeders in one fell swoop that day—it was roundup time. That ninth floor was a junkie floor—whether anybody knew it or not.

"I guess it was a matter of time—you really couldn't keep that kind of drug abuse secret for very long—your lifestyle would give you away. Not to mention the tracks."

Karen Johnson, in the Rochdale rental department, saw things from a building maintenance point of view: "The summer of 1969 was Speed Summer in Toronto. The people who were left in Rochdale saw themselves as a force that should be helping. They weren't assholes and didn't turn people away. They saw their duty and role to help where possible, and a lot of speed freaks were taken in. As a result there was an enormous amount of damage sustained by the building that summer. Rooms were totally devastated. When we went in we'd find rooms where people had shit for days and never flushed the toilet. It was all you could do not to throw up. There was rotting garbage, paranoid messages in paint or lipstick on the walls, spray-painted walls. Speed freaks lived bizarrely and did weird things."

But even Johnson admits that on occasion a quality individual could emerge from that scene. "Ron Day, he was a junkie but he was one of the most together junkies I ever met. He walked around in bare feet and did weird things but he managed his job. He was the 'mailman'—he distributed the mail from the mailbags to the boxes on the first floor. He was very reliable. We never had any complaints about the mail, or at least about the job that Ron Day had."

Rochdale was concerned only about certain drugs. It outlawed certain drugs—speed, heroin, coke—but actively supported the use of other "soft drugs." At a session of the Le Dain Commission, seven Rochdalians testified that while they absolutely supported the legalization of marijuana they vehemently opposed the use of speed. They went on to regale the commission with horror stories about eleven-year-old girls trying to cop speed at Rochdale.

Drugs were an important part of what Rochdale was all about. They weren't *everything*, but they were part of the searching, the questing for alternative ways of thought and life. They were part of the voyage of self-discovery that many Rochdalians had embarked upon. They were also dangerous, fun and a social bond. Rochdale seemed to be a living embodiment of Timothy Leary's new holy trinity—'turn on, tune in, drop out.'

However, not everyone in Rochdale used drugs. To some they were unnecessary and ruined the original intent of the college. For others, like Judy Keeler, the drug scene then was "baby stuff" in comparison with what is going on today. Steve Grant, a twenty-one-year-old drop-out from an applied chemistry course of studies, told writer LeBourdais that he "felt far more pressure to drink in the Waterloo college dorms than there is to do drugs here. It's like everything else—it's up to you. And unless you are causing other people problems, nobody interferes."

A survey conducted by Dr. Lionel P. Solursh produced the following rather interesting results, which contrasted with the assumption that *everyone* in Rochdale was involved with drugs at one level or another:

> 62% used cannabis either daily or weekly, 6.8% used it monthly, 18.2% used it less than monthly and 12.2% of the respondents did not use it at all. As regards the other drugs: 53.3% never used psychedelics, 2.6% used speed, 11% used heroin, 17.6% did not use alcohol.

After the first year of the college's life, the drug dealers expanded their businesses and the stakes were raised. When asked how much he made during his dealing days at Rochdale, Rosie Rowbotham answers, without blinking an eye, "From 1967 to January 1, 1974, I'd say $50 million passed through my hands." But he quickly adds, "At that time, there were some people selling both hard chemicals and smoke—they didn't differentiate. Me, I've never—even to this day—crossed that moral line. I never get any credit for it, but I know what moral lines I've never crossed.

"I dealt grass, hash, LSD and mescaline, but I stayed away from heroin, cocaine and speed. Once I even grabbed a pound of speed from a speeder who got it from the bikers. I put it in the shitter, mixed it up with my foot and said, 'You want to do a hit now?' and flushed it. Then I said, 'See you later. Get the fuck out of the building and I don't want to ever see you again.'

"Up to 1974, the only importing I had done was from America to Canada. It was just a hippie, freak trip. It wasn't like criminal. We were beatin' the Man and the system, but the system was bad—they were wrong. So we were doing something righteous and karmically good. It sounds a little naive, but, in my mind, I was making people spiritually aware enough to drop out of the technological world because nobody has any feelings for their next-door neighbours. That feeling is lost. You get it in small communities, but in cities, it's so cold.

"I liked doin' that, because it made people stop enough to think, 'So the leaders of the country say this, the state says this, the church says this. Is it true?' I want people to say, 'Well, let's question.' Maybe it's wrong to use an artificial substance to do that. But back in those times, everything was happening so fast that the only thing that got me thinkin' that way was to sit back, do a few tokes and start thinkin'."

As for Metro's finest, they knew that Rochdale was a high-stakes game. "It was big bucks, no doubt about it," says plainclothes officer Bob Waddell. "And the drug dealers knew it. They had the perfect haven. What better plan could you possibly have? They had an early warning system, they had stash rooms. There was no way of connecting any drugs to anybody. I mean who owned this building? To this day I still don't know who owned the damn building. They had the perfect location—at a busy intersection. These jokers had it made."

The structure and mechanics of drug dealing in Rochdale can be broken down into an internal operation involving the community itself and an external operation involving the outside world. The internal or in-house dealing operation was low-key and essentially community-oriented. An individual would purchase a quantity of drugs from someone in the building, then break up that amount and sell the smaller amounts to users in the building. It was essentially a domestic business with the traffic contained within Rochdale.

The real problems arose when the dealing took on an external nature. For one thing, those dealing to non-residents of Rochdale were involved with large amounts of drugs. Moreover, their businesses brought in the hordes of outsiders who caused so many problems for Rochdale. Some of the major dealers didn't even live in the building—they set up operations and had others run them. These were big businesses whose only concern was profit. The Rochdale community's hopes and aspirations didn't mean anything to these dealers. Rochdale was merely a useful base for them—a convenient fortress with a security system that protected them.

Rochdale's big dealers were highly organized and operated efficient enterprises. "When you're talking about big dealers and major quantities of dope in Rochdale," suggests resident Alex MacDonald, "and by major I mean hundreds of pounds and up, don't think about it in terms of dope, think of it in terms of logistics. Business management, financing, judgement, that kind of stuff. In fact the people who ran the major successful drug operations were just smart! You can't keep track of that much and make important judgement calls (to keep you out of jail and from being ripped off) by being stupid. These people were well-organized and smart.

"But at the same time you had the independents. There was a guy who lived across the hall from me who would sell pounds of hash in the stairwells and he'd have a pound of hash in each back pocket, right there."

In an effort to put as much distance between themselves and their illegal product, the dealers would hire young people—often teenage runaways—to guard their "stash rooms." Stash rooms (usually Kafkas) were used to store their goods. As rentals manager, Karen Johnson was well aware of how some of the building's rooms were being used.

"The dealers were renting rooms four, five, six, seven, even ten at a time. They'd do it under various assumed names. Sometimes they'd come in and say, 'I want to rent this room for such and such a friend.' Other times they would send in their people to rent 'for' them. It became very obvious to me.

"It got to the point where I was fairly perceptive about dealers and their tricks to get extra rooms. Mike Thornton, he was Rosie's partner—he was the one that didn't get caught, although he eventually did get busted in the States for something like thirty-two pounds. At one point he wanted a Zeus very badly. I liked him (although at that time I didn't know that he was Rosie's partner). He had been agitating to get this Zeus for quite a while. I had arranged for one through legitimate channels. One day he came to pay the rent on the Zeus and somebody in the room happened to mention that it was my birthday—ten minutes later Thornton comes back and says 'Happy birthday' and puts an ounce of blond Lebanese hash in my hand. I realized then I had been had. He tried three or four times after that, but I was wise to him by then."

As drug dealing grew in size and scope, it became an important, indeed a vital, part of the building's economy. "In terms of the black-market smoke trade," states Pat Phred, "Rochdale was probably one of the largest exporters of hash in North America for that period of time. Rochdale was a prime exporter of hash into the States, which was big news, especially since the dollar was at par.

"What did cannabis mean to Rochdale? It was the kind of economy that was thoroughly integrated through the social and spiritual fabric, all at the same time. But it *was* an economy. For example, when the building was low on a certain product, there'd be people pacing around. That's when you had your worst fights, cases of depression would break out. Now you'd think in strict drug terms, okay, people were out of drugs and they are going through withdrawal, but the truth of the matter was they weren't eatin' right either. The rent was backed up a few weeks, the groupies and the Rentals quit laying heavies on the dealers, right. 'Cause they said, 'Hey we need some lifeblood here.' Then bingo! All of a sudden something would come in and all the fights and feuds would be mended. Everybody would be busy again, workin', feelin' good."

As far as Phred is concerned, dealers had their own ethic and motivation beyond money. "You brought in these large amounts—cannabis and its friends. It's bulky and far less profitable than say heroin or coke. But you did it because you wanted it. It was more than a corporate thing. It wasn't just a business. It was, and I hesitate to use the phrase, it was a religion, good shit—it was like a sacrament!"

As the majority of Rochdalians saw it, there were basically two kinds of dealers: cool and uncool. The "cool" dealers were community-directed and, while certainly being entitled to a reasonable profit, money was not their only motivation. The "uncool" dealers were the exploiters interested in only one thing: the bottom line of profits.

Tony Zenker makes a distinction between dealers and pushers. "Pushers don't care what they sell or who they sell it to. It was just a matter of profit, profit, profit. Then, you had dealers who actually cared about their product, made a reasonable markup, kept the prices low for general consumption. It worked quite well for several years. The pushers—they were the people that handled everything from pot to smack. And smack and speed in the building were no-no's. They were so anti-social, those drugs.

"In all my time dealing, I never had a problem with collecting, rip-offs, nothing. Since 1969—that's nineteen years! You have to pay attention to what you're doing and not get locked into money. Greed is what takes most people down. Being a dealer and not a pusher, it wasn't a regular thing. When you needed money you did it. Otherwise I lived my life and had a good time. It wasn't money, money, money. I'd do the 500-pounds thing, then I wouldn't do anything for a month. Now if I were to do that every week, say, the pattern would show up and I'd probably get nailed."

Mention the "uncool dealers" to Bob Nasmith and you get back a torrent of abusive names. "Greedy, pig-shitfaced-goddam greedy-fuckhead-rip-off dealers who I despise more than anything else on earth were a big problem. To me the dealing aspect was very important. And the cool dealers had been an important part of the building, not only because of the dope and the good times, but because of the income it generated. That money was spread throughout the building and a lot of people benefited. Reagan notwithstanding, it was 'trickle down,' it was capitalism in the finest sense. I'm no Communist.

"But you got these people who were into making the dough, just hoarding it away. We're talkin' a lot of money. We're talkin' abuse of the building and zilch generosity, zilch idealogical sympatico. I despise them.

"The 'right' dealers felt they were part of the community and they shared the wealth—they liked the community they were living in. These dealers let the money filter down through the community. It was a period of survival for Rochdale during this dealer controversy. Rochdale had started out as this grand idealistic idea—this academic idea—some of which worked. But now at this time [1970] it became a question of survival; it came down to having a place to live and a way of life that was satisfying, which were getting harder and harder to find. A lot of the people who were coming through were mostly just trying to survive. They were not coming in from real comfortable homes looking for alternative education."

Rochdale's drug-dealing world was essentially a hierarchy. At the bottom you had the "nickel and dimers." These individuals sold small quantities to keep themselves in either dope or pocket money. They operated in the stairwells, in the lounges outside the building, anywhere they could move their product. Often these hustlers would keep watch on the dealers' stash rooms.

"Weird Waldo was the best nickel and dimer I've ever seen," claims Rochdale resident Horst. "He did it right in front of Rochdale, on the sidewalks, with the cop cars right there. He could sell a quarter-pound of weed in nickel and dimes in a day. You couldn't give him more than an ounce at a time because he'd get lost. I don't know how he did it. He did it for two years and never got busted. He found the victims, and he helped them smoke the stuff after they bought it. He could always pick up on the people from the Clarke Institute. Yeah, those weird chicks, he'd pick up on them, take them in The Rock, get them stoned to the tits and then dump them on somebody.

"The only time he got caught was when he tried to commit suicide on speed. He bought himself an ounce of speed, banged it up until he couldn't focus and he ate the rest. Then he went out for a hike and some hookers rescued him and took him to the hospital. A week later he phones me from the Clarke and says, 'Hey man, you got my keys?' He was definitely a Waldo. He had this wild electric hair, it looked like mattress stuffing, he never combed it. He was tall, skinny and he walked on a slant."

Next up the drug-dealing ladder were people who could cop larger amounts, say, a pound of grass or quarter pound of hash. These dealers would then cut up that amount, redistribute it and maintain a steady retail trade.

"Red" Rebel shakes his head in disbelief when he thinks back to the magnitude and complexity of the drug-dealing operation at The Rock.

"The only counter-culture," chuckles Red, "that I ever saw at Rochdale was around the sink. That place was the most capitalistic place I ever did see. It was wide open. There'd be these stash rooms that were just filled with dope. From floor to ceiling, hundreds of pounds of hash and pot. They used to keep the windows open because of the awesome smell. And those kids would be guarding the stashes. The big dealers would throw them some bread, loose change. And it was dangerous. This one time someone wanted into a stash room and went swinging out like Tarzan and around in through the window. It was nuts.

"Basically how things worked in the infrastructure was the dope filtered down through the building. From the large bulk quantities of hundreds of pounds, it came down to people at the five-pound level, and then there was another group at the pound level, and then down to ounces and so on. At each level there were a number of people involved and it really did seem to work out smoothly. You had people surviving by middling five-dollar deals. Do a few of those an hour and you've got a business going. Just wander down the hall and turn over a chunk of hash and pocket the five dollars."

"There were about 100 people bringing in large amounts into Rochdale," states Tony Zenker, one of the Rock's more trustworthy and reliable dealers. "Not all of it stayed there—some of it went out in large amounts, a lot was moved right there in the building. You had your social structure of who was doing what amounts and who you chose to deal with. Some people were honest—you could front them and they'd come back with the money; others you just couldn't trust out of your sight. After a while you learned who to trust and who not to trust.

"Each person bringing dope into the building had his own people. Each large dealer had his own organization, a chain of groupies and gofers. He himself didn't have that much handling to do. He never lived where the dope was kept because that's how large amounts were dealt with. Whereas at the pound level, with someone cutting it up into ounces, that usually ended up in the person's room and really that's where all the problems were.

"I'd buy for about $50 a pound and sell for $75—I made a reasonable profit and everybody was happy. I moved pounds—when you have that much you don't sit there and move bits and pieces. You find four or five people who have their own regular trade going on and you move pounds to them. It would last three to four days. In my personal dealing, I deal clean and simple. I don't deal to anybody I don't know. So the people who were moving it were all my friends."

At the pinnacle of the drug-dealing pyramid were the importers. These major-league players dealt in amounts that involved millions of dollars. The most celebrated of these dealers was Bob Rowbotham—aka "The Kid" and "Rosie." He came from Belleville and thrived in The Rock's drug hothouse.

"At that time, people who knew me from Belleville, Trenton, Picton and Kingston were coming up to Rochdale. I had a good reputation because I didn't fuck with things, so you knew what you got. Before they were just jocks, but now they were saying, 'Oh hey, remember how we didn't wanna talk to you three years ago because you were a freak? Well, listen. Now I am, too, so can you help me out?'

"Slowly I built a reputation of giving good counts and good quality and cheap price. You wanna buy an ounce? Fine. You wanna buy a quarter pound, you wanna buy a pound, you wanna buy two pounds, you wanna buy fifty hits, you wanna buy seventy-five hits. So that's how it happened. I never had it, but I could go and get it. But before six months passed, on a typical Friday night—and this is no exaggeration—there would be out of my door, down past here, around here through this door, out to the elevator, maybe thirty or forty people coming. And they'd be going to each other, 'What are you gettin?' Well, let's buy it together. Maybe we'll get it cheaper.' They don't even know who they are. They're just coming through."

Registrar Rick Waern watches the dream tower rise at Bloor and Huron streets in the spring of 1968.

Rochdale as it appears today — the Senator David A. Croll Apartments.

A stark warning in the southwest stairwell.

Billy Littler (lower right) supervises a guard-dog training session in the underground garage.

O, cannabis, we stand on guard for thee, as a Rochdale security guard takes a break.

"Badges? We don' need no steenkin' badges." Little John of the Rochdale security team.

Grass-cleaning party.

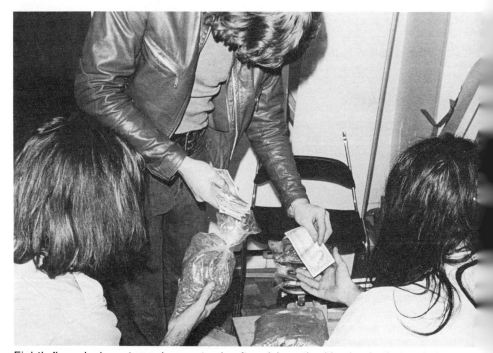
Eighth-floor dealers stage close-out sale after civic authorities begin their eviction crackdown.

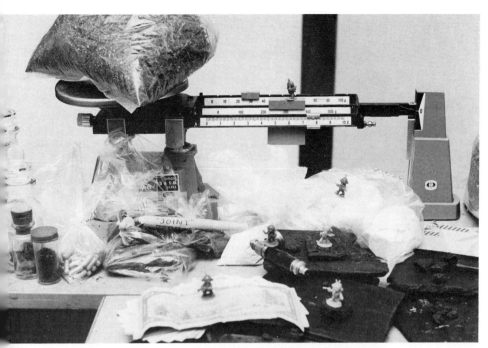

Psychedelic smorgasbord — Rochdale style.

Smoke gets in your eyes if you're at the receiving end of the Official Regal Sceptre of the Grand Duchy of Smeenskneeng — a Rochdale super-toke.

A geodesic zome (a variation of Buckminster Fuller's dome) under construction at the Rochdale farm.

Governing council meeting, circa 1971, in the second-floor lounge. Among those present are Israel Newell (far left in wheelchair), Pamela Berton (arm raised), Frank Cox (centre left) and Jay Boldizsar (seated in white).

Security staffer Charlie Taylor on patrol in Rochdale's lobby.

Key council member, the late Lionel Douglas, conducts a lesson in economic reality for the citizens of Rochdale. The blackboard illustrates the building's labyrinthine financial structure, with arrows leading to 341 — Rochdale's address at 341 Bloor St. W.

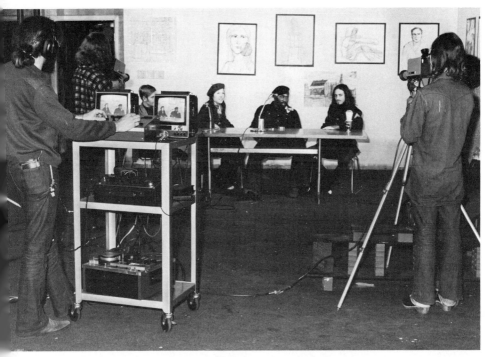

The second-floor video studio was able to send live telecasts via closed circuit to the entire building.

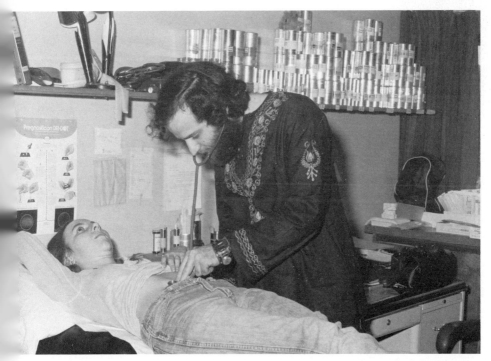

The doctor's clothes may have been unorthodox, but the treatment was first-rate at Rochdale's pioneering clinic.

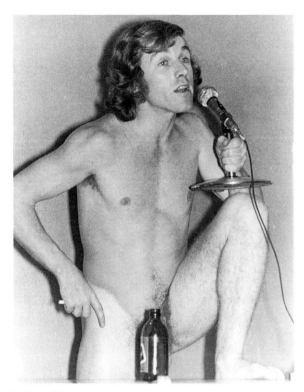

Council president Bob Nasmith addresses a general meeting of Rochdale
residents.

Another sunny afternoon in Rochdale's rooftop oasis.

Battle lines are drawn, as community guardians (hired by the receiver to maintain security after Rochdale's bankruptcy) attempt to occupy the lobby in 1973.

Rochdale's last act of public defiance — the burning in effigy of a community guardian (manikin centre).

The effigy in flames.

Rochdale supporter Pierre Berton shares a joke with council president Bob Nasmith at a Rochdale graduation ceremony in the spring of 1971 at the Yonge St. mall.

Welcome to my nightmare: another successful Rochdale graduate in Alice Cooper makeup proudly clutches her diploma.

Rochdale College

hereby confers upon

Alex MacDonald

the degree of

Master of Arts

together with all the rights, privileges and honours appertaining thereto, in consideration of the fulfilment of the prescribed contribution to higher learning as set forth in the official acts of the Council of the College.

In Testimony Whereof, we set our hand and seal on this day in the year of Our Lord nineteen hundred seventy-three.

President of the College

Chairman of the Council

Unidentified resident is forcibly removed in the wave of evictions that hits Rochdale in 1975.

City inspector surveys graffiti in the empty building.

At times Rochdale turned exporter to the hinterlands and supplied various parts of Canada with "the noble weed." 'Red' Rebel, a Californian junior high school teacher who got turfed for teaching Stokely Carmichael to his unsuspecting class of innocents and ended up being a blues singing, part-time dope dealer, gives us an idea of what a "dope-run" to the Prairies might have been like.

"I was running out of money and I was so into my music and the Rochdale thing that I didn't want to work. I was fronted three pounds of hash by these guys in The Rock. I took a train out to Saskatchewan with the three pounds. The destination was another ex-Rochdalian who had split to the Prairies to start a health food store—perfect isn't it? And this town was a college town and they were starving for smoke.

"I stayed with this guy for a few weeks until I sold all the stuff off. I'll tell ya, it was scary. I was living in this hippie crash pad with sixteen hippies. I was sleeping with the dope and the money under my pillow. There were some crazy people crashing there—grinding up asthma medicine and shooting up. This one guy was about thirty-five years old, a real loser-type hanging with sixteen-year-old kids. This crazy bastard would do anything to get off. I couldn't wait to get out of there.

"When I got back to Rochdale and paid everyone off, I pocketed a thousand dollars after expenses. Kept me going for another year."

The dealers often used young females as their "mules" or couriers. Bobbie Malone describes her experience as a "mule." "This one dealer I was living with—I'd tell you his name but the creep is still around and into the same business—he talked me into taking some hash out to the East Coast. I forget the exact amount, around three or four pounds of hash. I was pretty messed up at the time—drug-wise—and I needed the money so I agreed. The money wasn't shit—around $150, but still it was more than I had.

"I taped these thin compressed blocks of black hash to my body and flew out to the coast. It was like a dream. The fact that I did some speed before I left probably helped that. But I just floated through the trip. There were no borders to cross so you had just to keep cool and not attract too much attention. I did my prep-school bit, plaid skirt, white blouse and this school blazer I copped at a secondhand store. Okay, so the dark circles under my eyes didn't match, but it worked.

"I had some stuff to keep me going during the plane ride. Couldn't afford to crash while I was on delivery. So I finally make it to New Brunswick, meet the people, get the money.

"Now the thing is when I'm getting ready to split I can feel that something was going down with the two guys I had delivered to. They were in the next room and I could overhear what they were saying and it was, 'Maybe we should rip her off, she's only a chick, the guy's back in Toronto.' One of them was really into it, but the smarter of the two knew the character I was doing the run for was a mean sonofabitch and would track them down no matter what. So they let me go. I flew back to Toronto feeling like a total piece of shit. To some it sounds like a big fuckin' adventure, to me it was just survival."

On occasion, however, drug-dealing did have its moments of bizarre, black humour. Tony Phred remembers going to the airport "to meet this dude who was part of a Nepalese hash oil connection. It was pretty compact, this oil, and it was hidden in a pair of oversized, false-bottom sandals that this guy was wearing. They must have been the heaviest sandals in the world, with about a pound and a half of oil in each of them.

"Well, we're waiting for him on our side of the red Customs line and we notice that, as he's walking, every step he takes, the left sandal is leaving an imprint on the floor. The prophylactic that the oil was wrapped in must have expanded and burst, and the oil was soaking through the leather—but he didn't have a clue! We all waved to him and pointed to his sandal, but he didn't know what was up. And for some reason, neither did anyone else. I still don't know how he got away without being caught."

Getting the drug shipments into Rochdale was a world of high adventure on its own. "Bringing 500 pounds of marijuana across town in a Volkswagen," laughs Tony Zenker, "now *that* was fun. It all started out small for me, making just enough to have a little smoke for myself—from a couple of hits of acid it went to 500 pounds of pot. It just mushroomed.

"We'd be wheeling bales of it into the building. We made it in two trips. That particular lot we brought in through the back door of the cafeteria. We dumped it into shopping carts—it was still parcelled so they couldn't see what was inside. So we just wheeled it in. With 500 pounds [250 at a time] in the back of the Volkswagen, it's baled up so high and stacked so you can't even see out the windows barely. And if you get stopped for a regular traffic violation, there's no way in hell you can say anything. It's there—you're beat.

"We were dealing with these Newfoundlanders. They were based in the east end of Toronto. They would come through town and say, 'We've got this much, go over and get it and we'll be back in a few weeks or whatever to collect.' I didn't have transportation of my own, but my friend had this Volkswagen so we went over to this place on Eastern Avenue and picked up the bales like they had been through a garbage compactor. It took two trips to get it to The Rock. We took the back scat out, dumped it into those shopping carts and wheeled it into the elevator. That really was fun."

"The cops never had the brains to stop it going in," says Rosie disdainfully. "They were only interested in the number of busts coming out of the area. They never had the concept of stopping it going in. I'm sure there must have been some copper trying to do his homework, but they never really had a fuckin' idea. Y'know, police aren't that smart. They only learn through the process of repetition. But back then, they had virginal minds. They weren't that sharp.

"For instance, there was a narc car parked in the back alleyway off Huron Street. We loaded up our truck—a huge truck—with bushel baskets for the Etherea Restaurant. But we filled them three-quarters full of dope. And we'd go down to the food terminal at 5:30 in the morning and order all the carrots, green peppers, tomatoes and stuff we needed. Then we'd load up the baskets that had dope with vegetables over on top of it.

"So there's the police officer in the alleyway, having a cigar or feeding his face or whatever, and looking for whoever's bringing dope into the building. And we might have taken six, maybe eight hundred pounds past him in about a two-minute period, four feet from his face.

"We'd also take stuff into the underground parking lot. We had keys to it, and worked it so that we could trip the door. We knew when a special vehicle was coming. So when it came in, we could kick the door closed behind it and we could strip the car and get everything out in five minutes. Also, you do it in rush hour. The car's driving along Bloor Street, and suddenly it's there in the lane. You just make the turn, it's there and it's gone. The driver just fits the key, goes in there, closes the door and that's it. It's over—you're done."

As for Rochdale's clientele, there were two basic kinds of customers. One would be coming in to buy a substantial amount for an entire group. Malcolm, who grew up in the area, maintains that "anyone who wanted to get drugs went to people in the area

who then tended to go to Rochdale for their drugs. So after a
while, it turned out that you just went straight to Rochdale to get
your drugs. We'd buy pot and whatever else—your range of
drugs—from psychedelics right on down.

"At the time, I was going to high school. I had left home because
of problems with my parents. I was basically supporting myself,
and a small part of my income came from selling drugs. I didn't do
it as a business, but people who knew I had access to the place
came to me. It was easy money. We bought mainly for our
personal use. We didn't sell to others, or did on a very small scale.
You'd find a bunch of guys who want an ounce of hash and we'd
get our orders, go in and leave.

"Basically we'd go in and you'd know maybe between five and
ten people who had various types of hash. We weren't asked for ID
in the beginning—we just walked in. We went up to whatever
floor—certain floors were known for certain things at one
point—and you'd go in and ask for what you wanted.

"You'd ask whoever had Red Lebanese or Black Hash or
whatever, and you'd smoke a joint and talk about it. It really never
got to be hard-and-fast business. You'd discuss the merits of this
brand of hash versus that brand in a room down the hall. The guy
would say, 'All right, then, try this' and we'd have a toke and talk
about it. It was extremely easygoing. Basically, you did your
shopping, and whatever you liked, you bought. Then you left. We
never stood in long line-ups to buy drugs because we just knew
who to go to."

These customers were, by and large, proficient small-time
businessmen who came in, did their business and left. The less
attention, the better. It was the second kind of consumer that
caused the majority of headaches for Mother Rochdale—the
dreaded "bopper." Short for teeny-bopper, the term of disparage-
ment referred to the suburbanites who came to The Rock to cop
and have a weekend party.

James Johnson says he "first heard about Rochdale through a
bunch of friends. I was going to high school out in Cooksville. I
was in my final year in 1970. It was the time of the bellbottoms, we
were first in school to wear them. The same for smoking, we were
the first in school to get into that. I'd say back then about ten per
cent of the school was involved with drugs—grades eleven, twelve,
thirteen mostly. Some of the kids we knew would go down to
Rochdale and cop on the weekends and we found out about it the
same way it happened with Yorkville—word of mouth.

"There would be a bunch of us and on Friday night we'd all hop into a car and head down with this guy who knew somebody at Rochdale and we got to know those people as well. It was pretty free and open there that first year. It was before the heavy security trip came in—that was the decline of The Rock. We'd grab bags of pot—basically lids. If our regular guy didn't have it he would tell where we could score. There were so many places to go to get almost anything we wanted.

"We went for a couple of years straight, every Friday night, Saturday. A few times we ended up spending the whole weekend there, crashing out—that went over well with the parents—you'd get carried away and stay for the weekend. We would do some acid there—in fact we were heavy into acid then for a two-year period. You'd get all the colours of the rainbow, loony tunes, window pane, clear light—there was a lot of tripping to be done at Rochdale.

"It was like all the images you had seen and read about in California: Haight-Ashbury, the Electric Kool-Aid Acid Test, the Love Generation. It was very psychedelic, black lights everywhere. There was something very magical about it, something very mystical about it. There was a lot of painting on the walls, a mural in the hallway, graffiti everywhere, but really neat graffiti. It was like tripping into Wonderland—you didn't know what you were going to see or who you would run into. Different floors had different trips going, different ideologies—that was really wild as you tripped from floor to floor."

In Rochdale drugs and drug money meant power. Tony Phred: "Power at Rochdale was money. That would suggest how much you could do politically, how much support you could get. Take political groups like the Red Morning organization or the Maoists, they had political skills and organizational ability, but they didn't have the power because they didn't have the money. Money was the only real power at The Rock."

For all of its romantic, "outlaw-on-the-run" image, the world of the drug dealers had a seamy underbelly. Among certain dealers there seemed to be little truth to the adage that there was "honour among thieves"—rip-offs and burns were commonplace. As maintenance chief Brian Lumley indicates, it was an occupational hazard. "It was easy come, easy go. The dealer made an awful lot of money, but you could get ripped off for everything in one shot. More than once I heard a story about looking down the barrel of a gun and just giving them everything you had.

"I saw Security once when they caught someone who pulled off a rip-off like that. The lines flying around that room were like, 'Let's cut his finger off just to let him know who he's dealing with.' There were a couple of us in the room that weren't going to go along with anything like that. We actually ended up leaving the room. Pauline, who was the secretary and was very straight, said she was going to call the police if they didn't let the guy go, let him go right NOW! So they took the fellow out of the room and said they wouldn't hurt him and Pauline said that was good because if he was hurt she would guarantee that she would testify in court. They wouldn't do anything against her so they ended up letting him go. But they did take his car. The other guy [his partner] got away with the dope and the money. Security got the car and the dealer who got ripped off didn't get anything."

On another occasion, Karen Johnson in Rentals heard dogs being set on someone and confronted Rochdale vice-president Lionel Douglas about it. "I was absolutely outraged and had a big scene with Lionel. Somebody who had caused Security a lot of trouble with a rip-off or something was being worked over. I wouldn't stand for that and Lionel and I had a screeching match in the hall."

"I myself was never ripped off," announces Tony Zenker, "but there was some of that within Rochdale. If you allowed yourself to be ripped off or burnt, you deserved it for getting sloppy. Some people who I came up with, and did well, just got too high, so high they couldn't see. This one guy at several different stages got burned for five, ten thousand American. And I'll tell you this counterfeit money was so bad I could see it was bad even in the dim light of the hallway where I was standing. And it happened to him twice. Another time this same character stashed all of his drugs and a small quantity of money, about three thousand, in his garbage. His wife ended up throwing out the garbage. This poor bastard spent half a day in the garbage bin sorting through it looking for his goods and money. But the people at the bottom of the garbage chute, working in the bin, found it and didn't say anything. Actually the legend goes that one of the guys got hit on the head with the stuff when it came flying down the chute."

Drug dealing at The Rock reached its peak, or nadir, depending on your point of view, with the emergence of the sixth-floor dealing commune. Operated under the leadership of American "Big Al," the sixth floor was an island of lawlessness that symbolized to the authorities the depths of Rochdale's moral depravity and total disregard for the law of the land.

"With opposition growing to dealing to outsiders," states Peter Turner, who battled the sixth floor dealing commune during his presidential tenure, "some of the dealers got together. People like Big Al and Dale Grant felt they had to counter this opposition. The first thing they did—because they felt the Governing Council was starting to move against them—was to take over the Governing Council. They certainly had the money. They figured at $25 a membership, they could buy up the strength needed to run the council. They more or less formed a political movement to counter the opposition. They felt part of what they had to develop was PR—so they founded *Clearlight*, which was an alternative Rochdale *Daily*, to expound their views. So they had community news and articulated their philosophy. They aggressively questioned the activities of the council, suggesting we were mismanaging. We in our wisdom were silent—some of us tried to compromise. Ian Argue and Lionel Douglas attempted to talk to these people and they came back and said, 'But they only want a couple of members on council.'

"They did get one council member to step aside and put in Rosie. My response was to ignore Rosie at every council meeting he attended. I never once looked at him, I never once allowed him to get a word in. After three meetings he left and never returned. But they did build this very real opposition to us. Dale Grant had even drawn up impeachment papers.

"But shortly after that they figured that the best thing to do was to concentrate their enterprise. Since they had formed links with each other during this political movement, they figured it would best serve them to move into one floor together. This would restrict the traffic in the building (i.e., people wouldn't be going through the whole building looking to score drugs, but come to one central location), provide security and help them stop being the focus of Rochdale's anger.

"It had precisely the opposite effect. People started looking at this big huge closed door, and at the security guards they had placed there and realized there was an arrogance that could not be tolerated. Your typical scenario would be: someone approaches the door, the shutter window slides back: 'Yeah, what ya want?' 'Just want to buy something.' 'Okay, stand up against the wall, spread your legs.' They'd frisk you and then let you in. You'd be surrounded by these dealers. It increased the paranoia of the building.

"The biggest mistake the police ever made was raiding that floor, because in a few months there would have been so much pressure from within the community they would have had to move out on their own. Once when Big Al was displeased with some interference of mine, he threatened to kill me."

One segment of the Rochdale population in particular looked askance at the sixth floor operation—the big dealers. Rosie himself was based on the sixth floor, but he would have nothing to do with Big Al and his type.

"I was never involved in any dealing commune. I was always solo. The sixth-floor dealing commune was a crock of shit and that was on the other side of the floor. I was by myself in 617. I was my own island. The commune was an American version of garbage— the guns, the door, the lock, all that shit. It was part of the American culture I wasn't going to simulate."

Big Al and his fellow dealers—the total number was twenty to thirty people with a small auxiliary group—were simply too extreme for Rochdale by the summer of 1970.

Big Al himself was involved in more than one bloody incident. "Once Big Al met someone in Jamaica and this guy burnt him for $7,000," says resident T.J. "And later, by chance they met up again in Rochdale. There's a confrontation. Big Al unscrews the nozzle of a fire hose and says, 'Gimme the bread!' The other looks at the hose and goes flying down the hall and into the Ashram kitchen. He comes bolting out like a maniac and he's got a kitchen knife in his hand. He starts wielding it around. The two of them get into it and Al ends up losing two fingers. The blood was flying all over the place. The cops, of course, showed up. It was a bad scene.

"Al was definitely living out some sort of outlaw fantasy. I heard that he ended up getting killed in a dope deal gone bad. Figures."

"The guns were the limit for me," declares Bob Nasmith. "I know what they can do and wanted no part of them or the lifestyle that they brought in. So we started to apply the pressure. We'd call them into meetings, threaten to cut them off. Security was going to cut them off—Security would simply say nobody goes up to the sixth floor. It did get to the point—and you must remember when I say this what an anathema it was to us—but some of the people were ready to talk to the cops about these pricks because it was way out of line. Not just a couple of goofs with dogs, but guns, and guns suck!"

The situation clearly chafed Metro Police, who began observing the sixth floor, often from nearby buildings.

"The windows were blackened on the sixth floor and vinyl was put over the windows to keep prying eyes out," relates Nasmith. "It wasn't paranoid to think that there'd be cops in the Medical Arts building across the street or the Nu Sigma Nu house out back looking in. The cops had more than a rough idea where the action was."

After the summer of 1970 raids—events that will be covered in a later chapter—the floor was ravaged beyond recognition.

"It was like a ghost town," says Valerie Frith, who as a part of the rental office had to deal with the aftermath. "Rochdale had its own little ghost town on the sixth floor. Later on it was restored and part of it became a Christian commune. There was a period, the fall of '70–'71, there was no money available so it stayed in that torn-apart state. But we in Rentals had master keys so we could sneak in there. The destruction was phenomenal, it really was like a circle in hell, just unbelievable. There were no lights, no power, everything was black, even the windows had been painted over black and had vinyl attached. The destruction was unbelievable. Everything just hung from the ceiling, the walls had these little 'things' embedded in them so that as you went along in the dark your hand would touch them—it was quite fascinating. The sixth floor commune, it's a legend, part of the oral history of Rochdale. Everybody has his and her own version."

A dramatic example of how the Rochdale community was changing is evidenced by the transformation of the sixth floor. Frank Cox, an American draft dodger who came to Canada to attend the Strawberry Fields Festival, teamed up with Frank Burns to rehabilitate the sixth floor. They had their work cut out for them.

"Martin and I made a deal with Karen Johnson to get the sixth floor Ashram. So we cleaned it up. There was a telephone booth that was full of turkey shit, the sinks were plugged with vomit, the fridge had moldy oranges in it, there was food everywhere. When I was in there someone was showing porno flicks in the Ashram lounge. We changed it quite a bit from there, made it into a commune, a place to live."

The polarity between those who supported the dealers, either for selfish monetary reasons or on philosophical grounds, and those opposed to the "private enterprise sector" was heightened by the summer raids and subsequent riots. A growing number of Rochdalians felt exploited by an opportunistic segment of the population. The dissenting voices grew louder and louder as summer faded into fall. As general manager Bill King put it, it was "nothing less than a question of survival."

The college administration, sensing the turning of popular opinion, seized the moment and on September 5, evicted fifteen major dealers. On September 8, *The Toronto Star* reported a statement from King:

> "The dealers sort of closed themselves in in response to what was a building pressure from the residents," King said. "How long it will last I don't know. It was a voluntary thing.
>   ..."pressure arose because of large numbers of outsiders who came to buy drugs from the sixth floor.
>   "It was sort of creating an alienation within the community," King said.
>   He said there were between 10 and 12 pushers on the sixth floor during a peak period in August. Now there are "two or three smaller dealers who are selling out their inventory."
>   Most of the pushers were still living there, but "they are sort of retired," King said.

College president Peter Turner, reflecting back on the summer of 1970 in his book *There Can Be No Light Without Shadow* (published the following year), observed:

> The question of what to do or not do in the case of dealers in the building came to a standstill within the community when the raids began. The community waivered. Emotions and thoughts had been running high for some time on this subject and were mostly against the dealers. The raids shed new light on the question. Who were the police taking away? What and how much was being seized? The fact is they were seizing very little and often arresting people merely for possession. Suddenly, it seemed as though the community would unite against the police. Then it was pointed out that the dealers were not the ones going to jail – their internal clients were. The dealers were exposed as cowards, hiding behind the skirts of Rochdale and using the community for their own profit and protection and threatening the survival of the community. They were not heroes.
>   The referendum went against the dealers. Creating traffic from the outside by dealing was outlawed. To ban all visitors to the building penalized too many and would have been politically unfeasible. However, finding the dealers and proving a case against them before the Court of Appeals and then, after they were evicted,

hunting down the people they sent in as "fronts" to rent rooms and deal on their behalf was difficult, to say the least. The administration finally resorted to having the security guard on duty ask each visitor for the number of the room they were going to and the name of the person registered there. If they were unable to give the information, they could not enter. If a particular room proved to have a questionable number of visitors, security turned away all traffic to that room. If there was enough circumstantial evidence of dealing, it resulted in a room check, and the occupants of that room would find themselves before the Court of Appeals.

During this time, the governing council continued to make efforts to communicate with the police department to let them know we shared the same concern over possible violence. There ensued a number of mutually satisfactory discussions with the officials as well as the constables, sergeants and detectives of the police force.

The referendum that Turner refers to was an open vote held on September 12–13. The referendum asked Rochdalians to stand up and be counted. Where did Rochdale stand on the issue of dealers and dealing to outsiders? Did dealers have a place in college life? Did they help support the building's economy, and was that support worth the drain on the college? Was it worth all the negative publicity that would surely sink the college in the end? It was a critical moment in Rochdale's history.

"The referendum to prohibit dealing to outsiders in the early fall of 1970," reflects Alex MacDonald, "couldn't have possibly happened any earlier, like say the fall of '69. You had to live through the summer of '70 to get to that point. You had to survive the summer of '70 even to question the notion that some form of regulation of the private sector was necessary and indeed appropriate.

"But when the anti-dealing legislation was passed, most of the dealers just laughed and it was business as usual. But it did sink in because the idea had some support in the community. This wasn't a notion contrived by the bureaucrats. You can't just pass legislation like that—you need a social consensus, and it was there and growing all the time."

Israel Newell, who was involved in the counting, reveals that the two-day vote was actually going in favour of the dealers until the fallout from the last massive police raid began to filter through a concerned Rochdale citizenry.

"Part of the reason that the anti-dealing referendum was carried was because on the night after the first day of the referendum there was this big raid. It was a riot of some sort and a lot of people were traumatized by that particular raid. The vote on the first day was actually in favour of dealing to outsiders or at least leaving the dealers alone to do so. But after the raid, on that second-day vote, those who hadn't voted came pouring in and they said NO!

"I personally didn't see that the dealers had a legitimate function. It was illegal and they were, in the final analysis, destructive to the community."

CHAPTER 8

Dazed
and
Confused

When did the Sixties end? Was it December 6, 1969, the day the Rolling Stones, the world's greatest rock and roll band, threw a party at the Altamont Speedway? The day the cosmic boogie of the Woodstock nation dissipated into ugly mob violence and death, dragging down in its tow a generation's faith in itself and its ideals? That same week a former resident of the Haight-Ashbury, Charles Manson, went on trial with four others for the nightmarish ritual slaughter of actress Sharon Tate. The love train was derailed.

Or did the Sixties end on September 18, 1970, the day that Jimi Hendrix, that sweet black angel who had opened so many new musical horizons with an imagination that was as bold as love, asphyxiated in his own vomit? Or did flower-power wither three weeks later when we lost the Pearl—Janis Joplin—who OD'd in a Hollywood hotel room? Those two deaths hit the counter-culture with a sickening one-two thud. We were becoming numb. Something was slipping away.

Or perhaps we mark the end of the Sixties by the decade's favourite pop bellwether, the four young men from Liverpool who learned some good old American rock and roll and just happened to change the world while they were at it. In that case, it would be April 9, 1970, the day that Paul McCartney pulled the plug on the Fab Four by releasing an album he had been secretly working on at his farm in Scotland. Or perhaps it was December 31, 1970, the day that Paul filed an official suit in London's High Court to dissolve the Beatles.

Many cultural historians see June 17, 1972, and the Watergate break-in as the day the coffin lid closed on that unique decade, the Sixties.

Any of these dates would do; all of them are weighted with the obvious symbolism associated with the one event that ends an epoch—and the Sixties were an epoch—in cultural history.

Whenever it happened, the Sixties did turn into the seventies, and with that transition came a darkening of the vision. We moved from the Strawberry Alarm Clock to Black Sabbath, from *Surrealistic Pillow* to *Dark Side of the Moon*. Rock itself developed a tough, heavy sound that exalted power; the peace symbol finger sign was replaced by a clenched fist. We moved from body painting and making statements by throwing dollar bills onto the floor of the New York Stock Exchange to drug clinics and bombing induction centres. Even the Haight, the Mecca of the New Age, had degenerated into a heroin slum. Something had changed, something fundamental had changed. An innocence was lost.

John Lennon echoed a generational sentiment when he told *Rolling Stone* magazine in 1971, "The dream is over."

We see the same darkening of the vision at Rochdale through the early seventies. There was a new hard-bitten realism. Rochdale's general manager Brian Gilhuly articulated that realism when he told *The Globe and Mail* in the fall of 1970, "I think that what Rochdale was originally set up for turned out to be quite irrelevant. Very little of what people were saying in 1967 is more than laughable now. Nineteen sixty-seven was among other things the summer of love, good vibes and acid. It's a lot colder out there now."

The most obvious manifestation of the change in the texture of the times was the loss of life at Rochdale—the human carnage. No one ever accused Rochdale of being a home for choirboys and Girl Guides. It was a rough and tumble place.

It is difficult to say with certainty the number of unnatural deaths that occurred at Rochdale. The line between suicide, accident and murder was sometimes blurred.

On one occasion, according to security man T.J., a "suicide" had all the makings of an execution. "It didn't look like any suicide to us," says T.J. "The wrists definitely had rope burns and the way the body had landed, it looked like his hands were tied up from behind. But we didn't really get involved, besides discussing it amongst ourselves."

Security chief Billy Littler remembers another so-called suicide. "There was one chap, a resident, who fell. He was reported to be a suicide and I said, 'No, no, this is nonsense.' That stupid bastard was sitting on his window sill again, playing his guitar and he lost his balance. I had seen this guy and I had seen other people do the

same thing on other levels. They sit on their ledge looking out.
Now remember there were no balconies and no safety kind of
situation whatsoever. I knew this guy specifically, I had seen him
sitting on the edge strumming his guitar, one foot outside the
window and one foot inside. I'll never believe that guy committed
suicide. He was a true resident. Paid his rent. As far as it went he
was considered a 'good guy' by everyone in the building, or those
who knew him."

General consensus puts the total seven-year figure at one
murder and anywhere from six to eleven suicides. As for
overdoses, it's impossible to get an accurate estimate, due to the
reticent nature of the drug world. However, the Metro ambulance
department lists fifty-eight OD's with three DOA's (dead on
arrivals) for the period June 1, 1970, to March 31, 1971.

Much has been made of the many suicidal, drug-induced falls at
Rochdale, which may have been aided by poor window design. As
former resident Rico Gerussi notes, "The desk in the room
was built at the exact level of the window, and the window ledge
was slanted downward and out. If you sat on the desk, you could
drape your feet along the outside of the building—something that
would probably be totally illegal today."

Another resident, who wishes to be identified only as Brunnel,
adds that the desks had originally been fixed in place. "But all of
them were removed and changed around, because when people
moved in, they set the style themselves. They didn't want
standard, student-type lodgings, I guess. So when you removed
this desk from one of those windows, you had worse than your
standard balcony, because the ledge was at crotch level. So you
could easily trip out of the bloody thing.

"And often, from the room I was in—which faced south—I
leaned out the window to look at the corner of St. George and
Bloor, which was to the north. I was hanging my body more than
halfway out the window, so I could very easily have fallen out.
And I can imagine people who were rather stoned just falling
out."

But it was the "jumpers," those disturbed lonely people who
chose to end it all on the pavement outside of 341 Bloor Street
West, who attracted the most attention and the harsh glare of
publicity.

Rochdale's first casualty was Thomas Kelpe. Kelpe, a twenty-
one-year-old draft dodger from Phoenix, Arizona, leaped from the

sixteenth floor of The Rock on October 14, 1970. While searching his room, police discovered his U.S. Army induction card, dated July, 1969. At the time of his death, Kelpe was getting psychiatric help at the Clarke Institute.

From that very first jumping suicide, Rochdale became like the Golden Gate Bridge. The more media attention focused on the suicide jumps, the more the dislocated fringe element began looking at 341 Bloor Street as the place to end it all.

It was incidents such as these that compelled an anguished Dennis Lee to do anything necessary—to take any downtown route while walking or driving—to avoid catching even the briefest glimpse of the building he had helped to create. "For ten years," he sighs, "I could hardly walk by it, because I 'hemorrhaged' internally."

"People heard it was the place to take a leap," says T.J. "We had a basically fifteen- to twenty-five age group. That's the highest risk suicide age bracket. And we had an incredible amount of traffic—people staying a day, a week, a month, a year. And you had people who were lost. They didn't have anywhere else to go. These crashers used to just hang out. And I know some of them, when they were finally turfed out of Rochdale, well that was the end of the line for them. They had no place else to go so they took the big jump. There weren't that many—I think ten deaths over the years."

In February, 1973, Philip Hunter, a twenty-four-year-old Rochdale resident, plunged seventeen storeys to his death. At the inquest in July, coroner Alex Jones cast a further pall over the building by stating there was not enough evidence to determine whether the incident was an accident, suicide or murder. Hunter's father insisted that suicide was not in his son's nature and that Philip must have been unconscious and thrown from the roof, perhaps in a dispute over drugs. As in past inquests, the jury called for Rochdale's prompt closure.

T.J. remembers one particularly poignant incident involving a jumper. While patrolling the area of the second-floor patio, he spotted what he thought was a pile of dirty laundry, which turned out to be the body of a resident who had committed suicide. When the police arrived, they asked T.J. to identify the man, "but the body was in pretty bad shape. Even if it was my own brother, I couldn't have recognized him. Half his face was off and his hair was removed from his skull. It looked like the body had come from quite a ways up.

"So we went up to the top—the eighteenth floor—and started knocking on doors to see where he had jumped from, so we could determine his identity. Finally, we got down to the sixteenth floor and knocked on this door and there was no answer. I opened it with my passkey and we went in and found a pair of slippers by the open window and the stereo going with a set of headphones. It looked like this guy was sitting there listening to the music and then he just jumped.

"Later we found out he was a draft dodger and he'd been on LSD the previous night. And the day he jumped was the very day that President Nixon announced there would be no amnesty for draft dodgers—in other words, they'd be arrested and have to do something like five years in jail if they came home. We figured that must have triggered it. People who knew him said he was terribly depressed because he missed his family and wanted to go home very badly."

Sometimes religion took a grisly turn, especially in what Tony Phred calls "the Jump-for-Jesus crowd. There seemed to be one jumper per year—the great window-leapers of Rochdale! This group really hurt my headspace.

"I especially remember this one young runaway who came to the building—your basic runaway from a nice Rosedale family, probably overindulged. He was in there tripping out on LSD, and during one of his flippy trips, he runs into the Jesus freaks who decide they're going to pray the devil out of him. Well, that's fine and dandy. He confesses all his sins to Jesus, the weight is off his back and he doesn't have these problems, whatever it was that made him leave home.

"Two days later, he falls off the Jesus wagon and does another hit of acid. But this time around, he's fully convinced he's swallowed the devil. So he goes up to the laundromat on the eighteenth floor and makes this great leap out the window for Jesus. It's a sad commentary, because all those well-intentioned Jesus people did was pray that kid to his death."

"On the whole, the Christians weren't bad," says maintenance chief Brian Lumley, "although they did have some misconceptions about life in the real world. I let them get away with quite a bit—an awful lot more than a professional security outfit would have."

Cindy Lei took her own life when it looked like it was finally over for Rochdale. Lei was one of those Rochdalians who really plugged her entire being into The Rock (in her time she was the treasurer, an active force in Ed Con and the Toad Lane Tenants Association and a teacher of explorative choreography). By May of 1975 she had helped the skeletal remains of the Rochdale community cope with the last days. When she lost her final appeal on a rent arrears charge, she bailed out. For her, life without Rochdale didn't have much meaning.

Even though his figures are slightly off, Walt Houston makes a crucial point when he says, "A lot is said about the number of suicides connected with Rochdale—six or seven. But if you check the actual figures of all the people who actually died within the building, one was an old man who died of old age and another was a girl who lived in the building who committed suicide. None of the other people who died in there was from the building. They had heard it was a good place to kill themselves, so they went there to die. They went there because they knew they could go to the eighteenth floor or the roof and jump off. In any incident like that involving Rochdale, it usually took fifteen or twenty minutes to get an ambulance there."

More than one Rochdalian had the eerie experience of actually seeing someone in free flight. "I was high on acid once," says Rosie Rowbotham, "sittin' on the sixth floor when a guy fell out of the tenth floor window. And I actually had eye contact with him going by. It was really spooky, scary, because I couldn't reach out and help the guy. Then I saw him lying there and I couldn't look no more, because it was baggie time.

"Another time I had a rental car and I was coming in the back door because I had a key to the restaurant. These two old-clothes cops see me, but they're not waitin' for me. They're just hangin' around to roust people. I had nothing—maybe a couple dozen joints down my pants. So I get halfway up to the door and I hear the clunk, clunk, of their car doors and footsteps. I'm maybe ten feet away from the door when they go, 'Rosie, Rosie, stop!' Well, fuck that. I get the key out and I'm maybe two feet from the door when somebody fell from the eighteenth floor and landed on a car. He took off the whole top, the seats—everything's on the bottom. The guy's medically dead, but I can hear him going, 'Help, help,' and I don't know what's going on. And there's blood everywhere.

"Now the cops are ten feet on one side of this car and I'm ten feet on the other side. And when this guy lands in the middle, I open the door to Rochdale and close it. So these cops have come to roust a fuckin' hippie and they end up in ten tons of paperwork, a possible homicide or maybe a drug-induced suicide.

"Anyhow I went upstairs to sell a guy some hash and he said he had his car parked outside. I says, 'Is it a blue Camaro?' He says, 'Yeah,' and I says, 'C'mere with me!' He took a look down and I said, 'You don't wanna go near that fuckin' car.' "

Rochdale resident Brunnel "saw at least three out-of-the-window type of suicides. Other deaths, if it was a drug overdose or something like that, the ambulance just came and took people out. But these were more of an incident."

On December 18, twenty-two-year-old ex-Detroiter Maria Bulfoni took the plunge from the twelfth floor. For resident Red Rebel, it was "unbelievable, simply unbelievable. This friend of mine, he ran the second-floor cafeteria and he was up in his room, just laying down, reading and relaxing. When suddenly this complete stranger walks into his room, just opens the door and walks right in. She doesn't say anything to him. She walks through the room, opens the window and jumps out, just like that. His door obviously wasn't locked, but still you're lying there in your room and this incredible thing happens. I saw him about ten minutes later and he was just gone, know what I mean? Just gone! This Bulfoni woman just came into the building, didn't live there or nothing. Just walked in, decided she was going to die there and happened to choose my friend's room for her final act of desolation. This friend was devastated. He said Bulfoni was wrapped up in this big heavy coat and she looked bizarre to begin with. Just a strange, strange situation."

One of the key figures from the early days who could not bear to sever the Rochdale connection was Jim Garrard, the founder of Theatre Passe Muraille. While Lee shuddered from afar, Garrard was another witness to death. "This was in a real down-at-the-heels time when the pressure was being felt the most," he recalls. "I was playing cards on the second floor one morning at five or six o'clock and light snow was falling outside.

"There'd been a kid sitting up in the eighteenth-floor laundry room window periodically. He wasn't a Rochdalian, but he'd come in and sit in this window and God knows what he'd been thinking about. And I came out looking for cigarettes or something and I was standing in the lobby on the second floor, and I heard this noise behind me—kind of a clunk. And I turned around and, my God, this kid had fallen onto the patio. He was lying in half an inch of absolutely unbroken, white snow with this expanding halo of blood coming out from the back of his head.

"So here's the blood spreading out and the life's draining out of this poor kid who's got only a little bit of breath in him. The excitement, or whatever it was, must have travelled up, because all of a sudden, a whole stream—there must have been eight of them—of young girls was coming down the stairs from one commune or a bunch of them on the upper floors. They'd seen what had happened. It was a futile gesture, but they came out and laid their coats over the top of this kid. Eventually the ambulance came and the kid was taken away, and we all quit playing poker, because it was a real bummer."

Unnerving though the incident was, it did not shake Garrard's faith in Rochdale. "The thing is, people can commit suicide anywhere. This was somebody who had come to Rochdale to jump or—who knows?—maybe he was just feeling melancholy and thought that if he sat there, he would get some attention, which he didn't really get.

"The trouble is, when something like that happened in Rochdale, it became a major incident. People thought it was another bad thing about Rochdale. But if you really examine it closely, it was one of the good things about Rochdale. This kid had come there for some reason, and maybe he wished somebody would come and talk to him or some beautiful girl would come over and say, 'Let's go to a movie.' But the fact was, nobody bothered him. He wasn't put into the situation of a jumper on a ledge with people yelling 'Hey, kid, get down off there!' You were allowed to do pretty much what you wanted, as long as you didn't bother anybody else."

Still, suspicions about Rochdale's deaths persisted. Brunnel, in particular, remembers "a supposed jump from an eleventh-floor window by someone who was not a Rochdale resident. He'd come in to buy drugs or was a friend of someone there and he landed on a Toyota Celica at the back alley. I always figured that he'd been pushed out after coming in to buy some dope. But the dealers didn't have any for him and they just pushed him out the window, maybe because they didn't like him. I think that, because of the character of the people in the room where it happened and the types of rumours that went around, that was a possibility. At the time, there just didn't seem to be a good enough story to explain why this guy fell out the window."

The psychological effects of the drug culture were felt even by those who had helped to nurture it. Tony Zenker, a long-time dealer, remembers one of the MDA chemists who "started doing his own product and ended up committing suicide because he couldn't handle what came down. He tried suicide several times—once at The Rock and once by trying to jump off City Hall—but he was stopped in time. He finally got himself a room, mixed a special concoction and injected it. He was determined to go. He had looked around and he saw the damage that his drug had done to other people and he couldn't deal with that."

Another manner of death at Rochdale came via the misadventure route. The most publicized death in Rochdale's seven-year history had to be that of seventeen-year-old Kevin Yallop. Yallop was a North York teen who went to Rochdale on the night of March 18, 1971, along with three other teen friends, to obtain beer and/or drugs. The four had polished off a twenty-four-bottle case of beer early in the day and were on the hunt for more. They managed to get by the security desk because, according to college vice-president Lionel Douglas's testimony at the coroner's inquest, one of the teens was a former resident who was recognized by the security watch. In his search for more booze and drugs, Yallop went along the sixth floor indiscriminately knocking on doors, soliciting drugs. Trouble erupted when he knocked on the door of the apartment shared by nineteen-year-old Leona Crawley, her boyfriend Daniel Crowder and their five-month-old son, Jamie. Crowder told Yallop in no uncertain terms that they didn't sell drugs and ordered him to leave immediately.

According to Crawley, "Kevin was very violent that night. He was really looking for a fight." A scuffle did eventually break out when eighteen-year-old Rochdale resident Wolfgang Glaser confronted Yallop in the elevator lobby of the sixth floor. *The Toronto Star* picks up the story:

> Witnesses testified that the two youths were cautioned about the floor-to-ceiling windows, near which they were fighting, but they apparently didn't hear or ignored the warnings.
>
> They fell against the window and plunged six floors to the pavement on Bloor St. W. below. Both were taken by ambulance to Toronto General Hospital, where Yallop was pronounced dead.
>
> Glaser appeared at the inquest on crutches. He said he is recovering from his injuries, but cannot remember anything from about seven hours before the accident to about three days after it.
>
> In its verdict, the jury criticized "the building construction at Rochdale, whereby floor-depth windows of questionable strength are allowed in a public section of the building where there is likely to be a large number of people, with no protective guarding inside or outside the windows."

> The jury recommended that "immediate steps be taken to reconstruct all the windows and openings in such a way as to make it impossible to fall through the opening."

Eye witness Walt Houston narrowly avoided being hit by the two falling bodies. "I had someone almost land on me. I was coming in the front door of the building after going out to dinner one night. It was a real shock. At first, I thought someone had thrown a couple of bags of wet laundry out the window. We were approaching the door from the side and something went thump, thump in front of me. It takes you about five or ten seconds to realize it's two people who just went out a window. We looked up and saw that it was only the sixth floor they'd come from, so we realized there was a very good chance they were still alive. We got over to them really fast and did what we could in the way of first aid. There wasn't a great deal we could do, though—just wait for the ambulance to get there with the body boards to take them out. The second fellow wasn't too bad, although his legs and back were badly injured and he was on a cane for several years, because the guy who pulled him out the window broke his fall and he landed on him."

The coroner at the Yallop inquest, K.R. Baxter, called the incident a "sordid story of beer and drugs." Yallop, who had been using drugs since he was thirteen years old, was a product of "the social environment in which he lived," and the entire episode was a "sad commentary on the drug permissiveness of today." The most immediate result of the Yallop death was that Rochdale installed bars across the floor-to-ceiling windows in the elevator lobbies.

The Rock was the launching pad for a number of psychedelically inspired delusions of flight. *Toronto Sun* columnist Mark Bonokowski's obituary on Rochdale included the usual litany of horror stories like the headline which read "Girl on LSD Trip Jumps Four Floors." "No," he wrote, "the girl didn't die. She landed on the roof of a parked car, breaking her fall to the pavement. But she was only fourteen years old. A youth in the room said the girl was whipped up on acid. She started laughing, then crying. Finally she stripped off her clothes and dove naked out the window."

Rochdale's version of the flying fourteen year old was contained in resident Mary Anne Carswell's letter to the editor that appeared in *The Globe and Mail*.

As to the naked 14-year-old girl, yes, she was naked, 14, and high on drugs. No, she did not believe she could fly. Here's what actually happened. In the first place, the person she was visiting thought she was about 18. His room was on the 4th floor. She looked out of the window at one point and noticed a convertible, the hood up, parked directly under the window. She said she thought if she jumped out the window she'd bounce on the roof, like a trampoline, and not be hurt at all. Her host, anxious lest she be serious, went next door to get help. When he returned, his room was empty. The Rochdale security guard who found her reported that when he found her she was lying on the pavement, laughing.

It's remarkable that an environment such as Rochdale's, with its potential for hair-trigger violence, gave rise only to one murder in seven years. Despite the stream of severed fingers, busted heads, bloody knife wounds and rumoured drug-land assassinations, the police file lists the name of only one murder victim—Marika Sokolaski.

Sokolaski's body was found on December 6, 1971. She had been dead for two days. The twenty-two-year-old former model had left her husband two years earlier after falling in with Rochdale's speed community. With her four-year-old daughter in tow, the attractive brunette moved into an $85-a-month apartment at The Rock. Detective Crampton was one of the investigating officers at the murder.

"On December 4, 1971, there was an armed robbery in the vicinity of Rochdale. This was perpetrated by a young man who was not armed. He merely indicated to the teller that he was in fact armed by his hands in his pockets. And he got away with several thousand dollars. While he was on Bloor Street West, he was apprehended by responding police officers and he was taken into number 14 Division. I was in the holdup squad then and we were called to investigate.

"It was warm in the police station while I was questioning this young man. So he took off his outer garment and had just a T-shirt on. And the T-shirt was full of dried blood. We thought he was injured and asked to examine his head and his body. There were no injuries on his torso or his legs, but there was a head injury and we thought maybe the head injury had caused the blood. So we questioned him about this and he indicated to us that he had spent the last week or ten days in Rochdale to obtain drugs in order to satisfy his cravings. He was on LSD and speed. He also indicated to me that he had stabbed a woman in Rochdale, but he couldn't remember the floor and couldn't remember anything. Then he got quite concerned about this woman and wanted to know if she was living or dead, or if the police had received any complaint about this or taken anybody from Rochdale.

"So we left him for a few minutes and made some inquiries, which turned out negative. Bill [Wilson, his partner] and I decided at that point to go over to Rochdale ourselves. I phoned my contacts in security ahead of time and they met me and we got in through the doorway without incident. It didn't take very long to find the apartment, and there was a woman in the apartment—stone dead. Rigor mortis had set in and the place was a blood-spattered mess. The young man pleaded guilty to manslaughter and got eight years.

"The great majority of people at Rochdale were absolutely appalled that that [murder] could have happened. You're aware of the dream they had for Rochdale. Well, that murder was the beginning of the end of that dream—there's no question about it. They suddenly realized that in their midst they had people who were not psychologically attuned to the cause, but were using Rochdale for their own benefit. A lot of people bailed out as a result of that murder and the subsequent investigation of the chemist. They quickly realized that the police had not lied and they had concerns that were well-founded."

Rumblings calling for the end to this experiment-gone-awry began to be heard as Rochdale's dark side gained more and more publicity. It was little wonder that when a county court grand jury recommended closing Rochdale "as quickly as possible" the story was front-page news. The report presented to senior county court Judge Walter Martin read in part: "The people who advocate the continuation of this situation, whether educators, politicians or influential citizens, must somehow have their eyes opened to the truth of this unfortunate situation."

As scrutiny of Rochdale intensified, the news media took an even greater interest in the building's activities. But where residents had once welcomed reporters to examine the progressive experiments in culture and education, they now viewed outsiders with resentment and wariness. Most newspapers and broadcasters were content to base their view of Rochdale on revelations made at inquests or during the occasional press conference. However, television station CFTO was determined to get an insider's perspective, and in the fall of 1973, the assignment to go undercover for three weeks fell to a twenty-one-year-old newcomer named Tom Clark.

Clark, who has since risen to the position of political editor of CFTO, had grown up in Toronto and was generally familiar with Rochdale. But from early 1972 until mid-1973, he had worked in Montreal and was unaware of the extent of the building's deterioration. Even so, Clark was an ideal choice for the job, since he brought a fresh approach to the story, and his absence from Toronto TV screens meant it would be easier for him to live incognito in Rochdale.

"I was told to go into Rochdale, but not to file at all—just to spend three weeks there and, with whatever means I wanted, to come out with impressions of what was going on. I didn't know what to expect, quite frankly, and I was neither here nor there on the whole Rochdale issue. It wasn't part of my mythology at the time, and all I knew was that my new boss wanted to send me someplace because there had been some deaths there and the cops were all upset. There were no pre-conditions set and the story wasn't written before I went in there. The whole idea was that I was to get dressed in my old jeans and put on my red bandanna and go in and be part of the crowd. So that's what I did.

"Strangely enough, the cops were having a hell of a time getting somebody in undercover, but I managed to do what they couldn't. In fact, we made it a condition that the cops were not to be informed I was in there until after I had gotten in, because I didn't want any funny business prior to that. I was single at the time and my family knew that I was in there, but there was no need to contact them while I was inside. As long as things were going well, it was just another job—a weird job, but a job nonetheless.

"My cover story was that I worked part-time for Ontario Hydro as a lineman. I didn't use my real name, and I think I gave a false, out-of-town address and telephone number in Nova Scotia or New Brunswick. But they never once asked me for ID.

"Anyway, I was sitting in the interview with this older fellow who was obviously a bureaucrat from somewhere who ended up as the admissions officer at Rochdale, quite out of his element. I remember he was a very tall Englishman with sort of a tweedy, brown suit. All he needed was the golden retriever lying beside the desk and it would have been the perfect picture.

"And as he was asking me the questions and filling out the forms, without even looking up, he asked, 'And how do you like CFTO?' So I laughed and answered, 'Well, you've gotta be the only guy in Toronto who'd recognize me.' All of a sudden, he turned very serious and said, 'What do you think you're doing?'

And I said, 'I'm just doing my job. I'm coming in here to take a look around. I'm not going to do any damage or cause any alarm. I'm just an observer.' So he said, 'Okay. I won't tell anybody. But I have to warn you that if they find out you're a reporter, you're in a lot of trouble—not from me, but from the people in the building.' And he had me worried, because he kept on stressing the danger element from bikers and drug dealers. And he finished by saying, 'If you're discovered, get out of here as fast as you can and don't look back.'

"So that was my initiation and I moved in right away. I can't remember what floor I was on. But the set-up was my room and another room and a sort of little hallway leading to the door. There was another fellow in the next room, and he was a nice enough guy. But he was a bit wary of me and I returned the favour, being wary of him, although I tried to work on him quietly and gently.

"It turned out he wasn't involved in the criminal element, but boy—he sure knew his stuff. He showed me all the tricks of how to get rid of drugs and he knew who to buy drugs from. He also told me who you didn't buy your drugs from, so I asked, 'Why? Is it bad stuff?' And he said, 'No, no. But the other guys won't like it.' So that was the first hint I had that there was a fight for control of the drug trade and, obviously, some muscle being used to enforce it.

"The thing that struck me most was not the granola crowd or the flower-power crowd or the sex-drugs-and-rock-'n'-roll crowd, which were normal to me. What struck me as being strange in Rochdale was the people who just didn't fit—the bikers, for one. They were tough animals, these so-called security guards. You didn't get on an elevator until you passed under the gaze of one of those thugs. And that lent a sort of creepy air to the place, because without them there during parties or private moments, you didn't have a sense that this was a bad place. But the moment you walked outside of a room into a hallway and got on the elevator, your feeling was, 'What's going on here?'

"One time, there was a disagreement about something on our floor and I just happened to walk out and take a look. There were about six bikers there and it seemed to me that they didn't care who they were roughing up. There was obviously one central person that they were upset with, and anybody else who came out was also pushed around. I wasn't directly hit, but I sort of got caught in the crowd. That just reinforced the sense that you had to watch out in this place. Obviously, there were unwritten rules here that I hadn't learned, and if you were going to be a long-term resident, you had to learn those rules fast.

"Nobody but the so-called residents would venture past the elevator bank on the first floor. So anything that happened in this building was just happening in no-man's land. There was no cleaning and no maintenance to speak of. It was awful. My room was perfectly all right, but the common area was really kind of gross. One of the status symbols was how weird your animal was. Not too many people had them, but they were the talk of the place. So somebody would walk by with a pet python. It was definitely for show.

"There were no deaths while I was there, although there was one about a month before I went in. And I wasn't actually investigating that death, but I wanted to find out what people in the building were saying about it. I heard three or four different versions of what happened, and every single version said it was not a natural death, since someone had fallen off the roof or out of a window.

"One version said the death was an out-and-out murder over drugs that was meant to teach people a lesson. And there was also a creepy version that they had drugged this person and popped him so full of acid that if there had been an autopsy, drugs would have been determined as the cause of death. Another one was that he was being chased and ran and fell off the building. So what I'm saying is that despite all the inconsistencies in these versions, they were all basically foul play. Nobody was saying the guy willingly or accidentally took an overdose and died. What was interesting was that it wasn't necessarily true what people were saying about foul play. But it was certainly indicative of the thinking in the building.

"Throughout this whole time, I arranged to phone in and check in with my office every day. I would leave the building and walk from Bloor and St. George to St. Clair and Yonge, which was a big effort, but it gave me plenty of opportunities to look behind and see if anybody was following me. Then I would use a pay phone at St. Clair and Yonge and make my call. And from there I would head back.

"I did have this one other friend who would come in every now and again, usually on weekends. I felt I'd like to have one other person around who knew me, especially on a Friday or Saturday night when things would be nuts. It was good for me, too, to have another set of eyes looking at all this to see if I was off-base in my assessment of things.

"In the end, I spent just under three weeks in Rochdale. I left a couple of days early after I was found out because of something stupid. In the third week, I decided it was time for me to get some photographs of things that I wanted to talk about on the air. So I took out what I thought was a normal-looking camera, but in those surroundings was too expensive for a guy who was supposedly working part-time as a lineman.

"I was taking a picture of a bulletin board in a common room—half bulletins for meetings of various mystical, Eastern religious sects and half advertising for various types of dope and pills. And while I was shooting, two guys came around the corner. Fortunately, they weren't bikers, but they thought I was a cop, even though I said I wasn't. Finally, I had to admit I was taking pictures because I was a reporter. Ha! I should have said I was a cop, because they would have treated me a little better. So they got all upset at me and went off to tell their friends. And I took the opportunity to leave the building fast.

"I left behind nothing more than a small knapsack with a couple of shirts in it. Maybe I was being too cautious and maybe nothing much would have happened if I'd gone back for it. But my sense was that something would have happened. The threat would not have come from the experimental lifestylers or anything like that, but from the hard, professional element that would have felt very compromised and very threatened if they thought that a reporter had been living there and maybe finding out something about the deaths and the drug situation.

"As a result of my being in Rochdale, what we did in late '73 was a whole week or maybe even two weeks of special reports. I was only one part of it. Our police reporter also did a series of reports on police activity there—what the police thought, what their intelligence squads did and how the undercover cops operated. Another series came from the City Hall reporter who got the politicians' point of view.

"In my own case, it ended up as three separate stories where I detailed my experiences. I did the talking part in the studio, but we had some footage inside Rochdale because we sent a crew in and told them to shoot until they got thrown out. I also had an artist working with me to produce sketches.

"After the broadcasts, I had three telephone death threats. The station also had a couple. I was pretty worried for a couple of weeks. The threats I received didn't sound like crank calls. But then I thought about it and figured that if the mob was going to take out a contract, they weren't going to phone me first and tell me about it. After that, the story passed out of my hands because it was more of a police and City Hall thing. And I became more of a political reporter.

"The thing that I felt coming out of it was that I had seen an experiment that was turning sour in a violent way. So when I got out, I thought, 'If they shut this place down, they'll be doing a lot of kids in there a big favour, because this isn't working any more. It's not what they came for and it's not what they're looking to get. If it's summer camp they're looking for, there are lots of communes to join.' Misguided though it may have been, the original aim of Rochdale—at least as I understood it—had all but disappeared by the time I went in there."

C H A P T E R 9

I'd
Love to
Change the World

Through most of Rochdale's history, at any given time, approximately one hundred individuals controlled the political destiny of Rochdale. In order to be part of the political process proper you had to be a Rochdale member. Naturally, non-members made their opinions known and took part in Rochdale's democratic life, but the voting procedure itself was limited to members. When it came to politics, however, Rochdale was no different from the outside world—people just didn't care unless it directly affected their lives and their own little world.

Rochdale was a fascinating experiment in real participatory democracy. Power was constantly changing hands; at times the college's turnover rate resembled an unstable banana republic with one bloodless revolution after another.

From September to November, 1968, Rochdale was run by an administration headed by old Rochdalians such as general manager Bernie Bomers and registrar Jack Dimond.

In November, 1968, the first general meeting was held. According to the college charter, a twelve-member governing council was elected. Confusion set in from the outset as the college opted for a non-structured, rule-by-consensus approach. The college plunged into chaos.

In January, 1969, the governing council was fired and replaced by a new twelve-person council. Here's how *Maclean's* magazine writer Alan Edmonds depicted the meeting.

> At first, the management council consisted of any college members who wanted to help make decisions by consensus. Result: no decisions.
> In January a new 12-man council set out to hold open meetings at which college members could vote.
> The first was in a lounge on the second floor. About 100 people drifted in and out, so there were always about 60 people present, mostly on the floor. It rambled along for the better part of five hours

and at some point everyone spoke, except for a fat girl in slacks and sweater who wasn't wearing a bra and munched about a dozen candy bars as she leaned against the piano, which had the sheet music for Claire de Lune and the Royal Conservatory grade-four exams on the stand.

The assembled beards and beads, bell-bottoms and Boston accents dedicated to draft-dodging produced a nonstop parade of "points of order, Mr. Chairman," and mini-debates over who had been recognized by the chairman as the next speaker—though it wasn't always clear who the chairman was.

By invoking much democracy and rule of consensus, it was decided to decide not to decide anything, except for a few conditions of tenancy slightly more stringent than those in the average apartment building. Registrar Jack Dimond was moved to observe:

"Christ—it's the same tired old story. Look, if we want to get things done, we have to do unpleasant things, like writing things down and submitting them in advance to council meetings. Let's not kid ourselves that we're building a new and better world by getting 80 people together and embarking on interminable debates."

He then announced his resignation.

Later, he said he was not giving up on Rochdale; that he was not leaving a sinking ship; that his resignation had no significance beyond the fact that he was fed up with being bogged down in the detail of trying to run the college without the aid of an active, decisive council.

He also said he has the beginnings of a stomach ulcer.

In the spring of 1969, council attempted to deal with Rochdale's assorted problems: crashers, speed freaks, dealers, guns, bikers. The 1972 college catalogue dubs this council the "shadow council."

On April 2, 1969, Rochdale became a monarchy. King James I of Rochdale, aka Jim Garrard, explains. "The funniest part, I think, was when we decided to have a constitutional, parliamentary monarchy, because I'd always thought monarchies were kind of fun. So we stage this little number, but it was taken seriously. We actually operated as a monarchy for a while, and I was the king. I'm still the king of Rochdale, but I don't know how many people would take that seriously now.

"What it entailed was to convince the governing council that if we established royal protocols and had a monarchy, the powers of the monarchy would derive from the duly elected council. In that way, they could be taken back again. But it gave us a single decision-maker, and I was saying it would speed things up, because everything would be consensualized. And if people are dissatisfied with the consensualization that's going on, they can overthrow the monarch in some way, either through constitutional means or otherwise.

"So we had quite a lovely press conference in the empty shell where the bank is now. Lots of people came, and CBC-TV and radio were there. It ended up being mostly ceremonial. We wanted to have royal breakfasts, because that's when government would take place in my Zeus suite on the eighteenth floor. And Wu was quite prepared to order in good wines for breakfast every day. I think we could have justified the expense on the basis of the theatrical experience. And at the same time, there would have been some government going on. I had robes and I would show up and people would kiss the ring. But we retained the monarchy as a ceremonial kind of thing and went back to using the governing council."

In May, 1969, Maysay, a series of bulletins from "Rochdale's Liberation Front" called for the re-evaluation of Rochdale's relationship with its external management—the Toronto Student Management Corporation (TSMC). On May 31, 1969, Dennis Lee, one of the college's founders, resigned. Lee was but one of the many old Rochdalians who fled the building believing the Rochdale dream had no chance of surviving.

The following month, at a Gov Con meeting that lasted from 8 p.m. to 4 a.m., the fifth council of the year was fired, and on June 10, 1969, a new council, headed by twenty-six-year-old John Bradford, the former president of the University of Toronto graduate student's union and editor of the *Rochdale Bulletin* in 1967, was elected.

A new era was ushered in by Bradford's "get tough," law-and-order council, which initiated a thorough cleanup of speeders, crashers and bikers. Rentals was overhauled. Rents were collected. Hard drugs were banned. General administrative tightening up was reflected in cafeteria losses being cut. The press reacted to the change in government with encouraging headlines such as: "Rochdale Students Move To End Confusion." The June 13 edition of *The Globe and Mail* carried the following analysis:

A new 12-man council elected by residents of Rochdale College will be stronger on rules and discipline than its predecessors, the college's general manager predicted yesterday.

Bernard Bomers said he was confident that within a week the council will have produced a coherent long-term policy for

Rochdale. This will put the college on an orderly, pay-as-you-go basis without endangering its character as an educational institution, he said.

Mr. Bomers said the new council is generally agreed that some form of rules and discipline must be found to govern the college's operations. This was in contrast to former councils, which maintained residents must be allowed to do their own thing.

The new council began to set Rochdale's house in order, but at what cost? Kent Gooderham writes: "A particularly creative and exciting period of Rochdale's history ended in the spring of 1969, with the impeachment of council. 'All the most creative people left.' A very strong leader was asked to come and save the building. The residents were ready to admit that it was by that time in a deplorable state. Health inspections were being failed, equipment wasn't working. There was insufficient money and rentals were not being paid. The council took over the building and ran it in a dictatorial way.

"There followed a period when almost all seminars and all happenings ceased. The music left the halls. So, too, did the dog shit. Straight people were able to move into the building. The council meetings were stormy. The president shouted and residents shouted back. Any opposition to council policies was quickly squelched. Business that had been left undone was completed. The president had been asked to clean up Rochdale—to save Rochdale—and he proceeded to do just that."

On June 30, 1969, Rochdale finally cut its umbilical cord to its parent organization, the TSMC. June 30 was Rochdale's Day of Independence.

TSMC was the external management group that Campus Co-op established to oversee Rochdale. Although some of the TSMC board was partly made up of Rochdalians, and although the relationship between The Rock and TSMC was at first harmonious, the organization was still perceived as an outside authority. Rochdale, with its very vocal form of democracy, might have created the impression that it was a fully self-governing entity but, in actuality, TSMC pulled the important strings from behind the scenes, a fact Paul Evitts still remembers with some bitterness.

"Essentially, the management of the building's financial side and everything like that was in the hands of professional managers. What we found was we wanted to make decisions about things that were happening in the building, but we couldn't do it.

Management wasn't responsive. We couldn't even get financial information. We couldn't get the staff to do things. It was deliberately set up that way. We were supposed to stay off to one side and be kind of nice and basically pretend we were running the University of Toronto. They were the serious guys who were managing the building. Well, they were fucking it up. And the further we got into things, the more it was clear that they were doing a bad job of managing. And we weren't in a position to get the information we wanted.

"All the standard management things were being done very badly and were being done behind closed doors. The people managing the building were all in their mid-twenties; they'd never actually handled a large building like that before and this was the first time they'd been involved in a large development project like that. Now that I've had a chance to see a few other things, I recognize that a lot of the things that were going down there were fairly typical. But if I went back to the situation now with what I know now, I'd certainly find some way to postpone opening the building for a year."

When the Bradford-Evitts council assumed power, it asked to see TSMC's financial records. Suspicion had long been circulating that all was not as it should be. Even the University of Toronto student newspaper, the *Varsity*, published an article—"The Rochdale Papers"—that sympathized with Rochdale's plight and went so far as to allege financial mishandling on the part of TSMC and Campus Co-op. The writer questioned the "inflated mortgage" and original land cost.

From this point on Rochdale became embroiled in a civil war. On one side were Campus Co-op and its supporters, and on the other, the new Rochdale council and its backers who were pushing for Rochdale to be truly a self-determining project—a functioning, not a "paper" democracy. Accusations and counter-accusations flew; Rochdale owed Campus Co-op money; Campus Co-op was trying to subvert Rochdale by issuing 5,000 posters promoting open rental space in the building.

On June 30, 1969, the contract with TSMC (or the Toronto Student *Mis*management Corporation as it was nicknamed in the halls of Rochdale) expired and the council chose not to renew it. Rochdale was, of course, still bound to Campus Co-op and its Central Mortgage and Housing Corporation (CMHC) mortgage, but it was beginning to put some distance between itself and its disapproving parent. For its part, Campus Co-op wasn't too keen on being associated with the college, especially in light of the mounting problems and resulting bad publicity.

Minor skirmishes had erupted all summer long over trivial matters such as parking spaces and more serious issues such as rental rates and financial direction. But the council couldn't get bogged down in all the infighting because it had a more pressing matter at hand—November 1 was looming menacingly on the horizon. November 1 was the day that Rochdale's first mortgage payment of $26,000 was due to CMHC.

Exacerbating the financial situation was the fact that during the summer of 1969 Rochdale faced the "empties." In January of 1969 Rochdale's population was estimated to be around 1,250 (of which only 650 were students). From that high, the college's population dipped precariously to 400 by September of the year. The students who had spent their school year at 341 Bloor Street West, left either for the summer or for good.

Rochdale's fourteenth-floor commune, as commune co-founder Nicky Morrison explains, arose as a result of the "empties." "The fourteenth floor commune started in the spring of 1969 when all the students had finished their year and had moved out. I had been living there since the previous fall and had taken apartment 622 on Valentine's Day—that was the day that I actually became an official Rochdale resident. The building had emptied out and we were left there—about a hundred of us. A few of us talked about setting up something—a commune—and we decided the fourteenth floor would be a good place to do it. We moved up there, and once we were moved in we called a meeting and gathered everybody who was interested together. We started out with a dozen people. Michael Donaghy—I was living with him—and I became instrumental in setting the commune up.

"We did it originally to offset the emptying of the building—we thought if we could do this we could get more rent money coming in. It wasn't going to be regular students but they would be people who fit into the idea of what an alternate college was all about. The basic requirement was that you had to participate in the life and work of the commune. We had the greatest variety of people—a Swedish architect, lawyers, a fashion buyer from Simpsons, freaks."

"I had applied early to get into Rochdale," explains James Newell, "but I didn't move in until June 8, 1969. It was an interesting time for the building, in that the so-called filler students, those who used Rochdale as a place to live near the campus and didn't have any real involvement with the concept and the ideas of the place, were on their way out in June. And it was clear after the way the year went at Rochdale, they would not be back. Not only was it the end of the school year, but they would move on to some place sane and sensible. It was the end of the school year for me as well but I had the time and the energy to move. The building, though, became quite empty in June of 1969. It was a new crisis to face. At about this time the organizers woke up to the fact that they would have to start to make mortgage payments."

For Rochdale to work economically the building theoretically had to be one hundred per cent full during the school year and sixty to seventy per cent full during the summer. The actual occupancy was sixty per cent during the school year and down to thirty per cent in the summer. To compound matters, the rental department was in total disarray. When all the accounting was done, Rochdale had $40,000 in unpaid rent. Some $12,000 of that was eventually recovered via late payment. But the fact still remained that Rochdale was in very serious financial hot water. The college missed its first mortgage payment.

However, a reprieve came when CMHC delayed the foreclosure until a study could be conducted on Rochdale's future prospects (CMHC did accept a token payment of $1,500.). That report, when it finally appeared in February, 1970, was the first nail in Rochdale's coffin. To liberally paraphrase the report: "Rochdale hasn't got a hope in hell of succeeding financially."

Reverend Ian MacKenzie, one of the "old Rochdalians," recalls, "In mid-1969, just before I was president, CMHC was going to close us down. So we went down and met with the president of CMHC and he gave us a six-month moratorium on the mortgage payments. And then they did an investigation. It was during that period that we tried to do some stuff to see if we could reverse the way things had been going."

Given that bleak picture, and the fact that no one could come up with a viable alternative to save the building before it was lost, the Bradford council adopted the strategy of selling Rochdale—literally! It seemed like the only rational approach. Since only thirty to forty per cent of those at Rochdale were members committed to the project's educational and social ideals, why not sell the building, take the considerable profits and start fresh on a smaller scale with people who really cared and would attempt to make Rochdale work? However rational the plan sounded, it didn't stand a chance with Rochdale's constituency, whose response was, "Sell Mother Rochdale? Never!"

The question that lay at the heart of the matter was whether Rochdale was a building or a school of thought. If it was a school of thought, the sale of the physical building would not significantly mean the end of Rochdale; in fact, the true Rochdalians would be free of a millstone.

Paul Evitts was one of the governing council members who pushed hard for the sale of 341 Bloor Street West. "After looking at all the files and memos and cardboard boxes full of odds and ends, we came to the conclusion that not only was the management that we turfed out lousy, but also there was a lot of hidden stuff that we hadn't been aware of. The bottom line was that there was no way that Rochdale could work—period. The building was an albatross and aside from being ugly, it was dragging everything down with it.

"At that point we publicly announced we were going to sell the building. We got all sorts of interesting offers. The best one was from the nursing operator on Yorkville who was willing to give us his nursing home, plus a million bucks, plus space in the country. I think what we could have done—I don't remember if we had formal commitment on this from CMHC—was to get out of the building and take the embarrassment off the shoulders of CMHC. They'd basically forgive and forget, as far as the first chunk of the operation was concerned—because at that point we were talking about having been in operation for nine months. So it wouldn't have been a hell of a loss. The only catch was—and this was no problem because of the nature of the mortgage—that we had to be able to retain the existing CMHC mortgage for the nursing home operator to use the place as a nursing home."

"It didn't work out, though. We thought, 'God, this is great. This gives us all the opportunities—a farm in the country for the rural types, money to establish an educational program and space in Yorkville to do our community thing. For sure, this would be received with open arms by everybody.' But what we didn't realize was there was a large contingent of people who had come to regard Rochdale as Mother Rochdale, and somehow they saw this as a real threat. When we announced our plans, we got pulled into another general meeting like the one we'd set up when we took over. And we got turned down and turfed out.

In September, 1969, the Bradford council was replaced by a council dedicated to Rochdale the building. Anthropologist Kent

Gooderham describes the new attitude: "In their search for community and liminality,[1] the residents had lost the management of their lives to a group they later considered to be fascists. They threw out "big daddy" after he had put their home back into working order but threatened to take it from them.

"They replaced the most extreme members of the council and elected a new president who was dedicated to saving the residents' home. An interest in community and liminality began once more to permeate the building. Projects began to blossom. The library, the 'schop,' the art gallery, the *Daily*, all of which had been dormant for months, reappeared one after another. The council discussed and practiced—as far as they were able—horizontal management. Bureaucrats and politicians who were interested in keeping the building in shape at the expense of human relations came under severe attack. By April when the 'summer people' arrived, Rochdale was once again able to provide mind blowing experiences for many. The music was back and so were the police. Communal projects found many supporters and the shouts of corruption and mismanagement from reformers were beginning to appear."

According to Paul Evitts, "There was an interesting split. A lot of the people who showed up after the building opened and had been going for a while weren't people who had the inclination or the talent to carry off a lot of the visionary stuff we were talking about. They were marginal people like us, but they were looking for some sort of security and a place where they could shelter themselves from the world outside. It didn't matter what the bloody building looked like. It didn't matter what was genuinely going on in there—they didn't care. All they cared about was the fact that it was a crutch, it was whatever. And that's where the Mother Rochdale thing came from. It was essentially a haven and a hearth. Once that happened, I resigned and I'm pretty sure everybody else resigned around Christmas of 1969."

On the other side of the question were those who, like Pamela Berton, felt that "the building was an integral part of the community and to sell it would be to signal the end of Rochdale, the idea."

Kent Gooderham believes those on the council who wanted to sell Rochdale misread the underlying attachment the residents felt

---

[1]Gooderham defines liminality as "that 'structureless' time when participants are dead to the world outside and are being reborn into a new form."

for this ugly piece of concrete. "By November of 1969, it became clear that it was not financially feasible to keep the building, and the council proposed selling it. The college could then take what profit there might be and find quarters that would suit the lifestyle of the members, but which would be economically feasible. Rochdale members would not be in a position of running an apartment building for the benefit of straight students. The decision seemed to suit the ideology of the constituents but the council had misunderstood their mandate completely. The members had no intention of giving up their home and had little if any interest in finances. The president resigned, along with some other wise and powerful leaders. Once again 'all the best people left.' "

The nursing home idea was the most attractive of the sale offers, although the Ontario Government got in on the action when Stanley Randall, the minister for trade and development, announced on November 14 that the Ontario Government was thinking about buying Rochdale as a student residence. However, he added the tongue-in-cheek stipulation that "first we'll have to get a butterfly net and a couple guys in white coats to clean the place out."

As a self-sustaining organization Rochdale College did not depend on, indeed prided itself on its independence from, governmental support (outside the six million dollar mortgage, that is). It could generate income in three ways: rents, membership fees and fund raising. In view of the fact that a majority of Rochdalians were dead set against the proposed sale of the building, that rentals were screwed up and that membership was shaky at best, Rochdale had only one recourse. So, donning its mendicant's robe and stretching its palm out to the world, Rochdale became a fund raiser.

The most visible of Rochdale's fund-raising schemes was the infamous Rochdale Degree. It was Rochdale at its satirical best. You could order a B.A. in "Life's Tosses and Turns," an M.A. in "Absenteeism," and a Ph.D. in the venerable art and science of "Mind-Fucking." The college put out the following press release:

Rochdale is not an accredited degree granting institution in the usual morbid sense. However, we recently analyzed our situation and found that we were the largest college in North America that did not sell degrees. Feeling we might be missing out on something, we decided to peddle our papers.

We are selling degrees that can be used in the same way one might use other degrees. You can put them in your top drawer under your socks, nail them to your office wall to impress your patients, cut them into paper dolls, or write poetry on the back of them.

To get one of these fine pieces of paper you just answer the appropriate question and send the appropriate bread.

Degree	Question	Fee
B.A.	Name the first Prime Minister of Canada	$25.00
M.A.	Name the present Prime Minister of Canada	$50.00
Ph.D.	Name any Prime Minister of Canada	$100.00

Marshall McLuhan recently pointed out that a Ph.D. might very well be a sign of an atrophied head rather than a smart one. We already knew this but we figured we'd toss his name in to impress you if you're that kind of guy.

In view of this, we are also certifying people as Non-B.A.'s, Non-M.A.'s, and Non-Ph.D.'s. The requirements are as follows:

Degree	Question	Fee
Non-Ph.D.	Say Something	$25.00
Non-M.A.	Say Something Logical	$50.00
Non-B.A.	Say Something Useful	$100.00

Summary:
Make cheque payable to Rochdale College
341 Bloor Street West
Toronto 5, Ontario

Stan Bevington from Coach House Press was involved with the actual printing of the degrees. "Diplomas and degrees became a major source of income for the educational part of Rochdale. We must have printed up about a thousand. They were hand-made and hard to do. We made them that way because I deliberately didn't want just anybody to crank them out on a photocopier. I actually wanted the degree to be worth something, and I think now it has pretty good collectible value."

Valerie Frith handled the administrative part of the degree-selling scheme. "When I was selling degrees I was called the external affairs co-ordinator and registrar," says Frith. "The degree selling was by far the most successful of our money-raising schemes. We had the National Share the Wealth concept and so on but only the degree sales worked. I believe it was Ian Argue and Bill King who came up with National Share the Wealth and the degree-selling ideas.

"The degrees existed before I came along. They were joke degrees with the Queen on them, printed on good quality paper, very well printed. Most people understood them for what they were–jokes. People bought them for presents. Say you had a friend who was interested in bird watching, you'd buy him this Rochdale degree in bird watching. What people feared was that we were selling credentials to foreign countries and that people would actually try to set themselves up as doctors or dentists–but we never did that. At the time we did get a lot of mail from Asia enclosing $100 and requesting Doctors of Medicine, but we did not sell those degrees. It was a question of doing things that were quite conventional but doing them in an odd way.

"While I was handling the degrees I got orders every day. We were flooded with orders. We never realized a huge sum but we did have our rush periods, like at graduation time."

Bob Nasmith was the nude poster boy for the drive (one picture showed him as a flasher pitching degrees with a "Pssst, come here kid, ya wanna buy a degree" schtick). "There was an evangelical edge to the concept–a 'spread the good word' feeling," recalls Nasmith, "and it was a good joke to boot. I think when all was said and done, we broke even."

Alderman Tony O'Donohue was the recipient of a complimentary Ph.D. in political science. Even though he was disturbed by Rochdale's "making light of the educational process," he hung it on his office wall. The prime minister was also sent one, in order, as Ian Argue told the *Star*, "to encourage his interest in the college."

The degree-selling idea, which made it into publications such as *Rolling Stone* and the *Village Voice*, got off to a roaring start, bagging the college $6,000 the first month or so. But the requests petered out and eventually the campaign died a natural death.

For all their satirical value, the realistic-looking diplomas played a part in many a scam. Jack Dimond remembers receiving a long-distance telephone call in 1985 "from somebody in England who said he was a senior personnel officer and was interviewing somebody for a job. He said the guy had a master's degree from some British university, an MBA from Harvard and a Ph.D. in economics from the University of Toronto's Rochdale College. So I said, 'Oh, you've certainly got the right guy!' and told him what it was worth."

The degree-selling scheme was part of an overall umbrella concept appropriately titled National Share the Wealth With Rochdale, April 1 – 7. What could be more straightforward? "You've got the money Canada–we need it–please give it to us." The *Daily* outlined the campaign:

NATIONAL ROCHDALE WEEK
APRIL 1 – 7
We need something big; we need something good; we need something now. We've got it. *National Share The Wealth With Rochdale Week.* Get it? Here 'tis. . . .
1. Rochdale is not subsidized. All other post-elementary schools are (to the tune of about 95%)
2. We have really been torn up by most media and as a result, must improve our image by letting people know that Rochdale is extremely important . . . by letting them know the good things that happen here and by making them aware of the fantastic potential that is ours.
3. We ourselves must become more aware of our position as an educational situation . . . and make others aware of it.
4. We must increase our credibility with CMHC who can think of us as a $5,000,000 mortgage. THIS IS SERIOUS. Rochdale could very easily be sunk without a ripple unless we make every effort to get together, to tell our story, and to make it work.
5. There is a continuing need to attract future residents and members, to create a summer programme and corresponding higher occupancy rate.

THIS IS A PEOPLE PLACE, WE WILL NEVER HAVE ENOUGH INVOLVED SUPPORTERS, WITH US AND FOR US, UNLESS WE CAN OFFER THEM SOMETHING WORTHWHILE . . . SOMETHING THAT CANNOT BE DONE ELSEWHERE, SOMETHING THAT WE CAN DO BETTER.

We are working on it now and need the help of everyone. We, Rochdale, can share the wealth. Can? Shit! must. . . .

Canada has been divided into 7 parts, each with a co-ordinator:
Alberta, B.C., Yukon — Ralph Osborne
Saskatchewan, Manitoba — Linda Bomphrey
Eastern and Northern Ontario — Rosie
Western Ontario — Ken East
Quebec, Maritimes — Michael Lebeau
Toronto — Ian Argue, Jim Garrard
Rochdale — Dan McCue

In each of these areas we are attempting to find people who will organize groups to raise money for us. We will provide them with information, ideas, sample publicity handouts, speakers, Rochdollars, etc.

Interest must be generated and maintained through April Fools' Day when the NATIONAL SHARE THE WEALTH WITH ROCHDALE WEEK begins.

Publicity is important, but what we really need is $ $ . . . so badly we can taste it. People, if you can raise money, if you have money raising ideas . . . get together with any of the people who are co-ordinating or come down to 208–210.

Here are some of the things that we have been working on.
1. Speakers for anyone who wants to listen.
2. Benefit Concerts.
3. The biggest bloody open house that Rochdale has ever had. Something to do 24 hours a day. Play on and on. Bazaars, auctions, marathon poker games, Rochdale buttons and posters.
ROCHDALE IS NATIONAL—dig it.

The Share the Wealth campaign took a number of Rochdale leaders across the country to drum up financial support for the beleaguered college. Bob Nasmith was one such leader.

"It was a wonderful idea. Just to send people around spreading the word about Rochdale. I took Passe Muraille down to Brock University on the Niagara Peninsula and we put on a couple of shows there. It was wildly successful and as a result Brock University started a liaison with Passe Muraille that lasted for a number of years."

The Rochdalians spoke to college crowds, high school crowds, whoever would lend an ear and maybe a buck or two. One college, for example, cashed in 125,000 beer bottles, bringing $2,500 into the Rochdale coffers.

To many of these students, Rochdale was a guiding light, an example whose success was seminal to the development and growth of the Canadian counter-culture as a whole. If Rochdale didn't make it, it would be that much more difficult for anyone else to follow in its path.

Lionel Douglas, college vice-president and a major strategist, made an articulate plea for help in the *Star*'s editorial pages:

Share the Wealth (urp) with Radical Rochdale College

. . . Rochdale is radical only in the sense that 'radical' means "of roots."

First principles

The so-called "hippy" culture is an attempt to adhere to and build on the root premises and first principles of our culture. We are the children of war who first recognized war as economic sham. It has been said that we are rebelling against "do as I say, not as I do"; we are attempting to "get ourselves together" to do as we say, to replace ambivalent and lugubrious self-analysis with a healthy performance based on self-respect.

Our education then, is going back to the original role of the university which was, if anyone remembers, "to create the whole man." Rochdale is an education in attitude and civilization.

Not everyone in Rochdale is a student and member, some are both, some are neither, some are the former, but not the latter, and some the other way 'round.

—anonymous adolescent poet

Active members of the college are the baby-sitters to a goodly proportion of the post-hippy sub-generation. These are the 14- to 18-year-old kids who flow through the building constantly, especially the screwed-up ones. Our clinic treats more of them on bad trips, etc. than all of the major hospitals combined. We are trying to learn and at the same time teach these kids a cultural concept—which two world wars and the concomitant acceleration and chaos of 20th century life have almost obliterated—the idea of "enough." In other words a true and functional sense of proportion as applied to every aspect of life, social and economic.

We are serious, but realize the great danger in taking ourselves too seriously. Humour is a great non-violent revolutionary tool, albeit perhaps a uniquely Canadian one, but nevertheless one which we feel is more appropriate to the problem than political whining or rampant bloodshed.

Rochdale exists in Toronto for good reason. This is one of the few, indeed perhaps the only city left in North America where there is a stable enough environment for true evolutionary cultural growth and regeneration.

. . . Inadequate first year budgeting and cheap construction have cost us a lot of money, and we're virtually at begging point; we can afford to keep ourselves day to day, but like many families we can't meet our inflation-time debts.

We're not proud, though; we think we have something useful, to all of us, right now, and we're coming out to beg for help (moan, carp, greep)—April 1-7, National Share the Wealth with Rochdale Week. Urp.

Lionel Douglas, Toronto

Despite the clean-up instituted by the Bradford-Evitts council, despite the rallying effort evidenced in schemes like National Share the Wealth, Rochdale was still going through difficult times. Many considered 1969 to be the equivalent of the college's Dark Ages.

One of the victims of the entire process of decline was the educational component. According to some estimates, 60 per cent of all seminars were discontinued. The "free education" simply wasn't working.

Maclean's magazine wrote:

Education was to have been by seminar. The "resource person"—
philosopher, economist, sociologist, academic—would provide the
information and cover the areas chosen by a consensus of students.
A dozen seminars started.

There were no plans for diplomas; no degrees. The hope was
simply that, over the years, Rochdale "graduates" would so amply
demonstrate their abilities that attendance alone would earn any
recognition desired.

By Christmas, most seminars had failed, or were in limbo. "They
were too democratic," says Registrar Jack Dimond. "Students don't
know what there is to know and must have some direction. There
was no discipline: anyone could join in at any time. Then everyone
got caught up in the growing pains of the building."

By March, however, things had looked up. Some seminars were
reviving. Others had come into being spontaneously. These
included groups studying music, real estate (for a back-to-nature
movement), film making, ceramics, witchcraft, primitive religions,
revolution, drama, yoga, cooking and something called The Utopian
Research Institute.

Democracy wasn't the only thing to kill seminars. As Bernie
Bomers says: "Before Rochdale, it was easy for people to say that
external conditions prevent your genius from blossoming. Then they
come here, get the freedom and discover they still can't write like
Mailer or paint like Pollock or blow horn like Miles Davis and it's a big
disappointment. It's hard to cope with."

For Rochdalians still interested in the educational experiment,
it was a long process of self-discovery. *Maclean's* offered the
example of Mary Trew:

Mary Trew, 20, is a Rochdale student. She moved in last September
and began seminars in philosophy, sociology, physics, art and
conversational French. After five months she said she had learned
very little in the strict academic sense.

"I think I did quite well in high school, but by the time I graduated
last year I'd had it with the formal education thing. Most of the other
kids respected the whole authority structure, the parents and the
teachers who wanted them to get good marks.

"From when you are five years old the system is teaching you that
you have to be told what to learn and how to learn and when to learn,
and that's why the situation at Rochdale is so difficult for most
people.

"You are confronted with this void where there's no one to tell you
what to do and where to go. For the first three weeks I was very keen
on the whole idea of seminars, because there was nobody telling me
I had to do this or that and why. But I gave up on it. It was difficult to
handle all that freedom. I didn't want to be told and yet I had nowhere
to go; I had nothing to rebel against, and nothing to follow.

"But it's so necessary to go through this. If I'd confronted this void as a schoolgirl and had had to take responsibility for myself, it wouldn't be happening now, this flailing around looking for directions and interests.

"I didn't do anything academically for five months. But it wasn't wasteful. I more or less sat around and talked to people, learned to get along with others, how to manage human relationships. I read an awful lot."

Mary Trew is now working as a waitress in the college restaurant to earn her keep and has plugged back into the philosophy and sociology seminars. She says she has a self-imposed regimen; that she doesn't care about getting education for a job; that she just wants to be a good human being and that Rochdale will help.

However, people were still being drawn to Rochdale by the promise of a liberated, enlightened education. "My hometown is Windsor," relates Carol Popkey, "and I had finished university at the University of Windsor. I was working at the Browndale residential treatment centre. There was a couple working there, Bill and Chris King, and they had heard about Rochdale. I wanted to leave home and leave Windsor, so we got into discussions about Rochdale. And from the little bit of printed material they had, I thought it looked great. So the three of us moved up there together in May of 1969. In 1969, I was twenty years old.

"I was interested because of my conversations with Bill and Chris King and our idea of what free university should be. I'd done some reading about Summerhill in England, and working at Browndale meant I was involved with the education of the kids in the house who couldn't go to a regular school. I had a BA in psychology, but I thought there were other things I'd like to explore, like Rochdale. But Rochdale wasn't anything like what I expected or anything like the impression we'd gotten from the printed material."

A significant number of Rochdalians still believed in that educational aspect, and they applied pressure to the governing council. This salvo fired in the January 20, 1969, *Daily* was aimed at the college administration:

WHATEVER HAPPENED TO ROCHDALE COLLEGE???????
(The experimental educational institute that never was)
Rochdale College: that glamourous institution of *Toronto Life*, *Time* and *Newsweek*. Of the networks, of the [*New York*] *Times*. Described by the establishment as "an exciting educational experiment." How smugly they can say that because there is no threat here to their system.

Because Rochdale is an inert mass on Bloor Street, inhabited by misguided idealists, hippies and fucked up kids. If you think this is experimentation, brother, you are kidding only yourself. Rochdale is only a twisted rerun of all the hangups it was supposed to avoid.

Why? Why haven't the people who first came here to make it a place of educational innovation gotten their head together? Why does our bureaucracy so carefully succeed in mismanaging the finances, stifling creativity and, above all, in alienating the people from themselves? Why does the management work on the buddy system, with everyone patting themselves on the back, instead of looking self-critically at what they are doing and how they are doing it?

Why do some people live very nicely on large salaries, despite the fact that they are directly responsible for Rochdale being continually over budget? Why are people committed to Rochdale forced to do all of the shit work, picking up the crumbs after the administration has taken its share?

Why, Mr. Dimond, is there no money in the Education Fund?

Why, Mr. Roberts and Mr. Bomers, is the food operation allowed to overspend to the tune of $13,000 in the first few months of operation, with nobody being called to task?

Why, instead of having an intelligent admissions policy, has Rochdale been filled with paranoids, schitzoids, neurotics and bewildered kids?

Why does the place smell?

After several months the patronizing reply of "Well, I'm amazed that it has got this far so quickly . . . at least two years I thought it'd be" . . . starts to lose some of its power. It is rapidly becoming obvious that we have created a structure that is going in entirely the wrong direction, and that is strengthening itself as time passes and, if not soon replaced, will lead to the demise of the Experiment and of the conventional apartment and dormitory. . . .

We need a separation of the building administration and the educational programme.

The Education Committee must be formed. . . .

In late 1969 Sir Basil Nardley-Stodes, the fictional editor of the *Daily*, suggested forming a permanent education council. It would take a full year, but Sir Basil would see his wish fulfilled.

The original idealism and spirit that refused to let the educational side of the college get steamrolled by commercial considerations appeared to be alive after all. How long it could survive was another matter entirely.

C H A P T E R 10

I
Fought
the Law

Realizing that Rochdale was obviously a unique policing situation that called for more than brute force and intimidation, Metro Toronto Police established a community relations team in the building. Perhaps "team" might be exaggerating in that the "team" consisted of one individual—Dean Audley.

Audley explains his position: "What I found was that the majority of people in society did not understand what was happening. I didn't understand either, but I got to know a lot of the people there. It was a whole learning experience for society. The kids manifested the craziness that was happening at that time, and I was sent there to hopefully find out how to adapt to the changes that were taking place. My job was to go into Yorkville and Rochdale as a police officer—not in an undercover capacity in any way—to explain to them what the law was and what we had to do. But mainly I wanted to find out how we could assist the kids."

In time, others were added to the Rochdale detail. Ross Prasky joined Dean Audley in late 1969. "I was in 52 Division downtown in 1964 and left there in late 1972. We saw the old homes coming down on Bloor Street and we saw Rochdale going up. And then, there it was and all of a sudden it was a big problem.

"In the latter part of 1969 I was working in uniform in 52 Division, riding motorcycle. They asked if anybody wanted to be involved in a new program in Yorkville, which was in its heyday in those days. I joined up with another copper named Dean Audley and all of a sudden I found I was inside Rochdale on a daily basis. That went on from late 1969 to late 1972. I was a constable at the time, and Deputy Chief Jack Ackroyd was starting a new program within the Toronto force called Community Service. It has since been established as a program throughout the entire force—it's called Community Relations now.

"We tried to bridge the gap between the uniformed guys working the streets—working Rochdale and working Yorkville—and a large collection of people who had gathered in Yorkville and places like Rochdale. We tried to work a sort of middle ground with the uniformed officers because they had an attitude about drugs, runaways, long hair and that kind of thing. On the other hand, we found ourselves facing a community [Rochdale] that was very anti-police. And, of course, there had been major confrontations.

"We wore our uniforms on occasion, but more often than not, it was a pair of jeans, a T-shirt and a jacket. We were in and out of Yorkville and Rochdale on a daily basis. Everybody knew us as cops. There was never any intent that we should be undercover, although we were accused of that on both sides. Some of our own people wanted us to work undercover, and some Rochdale people accused us of being undercover. But we were always straight and up-front and easily identified because we were there every day. Everybody got to know us as the two cops from 52 Division.

"Some officers got the mistaken impression we were defending the Rochdale people or trying to clean up their image. We were definitely accused of changing sides. We had to work out some very difficult situations sometimes.

"We were able to do some things that uniformed coppers at 52 were not able to do. For example, if we got an inquiry from some mum saying, 'My daughter's in Rochdale. It's a terrible place. We want you to do something,' the uniformed guys couldn't approach the building. But we could make a phone call from our office to someone in authority at Rochdale and say, 'It's us again. We've got to know about so-and-so. She lives on the sixth floor. Tell her to call her mother right away.' And if she was under-age, we had a working relationship with them and they saw it was to their benefit not to allow fourteen-year-olds to live there.

"What we tried to do was stop the polarity that caused riots in other cities. And that clearly helped smooth relations with the people at Rochdale."

As one might expect from a building like Rochdale, its relations with the police were strained and for the most part antagonistic. By posting various policemen's "mugshots" on the security office bulletin board, Rochdale was making it crystal clear just exactly who the "wanted men" were.

"It was mostly the drug squad guys who had their pictures posted," says Ross Prasky, "although on occasion our pictures [the community relations cops] were put up and we'd go by and draw mustaches on them."

Sergeant Dan Marshall, a drug squad constable at the time, didn't know quite what to make of the "honour." "They were candid shots, quite good ones actually. None of us knew when or where the pictures were taken. But they had the pictures up there and who we were underneath and to beware of the local narcs. I remember going in there to the lobby and seeing my picture looking back at me and thinking to myself, 'Holy smokes! I made it! I'm famous!' As other fellas came along, they took our pictures down and put other pictures up and they kept changing them. But we were up there for a long time."

In an effort to stem the growing drug trade, the police conducted a number of raids on known drug dealers in the building. These raids were fraught with difficulties, not the least of which was getting in and out of the building.

"The problems began as soon as you entered the building," states thirty-seven-year veteran Sergeant George Crease. "The biker-types who were involved with Rochdale's inner security controlled the elevators. So you'd be in the place conducting a raid, you'd get into the elevators and you'd get halfway between floors and the power would go off, the alarms would be off and you'd be stuck in the elevator. Meanwhile all the stuff is being moved from one location to another, and your warrant says one room when it's really in another, so it wasn't any good even before you started.

"So we had to look at other methods to get in. Sometimes we'd get to the floor before the alarms went off, and the residents' dogs would come running down on us. We'd get to a location and that person would be in another apartment, or he'd have his stash in another room and we wouldn't have a warrant for that room.

"The most dangerous part was coming down the stairwell. They'd throw bags of dog excrement (we suspected they even used human excrement), they'd throw ten-gallon buckets of paint, bricks, brick-bats—it would be like shrapnel flying around those stairwells. You'd be trying to get down with the handcuffed prisoners. It was lucky none was killed. A few of us did get hit with paint and pieces of brick, but none to my knowledge was ever hurt seriously; just bruises, barked shins, that sort of thing.

"We never did get much on those raids. The bigger busts were when we knew where the stash was. The biggest haul I was involved with was six burlap bags of marijuana. Usually it was a case of whatever was around, stuff under mattresses, that sort of thing, small quantities.

"There wasn't any police officer who ever went into a Rochdale raid that wasn't shaking at least a little in his boots thinking, 'Am I going to come out of this with my head on?' It was mostly because of the debris they were throwing from the roof and in the stairwells.

"Getting out was the difficult part. We would exit en masse. We'd count heads from top to bottom. We didn't want to come out piecemeal. Sometimes you'd get trapped in the dark hallways when they turned off the power. Any policeman who went on a raid without his flashlight was stupid. Initially they'd turn off the lights and you'd hear the dogs running down the corridor, barking and carrying on. That would get you a little uptight but a good swift kick or a wallop on the head with a crowbar and the dogs would go yipping off down the hall. You'd get heck from the people who owned the dogs, but if they were attacking you, what are you going to do?"

"They'd shut the light off, close the elevators and pull the fire alarms," says Sgt. Dan Marshall. "You'd run up the stairs and they'd throw ball bearings down the stairs and smoke bombs. It even got as far as tear gas in the stairwells. So it was almost impossible to get in there and get a good pinch. And when you got to the doors, all the markings were removed anyway. So if you were going to apartment 602, there was no 602. They were all blank doors. You wouldn't know which door to knock down if you had a sledgehammer or a warrant to get in there.

"The raids were usually unsuccessful. Or if they were successful you'd make a seizure, but there was nobody to go with it. All you had to do was park a police car out in front of that place for any reason, and you'd have fifty to a hundred people milling around."

"I was involved with all of the raids," says Officer Bob Waddell. "You'd get forty or fifty guys, you'd sneak up so they wouldn't see you coming. Then we would take a small cadre of individuals in plainclothes and try to get to the back stairwell and up to the floor we wanted. If anyone spotted you, they'd be off in a flash, pushing the buzzer, the alarms, and then you really took off. That got ten, twelve, fifteen into the building, but then your element of surprise was gone and your support system followed.

"I can recall being on one of the floors and the power went off and we were trapped in a pitch-black room, about six of us. The hallway was jammed with people. We were up too high to jump out the window, so the only way out was through the hallway in the dark squeezing by all these people—and let me tell you these people hated us. If anyone had a little pick or a knife, who would know? What fun they would have sticking one of us. It was a very stressful situation.

"Then it got to the point where the Emergency Task Force got involved and the raids got bigger and bigger, and then they stopped. It got to be too much of a political thing to go into Rochdale. I don't think we ever got out of there with more than a couple of pounds maybe, a few pounds of this or that."

Police Chief Adamson believes that "Rochdale was a terror to the neighbourhood—and I don't minimize that word. People in that area were really concerned about those individuals who looked as if they weren't from this world."

Adamson's first visit to 341 Bloor Street West was memorable. "As you know, if the police were to conduct a drug raid there, the alarms were sounded, the elevators were shut down and the police officers were forced to walk to whatever floor where they suspected the drugs were. That was my first experience. I went there, the alarm rang and I had to walk to the seventeenth floor for my first meeting with the council. On the way up, the women stopped and urinated on the floor. One lady lifted her dress and had a complete bowel movement in front of me and told me what they thought of me. I guess a dozen of them followed me up and followed me down. That was my worst experience. That was their version of hello."

"I've been on the outside a few times when drug raids occurred or something happened where police had to be called. You'd have people up on the fifteenth or sixteenth floor dropping Coke bottles filled with sand down on the police cars. I can recall being over there one night when those pop bottles were coming out of the windows like no tomorrow. We had several windshields smashed, and the bottles were landing on the sidewalk and the glass was spraying around. People were screaming and cursing and swearing out the windows."

From the police department's point of view, Rochdale was a drug distribution centre for all of North America. It may have had its greatest influence in the southern Ontario-Golden Horseshoe area, but The Rock was an international phenomenon. Inspector John Wilson, chief of the Metro Morality Squad, told the *Star* that "such is the fame of Rochdale that dealers come in from California, Detroit, New York, Chicago."

According to Police Chief Adamson, Metro suffered terrible notoriety as a result of Rochdale. "I can recall being the chairman at an international police chiefs' convention on crime prevention," says Adamson. "I remember most of the questions that were asked of me had nothing to do with crime prevention; nearly all of the questions centred on Rochdale. Obviously Rochdale had an international reputation among the police forces."

"It was on national TV and in the press constantly," adds Ackroyd, "and Rochdale-related arrests were being made all over Canada and the States. That certainly added to the notoriety. Whenever we had visiting police chiefs, they would invariably ask to see Rochdale."

"It was a first in our police experience," explains Inspector Crampton. "We realized that once these people got a grip and took hold, they were extremely well organized. I'm talking about a small core of them, not the overall population. They had international contacts and had suppliers for arms and drugs worldwide. It would be nothing for us when we executed a warrant to find literature from Hong Kong, Quebec, South America, Cuba, the United States, Africa and even Ireland where the IRA were very strong and very powerful at that time. That gave us fits. As a result of that, we worked with Interpol and the United States Secret Service and the FBI and many other organizations throughout the world. We exchanged a tremendous amount of intelligence data that was extremely helpful to all parties. Once intelligence got flowing, we were able to nip a lot of things in the bud and cut off the source of supply. It was the beginning of a wonderful relationship with a lot of police organizations elsewhere."

Rochdale's drug-dealing community would concur with the police chief's depiction of the international scope of the Rochdale reputation. Word of Rochdale filtered through the underground drug-dealing network, as Rosie tells us, "by word of mouth. I'd run into people I knew when I was going to a concert in the Palladium or Hollywood Bowl. I'd ask them how they knew about Rochdale, and they'd say, 'Oh, we heard about it down here.' It was known all over the place—mostly by word of mouth.

"In Southern California, all the major dealers knew that Rochdale was happening because we were down there buyin' blocks and blocks of pot. People in Florida knew about it. Ann Arbor knew about it. Madison, Wisconsin, was the centre for the drug scene there—and they knew about it. Montreal, Vancouver and New York always knew about it. It became a happening—not as well known commercially as the Strip in Los Angeles or Greenwich Village. But to the sub-culture, it was known as much as any other place. It was well known to the people who mattered."

Even Rochdale's "innocents"—those not involved with the drug trade—paid the price for being associated with The Rock. "On one occasion I went home to visit my aunt in Detroit," says Carol Popkey. "When you're a Windsor resident, crossing the Windsor-Detroit border is no big deal at all. But in my suitcase were a couple of *Rochdailies*—I didn't think a thing about it. I also had a letter that my dad had written to me in Toronto. So I was crossing to go to my aunt's for a couple of days, and the guards looked through my suitcase and pulled this stuff out. And they hauled me in! It was the first time in my life I'd ever been hauled in.

"They questioned me and said, 'Do your parents know about this?' I said, 'Yeah, they know I live there.' And they called my aunt to be sure that's where I was really going. I'd never had a problem before crossing the border. I was surprised they even knew about Rochdale—it was the Americans, not the Canadians. I had no idea what was going on in their minds."

During this period, Rochdale's residents felt considerable strain because of the heightened police vigilance and the constant searches. Resident Judy Keeler bitterly remembers being harassed and "subjected to what I would call very nasty, sexist and ugly remarks. I'd been invited to a feminist party that was a pot-luck dinner, and we were supposed to bring food. So I had a basket with me and was walking down the laneway behind Rochdale to get on the College Street streetcar.

"Suddenly, this car started curb-crawling alongside me and then pushed me right over to the wall. I was terrified because there were two very large men in that car and I didn't know they were police. One of them turned to me and said, 'Hey, sweetheart! What have you got in that basket?' The first thing I thought was where I could run to, because these guys were really awful. But there was nowhere to hide. So they took my basket, and when they found out I was carrying a meatloaf, they backed off.

"But in the meantime, I had walked to the back of their car and memorized their licence-plate number and then I asked them for their badge numbers, which they hated. And as soon as I got down to the dinner party, I was so upset that I immediately phoned the police department and asked to speak to a policewoman to place a complaint. Well, of course, they never found the car or those two men!"

Judging by Reg Hartt's experience, even the average cop on an American street knew about Rochdale. Hartt was spending time in California in January of 1970. "I was hitch-hiking one day in Los Angeles, which you can't do there. So the Los Angeles police pulled up and interrogated me and asked me where I was from. I told them I was from Toronto, but all I had for ID was a library card. They asked me what I was doing in Toronto and I said I was showing films at Rochdale College. They said, 'You mean Canada's Communist training centre?' At that point, I figured that if the Los Angeles police knew about it, then it was the one place on earth that was probably THE place to be."

"They walked in and out of there," says Sgt. George Crease, leader of the specially formed Rochdale Squad, "like they were walking into Eaton's to buy a pair of socks." Chief Adamson admits that "some police officers were unhappy and some of them even spoke to me. But in the final analysis you have to take a mature, effective stance to correct these types of things. And that is what [Deputy Police Chief] Jack Ackroyd was trying to do."

Of the department's policy not to mount a massive "clean them all out of there" raid, Ackroyd says, "I think the troops were never happy with me on that score. They never accepted that. I'm not critical of them, because they just didn't know the game plan or what we were trying to accomplish [by using peaceful dialogue]. There was no way of really communicating that. And they were the ones on the firing line. They were the ones who, every time they went in the door, were having bricks thrown at them. Sure, they were dying to go in there and raid the place. One time, when we thought we were going to go in there [for an all-out raid] under receivership, I had 200 phone calls from policemen willing to come back on their day off just to get in there and kick ass."

"The frustration was very real," states Ross Prasky. "At the same time I think it would have been really bizarre to attempt to clean out that building. I mean a small house where dope dealers are is no problem. But we'd never been confronted with a bloody great apartment building that had been turned over to drug dealers—every one of them regarded by many people as assholes. It was absurd to think you could take that size under any circumstances.

"The truth of the matter was that there were a lot of street people and a lot of crazies who wound up there from all over North America and Europe. And they were dangerous, as well, because as a group they fed on each other's energy and each other's misinformation and focused it on the police. So the idea of going in and cleaning everybody out was just ludicrous."

Even nearly twenty years later Bob Waddell's voice registers incredulity when he thinks about why Rochdale was allowed to stay wide open as long as it was. "To me it was incredible that the powers that be, with the information we had on the place, didn't do something. The numbers were staggering—both the arrests and the quantity of dope. What I always wanted to do was to surround the place and get absolutely everything out of the building. Just empty the place. Pile the stuff out in the street. Then everyone could see with their own eyes just what kind of stuff this building was supporting with taxpayers' money."

Even though the stakes were high, both Rochdale and the police seemed to take particular relish in playing cat and mouse games with each other.

"My partner King and I used to go to the front of the building on purpose," relates Bob Waddell, "just so they would flush their toilets. We did that for years. Or we would go up to the doors without a search warrant, knock and say, 'Hi, we're the police,' and you'd hear this mad scrambling and the toilet flushing. We'd piss them off that way. There was a lot of game playing. You'd have some of them pretending they were smuggling stuff out and when you grabbed them it'd turn out to be wood shavings or alfalfa. Smart-ass stuff. Generally they knew they were safe if they stayed within the perimeter of the building. Because to tell you the truth, to bust someone out in front of Rochdale was to take your own life into your hands."

"We used to pick up kids hitch-hiking," continues Waddell. "We'd ask them, 'Where you going?' and they'd say, 'We're going to Rochdale.' 'Oh yeah? What are you doing, going to buy drugs, well you better be careful.' And they'd say, 'Ya, we know, King and Waddell are around.' They'd know about us because their friends had been talking to them. And we'd say, 'Oh yeah, well hop in and we'll give you a ride there.' We arrested people after picking them up hitch-hiking. We let them score, pick them back up and take them directly to the station.

"You had to have a sense of humour. It was cowboys and Indians. It was great, a lot of fun. It was the most fun time in my

whole life in that six- or seven-year period I worked out of
Rochdale. If you were a fisherman and you could go to a lake and
constantly catch fish no matter what the weather was like, no
matter what day it was, wouldn't you have fun? That's what it was
like. We arrested over a thousand people. No one else ever
approached that number.

"We arrested a cross-section of people. Your drug dealers in
those days were middle class or from well-to-do families. They
were from families that fed them every night. They weren't really
drug dealers. They were kids who pooled their money and divvied
it up. They weren't hard-core criminals as such. Instead of booze,
it was drugs. They were regular kids.

"It was difficult to apprehend anyone that was dealing drugs
out of Rochdale. It was easy to get the people that were buying
drugs from the dealers but it was difficult to identify the actual
suppliers and to identify exactly where they were dealing the drugs
from in the building.

"We could tell where somebody [who'd come to buy drugs] was
from by looking at the dealership sticker on the back of the car.
Say three or four young people come in from Hamilton and they
park outside Rochdale. Two get out and walk towards the
building, two stay in the car, cigarettes are lit up, the windows fog
over. Then forty-five minutes later the other two would come out
looking furtively to the left and right. They'd have something
under their coats. Then they'd speed out of there, and we'd take
off after them with our red police toplight flashing. At which time
the windows were rolled down and something was thrown out of
the window. So we didn't have to search too much—it would be all
over the road and we would pick it up. That was how easy it
was.

"In fact at one time we asked our boss if we could have an
undercover bus instead of a car. There were just so many of them.
There would be ten to fifteen possibilities sitting around the
building waiting for drugs. I don't know how many charges we
laid in that period of five years or so, but during that period we got
very adept at being able to pick out not only who was buying
drugs, but how much they were picking up. So you wouldn't waste
your time on the ounce players. Sometimes there would be so
many cars waiting for people to come back with the drugs and
make their quick getaway that we had to pick and choose and
hopefully get the ones with the pounds. If you had a bus and lots of

pairs of handcuffs, you'd be able to chain them to the seats and take a whole busload down to the station instead of two-three at a time.

"I'll tell you how bad it was. There was another team that started shortly after us—Mike Burke, Danny Marshall, and Donnie Young. These guys worked out of 14 Division but we were all down at 52 a lot because that's the area Rochdale was in. I can recall Burke and his partner were down at 52 and it was eight or nine in the evening. I said, 'Let's have a bet, a contest to see who can bust the most people at Rochdale—loser buys dinner.' It ended up we had fourteen and they had eleven. It was a fishing hole. It got to the point where they wouldn't let us go in anymore. It became a political thing. But I'm sure we arrested more people coming out of Rochdale than anyone else."

Sometimes the Rochdalians were more sophisticated than the "got ya" mentality of running out of the building with a bag of woodshavings under an overcoat. Tripper recalls one night on the roof. "Someone, I think it was an American, had gotten ahold of a flaregun—one of those regulation army suckers. Now we knew the fuckin' pigs were over the other side in the parking lot in the other building on the stake-out. It was a twenty-four-hour thing. It was weird to always feel these eyes at the back of your head. Like being under constant observation. So this one clear night we know the coppers are across the street in the parking lot. All of a sudden this guy pulls out the flare and fires it into the sky. Well, let me tell ya it was like goddam day out there. It was funny, this flare comes floating down in a parachute. The coppers scrambled like hell to get into the dark. It was an effective move. I heard the cops later were so freaked they really thought this was it—that the machine gun would follow. But it was more of a head game. You know, tit for tat."

The cops' head games with The Rock often had an underlying method in the madness. "We used to drive our cars there just to aggravate them." recalls Dan Marshall. "We used to take the regular police cars and we'd roar up in front of Rochdale and slam on the brakes and jump out of the cars and yell, 'Nobody move! It's the police!' And everybody'd be runnin' all over the place and runnin' up and down the streets and throwin' drugs on the ground. And we'd just get in the cars and drive away—just to see their reaction. And, of course, everybody'd be all hyper and everything else. And it would be a great time! Then, just as we took off, we'd get our undercover guys to come in and stand around with the people out front. Everybody'd be saying, 'Oh, did they catch so-and-so?' And they'd pick up a name here and there, and pick up a face here and there. I mean, you've gotta have a reason for doing things—beyond the fun factor.

"We had to outsmart them. What we used to do was get their telephone numbers. Somebody might be arrested and you'd come up with a telephone book that would have 'Joe—Rochdale' in it and his telephone number. So we invented dial-a-pinch. One of the most notable dial-a-pinches that I got was the group of us set up in a hotel not very far from here [Strachan Avenue]. We rented a room and called up the telephone number at Rochdale. A guy answered the telephone and we gave him all the referrals. We didn't have to worry about him checking with the guy I got the referral from, because he was in the Don Jail and wasn't available at a telephone.

"So I made a deal to buy three pounds of hash oil. We sat in the room and talked for a while and watched part of a hockey game on the tube. And we were shootin' the breeze and we made all kinds of arrangements to go out drinking. We were really going to party it up. So he finally went out and came back with another fella—a younger guy. I pulled out the money and put it on the bed, and the guy had all of the stuff concealed inside camera cases and he put it on the bed.

"Then the door gets knocked down and in come the troops and they arrest the three of us. We're taken off to 14 Division and we're sat down in an office. The dealer immediately comes forward and says, 'I'm declaring diplomatic immunity.' Everybody looks at him and says, 'Who is this guy?' So he pulls out his identification and he was the counsellor for the Dominican Republic and he was stationed in the United States. He did have diplomatic immunity in the U.S., but not in Canada. He wanted to phone Trudeau, he wanted to phone everybody. He had names comin' out of him like you wouldn't believe.

"He was also blaming the whole deal on me—that it was my drugs and I was trying to sell to him, and all this kinda stuff. Then they marched me in and said, 'Is this the guy?' 'Yup, that's him! He was trying to sell the drugs to us! It was my money and his drugs!' He'd switched it all, you see. And they said to me, 'Why don't you introduce yourself to this guy?' So I went over and pulled out my badge. He looked at the badge, looked at it again and collapsed on the floor.

"Anyway, he appeared for his first time in court. He got bail. Nobody's ever heard from him since. The drugs are still being held as evidence, and that's a lot of years ago."

Among the more hair-raising incidents was a high-speed chase around Queen's Park with Bob Waddell and his partner in pursuit of a car full of marijuana. "When you're southbound on that road," says Waddell, "you go over a bridge with the university below you. Well, these guys were going lickety-split, and we're right behind them, when suddenly, they throw the grass out the window of their car. But it hit the railing of the bridge—five or six pounds of it. And since I was the passenger in our unmarked squad car, I jumped out to grab it for evidence while we were still moving. Well, it hits my partner and breaks open and the wind spreads it all over the inside of the car and all over my partner and me. We look like a couple of scarecrows with grass sticking up all over the place.

"But we go on with the chase and finally stop them at College Street near what was the old 52 Division police station. Well, we're covered with weed and everything, and the police in the building are looking out to see what's going on—and here are these two scarecrows apprehending a couple of guys. It was crazy, just crazy."

Community relations officer Dean Audley also remembers how one seemingly innocuous incident triggered a near-riot. "What happened was that there was something thrown at a police car. I think there was a detective unit driving by along Bloor St. and a pop bottle was thrown through a windshield. So the car stopped and one of the police went into the main lobby. An arrest was made and when the residents started milling around, the officer called for assistance. Residents started leaving the building, and what we had was a confrontation of people—police on one side and young people on the other.

"I was called and the other fellows were called, and by the time we got there, they had started calling in the troops. It looked like it was going to be one hell of a confrontation. We ended up with all sorts of uniformed officers in cars outside the building wanting to go in and do whatever they thought they could do to close the building down, which was physically impossible. Meanwhile, the residents were ready to do battle with the cops, whom they hated. And there I was, running back and forth as a go-between. By working back and forth, we would move off a few police officers at a time. And the ultimate saw-off was that we called the police off. Gradually, we avoided what could easily have been a bloodbath, because both police and young people were ready to get it on."

The Rochdale cauldron, heating up through months and months of pent-up frustration and repressed hostilities on both sides, finally exploded into violence on the night of August 15, 1970. The headlines told the story to the rest of the city the next day: 1,500 PEOPLE CONFRONT 150 POLICEMEN AT ROCHDALE IN NEAR-RIOT AFTER ARREST; 1,000 BATTLE POLICE AT ROCHDALE; MOB INJURES 3 POLICEMEN AFTER ROCHDALE DRUGS RAID. *The Toronto Star*'s account gave the following details:

> Three Metro policemen were hurt fighting members of an unruly mob of more than 1,000 young people who poured onto Bloor St. W. in front of Rochdale College Saturday night to protest a police drug raid in the building.
> College residents screamed threats at about 25 policemen called to the scene, and hurled bottles, stones, water and a live cat from windows of the student-owned co-operative.
> Rochdale dwellers were angered by the way six Metro and RCMP detectives searched a 15th floor apartment for drugs, said Michael Eleser, a member of the college's security force, which later attempted to calm the mob.

There were, as you might expect, two sides to the story. Here's Metro's account according to official police reports filed the night of the riot:

> At 9:30 p.m. Saturday August 15th, 1970, the R.C.M.P. Drug Squad, assisted by Metro Drug Squad and members of the Morality Bureau executed a warrant to search for drugs at 341 Bloor St. W. Apt. 1509P (Rochdale College). The search of this apartment proved negative; however when they were walking down the stairs at the ninth level they arrested one Robert Edward ANDERER 20 yrs. 341 Bloor St. W. (Born U.S.A.) for possession of narcotics (hashish)
> . . . .
> It appears that by this time a large number of the college residents had gathered and were trying to block the paths of the drug squad members who had the prisoner. Calls by this time had been put into the radio room to assist the police at this location. Units from 52, 14, 13, and the E.T.F. had responded.
> A very large crowd had gathered by this time and the college residents began to throw things from various heights of the building (bottles and rocks). Some of these objects struck the police vehicles and also the police officers. . . .

Needless to say the Rochdale residents saw things from a somewhat different perspective: "The massive police raids were never executed for the purpose of finding drugs," states Alex MacDonald, blunt and to the point as usual. "They were executed for the purpose of generating negative publicity for Rochdale. They sent in a hundred policemen to knock down seventeen doors, trash people's living quarters. And for what? A couple of ounces or a chunk of hash and a couple of resisting arrests."

According to resident Alex Martin, it was the police force's heavy handedness that ignited the riot. "The cops surrounded the building and we were throwing stones and stuff off the roof onto their cars. It was neat. They were stupid to park their cars so close to the building. They came into the building and they were pretty heavy handed. There were riots because they came with so many—I mean 200 cops pouring into the building is bound to get people excited. This guy would be asleep in his bed when, smash, an axe comes through the door. They could have kicked it in but they preferred the heavy-handed approach.

"The August 15th raid was on Delajinski's place—everyone called him Del. He was on the eighth floor. They raided his place and the people in the building rebelled and started to pour out into the street. There was a lot of pushing and shoving. There was a feeling of, I don't know, injustice. They were wrong and they were brutal about it."

Part of the fallout resulting from the August 15th raid was the increased pressure brought to bear on the college by the civic authorities. Metro Toronto realized that Rochdale, to a large degree, was a federal problem, but the fact was that this highly volatile piece of property was within Metro, and Metro had to live with it. If something was going to be done about 341 Bloor Street, Metro would have to accelerate its anti-Rochdale campaign. As a result, the running battle between the municipal government and the delinquent college escalated dramatically in the aftermath of August 15.

On August 19, the Toronto building department sent a letter to Rochdale ordering fifty-one repair and clean-up jobs. The department had conducted an inspection of the building from July 29 to August 4 and found an assortment of things to complain about, including overcrowding, littering, scribbling on the walls, abused fixtures and carpeting, two motorcycles in apartments. The building department followed up with a confidential appeal to the CMHC for help to alleviate "the apparent poor management control and housekeeping" at Rochdale.

For its part Rochdale was at least officially trying to do its best to clean up its act. On August 18, Peter Turner's council evicted 150 U.S. transients and one permanent resident. The transients were Americans returning home from the Strawberry Fields Rock Festival, which had drawn 50,000 people to Mosport Park the previous weekend. Many residents felt that the Americans were the spark that set the building off on the night of the 15th. Turner tried to convince the public, through the newspapers, that Rochdale did not condone the violence on either side. The raid may have been calculated and unnecessary, he argued, but Rochdale had no right to throw bottles, stones and dangerous debris in retaliation.

"We were," says Turner, "at one and the same time trying to protect both the police and the community. We had our people throwing bricks, cinderblocks off the top of the building. We had to stop them from throwing fire extinguishers out the windows. Imagine the chaos if those had started exploding all over the place."

The authorities struck again on August 21 when forty police hit the building, sealing off exits and rushing up to the fifth floor with warrants. Six residents were charged with various drug offences, but, unlike the previous raid, this one came off without incident. Still, the point was clear: the party's over.

The police weren't finished with The Rock yet. They made it three in a row when they stormed the building for their third major raid in three weeks the night of September 11. This time they were aiming for the heart of the beast—the sixth floor dealing commune. According to police records:

On September 11th, 1970, about 9:30 p.m., officers from this department, accompanied by members of the R.C.M. Police executed orders for search on Apartments 604, 606, 607, 609 and 619, Rochdale. When they entered the building from the rear, the alarm rang instantly. They proceeded to the sixth floor, via the stairs, accompanied by the security man. The doors leading to the sixth floor apartments were forced. Ten persons were arrested for trafficking and possession of marijuana, hashish, and offensive weapons and also obstructing police. Uniform members entered via the front entrance, and immediately debris in large quantities was thrown from the windows. Due to normally heavy traffic on Bloor Street at this time of night, a large crowd of pedestrians congregated.

An unknown person placed a call to the police dispatcher, resulting in the arrival of several more police autos. As a result, eight of these autos suffered considerable damage such as broken headlights, window and body dents. Some of the damage was caused by falling debris thrown out of the windows and by rocks thrown from the ground. One motorcycle suffered damage for which

a male person was arrested on a charge of malicious damage. The
usual name calling and the utter lack of co-operation from the
residents were apparent, as on other occasions. A quantity of
marijuana and hashish was seized; also several glass jars of
unknown substances believed to be drugs or materials used in
drugs on the street.

Amid the din of screeching tires, wailing sirens, smashing
bottles and screaming, Rochdalians were buzzing with the sense
of exhilaration that comes pulsating into a body when the
restraints have finally been thrown off, the preliminary jabbing is
over and you wade in with your fists flying.

"We closed Bloor Street that night," remembers a still-defiant
Alex Martin. "We closed it right down. We sat down on Bloor
Street until they brought in the heavy-duty riot squad and
physically moved us. We sat on Bloor Street right across from the
church. We must have brought the street to a complete halt for at
least an hour. It was pretty wild out there. The cops were laying
beatings on people pretty heavy. I remember this one guy, Don, he
got it bad. There was lots of blood, cracked skulls—they were out
there bashing heads.

"Me, I hated the cops then. I saw them as invaders, the enemy
coming into our home. They weren't there to do their jobs—maybe
some of them, the on-the-street constables—but the higher-ups,
I hate to use the term, but they were so neo-Nazi, so fascist
about it.

"There was a real sense of exhilaration out on Bloor Street that
night. We were winning and we weren't going to take anymore
shit! But then I saw this cop getting hit in the head with a brick. He
was wearing a soft cap, so he crumpled right to the ground. He was
hurt bad, bleeding. Another cop went over to help him and then I
saw that it was getting out of hand and it wasn't so much fun
anymore.

"I was threatened by King or Waddell—I always mixed the two
of them up—during the September 11 riot. They were coming
down the stairwell and I was being real mouthy. Waddell was
carrying an axe and he pinned me with it against the wall and
threatened me with the axe. It was all show, but still he scared the
living shit out of me. This other cop pulled him off and said
something like, 'You don't want to do that,' and he said, 'All right,
you little prick, get out of here and keep your big mouth shut.' I
was shitting myself."

Another recipient of the police's strong-arm tactics was Bob
Nasmith, a Canadian who had fought for the U.S. in the Vietnam
War and was no stranger to violence. "On one occasion, I was on
security when the police came in," he says. "It was early in the
morning and they just started charging up to the rooms, with me
swept alongside them. And as we were going into one of the
stairwells, I said, 'Excuse me,' and reached over and pulled one of
the fire alarms.

"One cop—a nice, old guy, a big guy—turned to me and said,
'You shouldn't have done that,' and he gave me a few good
whacks. Then a couple of other cops jumped in and gave me some
more good whacks. I took a swing at them and they kicked the shit
out of me—and that was fine. No problem. I had fucked up by
their standards and they kicked the shit out of me. What could I
do? Fair's fair."

After the disastrous summer of 1970, Rochdale decided to take
a different tack in dealing with the authorities. Led by Peter
Turner, Rochdale the political animal adopted a more mature,
adult approach in dealing with Ottawa and the CMHC. With
other council members in tow, he headed for Ottawa to discuss
Rochdale with the appropriate officials and civil servants. By
upgrading The Rock's presentation, Turner hoped to convince the
powers that be that despite all of its financial and social woes,
Rochdale was still important, still a viable youth concept. "Take a
look at us—we're serious young people—don't abandon us in our
hour of need," was the plea.

Turner knew that a concentrated effort to change Rochdale's
very negative public perception was mandatory for the college's
survival. To that end, Rochdale council held town-hall-type
meetings to discuss the situation with the community at large. The
council went on a number of PR trips to nearby college campuses.
No sooner did a negative, usually erroneous, piece on the college
appear in the press than Rochdale would react with a stream of
letters to the editor. Some of the rebuttals were published, like that
of Pamela Berton's in the *Telegram*:

> I am writing this in reply to the letter (The Rochdale Experiment has
> destroyed itself, September 25) which condemned Rochdale
> College. It is only another of the instances of bad publicity which
> have plagued Rochdale from its opening. I am not a 'hippie,' I am not
> a drug addict. I pay my rent. I am not an exception . . . I would like to
> remind the letter-writer that Rochdale is like life—you get out of it
> what you put in.

So concerned was Rochdale with its public image that it made sure the newspapers were contacted if a raid was being conducted. Veteran *Toronto Star* police reporter Jocko Thomas recalls, "Newspapers mostly waited for tips from the inside. Rochdale had its own sort of public-relations people who would tip us off if there was a raid. They wanted to get pictures of the police into the papers, pictures that would reflect badly on the police. Sometimes there were unpleasantries between photographers and the police who tried to keep them out while they were inside."

For their part the police stepped up their raiding campaign on Rochdale. The raids continued unabated through the fall of 1970 right through 1971. The frequency and the net results of the raids prompted a reaction from author Pierre Berton, who charged in letters to the editors of all three Toronto dailies that police were on a "fishing expedition" in raids that were "highly unproductive." Berton protested in "the strongest possible terms the incredible mass police raid."

Deputy Police Chief Jack Ackroyd denied the charges of harassing Rochdale but added that the raids would end eventually. Closer to the mark was Berton's assertion that the raids "produced such picayune results."

As for the residents, the raids became a way of life. For resident Murray Campbell, the raids were "taken as ordinary. As I recall, they happened weekly on Friday morning around three o'clock, especially during the summer of 1971. Bells would go off, and I was told that this was because the fire alarm system had been rewired as an internal early warning system. Since I wasn't a dealer, I had nothing to hide and wasn't tied in to anyone who was. So when I heard the bells, I'd go back to sleep. I think about it now—I'm on the fourteenth floor, I hear fire bells going off, and I roll over and go back to sleep. I was a little cavalier with my life, if nothing else. If there had been a real fire, I don't know what would have happened. But I guess it illustrates the ability of someone to incorporate incredible experiences and make them seem normal. This to me was normal—a police raid every Friday morning.

"You could hear doors being broken in on the floor above and the floor below. You could hear slam, slam, slam! And then the next morning, you'd go out and there would be a succession of broken doors lined up to be taken away as garbage. Police had come in and busted doors with axes, I assumed.

"The only time I call recall bothering to get up was when something extraordinary happened. It strikes me that it was the first time the police used Chicago-style riot gear. I watched from a higher floor at three in the morning and there were kids out and the ordinary sort of police presence that accompanied these things. And all of a sudden, a bus from the service station at Bloor and St. George pulled up, and these guys got off in their riot gear. The crowd below started laughing and said, 'Look! Real pigs! Real pigs!' And these guys stood around with everybody laughing and pointing at them and eventually got back on the bus and drove away."

There was a feeling, at least within the more radical segment of the Rochdale population, that at times the police raids masked other political intentions on the part of the authorities. For example, as the events of October, 1970, unfolded in Canada—the kidnapping of senior British Trade Commissioner James Cross and Quebec Labour Minister Pierre LaPorte by the FLQ, and the subsequent invocation of the War Measures Act by Prime Minister Trudeau—some, like Rosie Rowbotham, felt the raids were a front.

"In October of 1970, they came in under the War Measures Act," says Rosie, "with one soldier, one RCMP officer and eighty regular police under the martial law. But it was crazy—it was all just an excuse for beatin' us. And in the end, they came out with only five dollars worth of pot."

Still, the raids did have their comical side, and Peter Turner remembers one attempt in particular to defuse tension through humour. "It came to a point where we said, 'Look we keep having all these raids, so the next time the cops come, why don't we bake a cake and throw a party? Well, for the next raid, the fourteenth floor had baked this big cake and we had huge amounts of confetti and there were these two-foot-high red letters over the door saying 'Welcome 52 Division!' We all stood around shouting and singing at the top of our voices, 'Happy bustday to you, happy bustday to you.' You had these half dozen cops surrounded by all these confetti-throwing freaks and revellers eating cake and all this fun-loving hysteria. After they had finished busting this room—they demolished it—people threw confetti at them and got their aggressions out. It freaked the cops out, but it worked. But the press wouldn't handle it. I was furious. We had called the press to come down because we were being raided but they never came once."

The authorities believed that under the glare of the spotlight of public scrutiny Rochdale would reveal its true face. However, outside of the negative publicity angle, the raids didn't work. They were dangerous and destructive and, even after inflating the numbers of drugs seized and arrests made, the police themselves felt they were unproductive.

Julian Fantino, part of the Rochdale drug investigation unit, states, "Over time it became very dangerous to commence any operation within Rochdale. Raids became extremely dangerous. Each time the frustrations became greater and greater and certainly the hazards became greater and greater. Almost from the outset of my police service, I was sensitive to the reputation that Rochdale had in police circles. It was a formidable problem as far as drugs went. The fact of the matter was we weren't busting either the number of dealers or quantities of dope to justify the risk."

At City Hall, the question of the Rochdale raids was hotly contested. "I think I was there when two of them were on," recalls Alderman Tony O'Donohue. "There was a whole lot of screaming and shouting and insults and very inventive profanity. It was difficult for the police to go in there. Most of the police were afraid because of the stabbing problem. It got so that I would not go in there at all after a while because I was told that fellows like me were going to be done in—literally done in. So I just took their insults from a distance. But these police were brave people to go in, because there certainly was nobody in there who was at all favourably disposed to them. It was total bedlam and chaos to have a raid on Rochdale."

Reform Alderman Allan Sparrow felt that the raids were a "make-work project" for the police. "For the police, Rochdale was just a boon. It allowed them to increase the number of charges they laid and to create a climate of apprehension about the downtown which wasn't shared by downtown residents, but was widely reported in the media. It helped keep their crime statistics up for the year so they could ask for even more cops to hassle even more people. So it was a wonderful make-work project for them, and they went after it assiduously. They mined it as if it were a gold mine, to the point where people in Rochdale were complaining that anybody coming in or out of Rochdale was being harassed needlessly."

Clearly, new tactics were required. After some deliberation, police officials decided that, rather than raid the building in periodic sweeps, they could accomplish more by surrounding Rochdale at all hours and conducting searches of almost everyone entering or leaving the premises. That responsibility fell to the morality squad and, finally, to George Crease.

"What we did was peripheral surveillance from the middle of January until the end of April, 1973," recalls Crease. "We stopped people coming in and out of the building as best we could. And in doing so, we pretty well stopped the drug trade in Rochdale, although some dealers did set up satellite operations in apartments elsewhere in the downtown area.

"When they asked me to form the squad, I asked if I could pick my own men and they said yes. I hand-picked them from the morality squad in 52 Division and the odd man from 51 Division. Some of them didn't particularly care for the assignment, but if I said 'I want you,' they came. I started out with eight men but after a month, I realized that wasn't enough, so I ended up with twelve. I was promised three cars but, except for the use of one of the inspector's cars, I ended up with only one—and that turned out to be an old Volkswagen that hardly ran.

"What I was looking for were policemen who could get out there and hustle. I didn't want any shining stars, though. I needed guys who would go in there and muck it out, get the people right off the street. If we hadn't had that kind of policeman, we couldn't have done what we did. Some of the investigators who had worked out of Rochdale were good, but I didn't want that type. I wanted street cops—street-wise guys who wouldn't be afraid of civil complaints.

"We'd walk up to them as soon as we saw them come out of Rochdale, whip them into the car—and zip! They're gone! No hassle. Even if they didn't co-operate, they were put into the car. By doing that, we seldom caused a disturbance on the street. It was like picking flowers—one, two, three!

"We worked the periphery like that for six or eight weeks before the people in Rochdale realized what we were up to. Then, of course, the word got out that we had this special squad and things got thinner and thinner, until there was next to nothing. So we ended up being not a permanent fixture, but a sort of temporary emergency squad."

C H A P T E R   11

The
Beat
Goes On

To those running Rochdale, it must have seemed as if they were caught in a vise, being squeezed on all fronts: the police, crusading politicians, the newspapers—all were screaming for the head of Rochdale College. The enemies of The Rock decided to attack their nemesis at its most vulnerable spot—the mortgage. The Rochdale politicos had become, in the course of their battles with officialdom, wily opponents, but their wiles and skills would do them little good when they faced the incontrovertible truth—the mortgage had to be paid. Even seasoned veterans like Peter Turner, who resigned on October 30, 1970, because he feared "burning himself out," couldn't extricate Rochdale from its mortgage obligations.

Of all the threats to Rochdale's existence, the foreclosure of the college mortgage by the CMHC was by far the most serious. The first salvo in the war was fired by one of the crusading anti-Rochdale politicians—Toronto Alderman Tony O'Donohue. He appealed to the federal government to "put an end to this madness" of Rochdale College and to convert its Bloor Street building to a police college or a home for the aged. In a letter addressed to Robert Andras, the minister responsible for housing, O'Donohue likened the three-year-old building to a "drug supermarket," a building that had deteriorated from its original academic principles and goals to become a "haven for the sick, the drug user, the drug pusher—an eighteen-storey flophouse."

O'Donohue's letter to Ottawa received extensive coverage in the Toronto dailies. Ottawa, in particular Robert Andras, wasted no time in responding to the alderman. Andras admitted that Rochdale wasn't working and that something had to be done about the situation. The college was $260,000 in arrears on its mortgage. However, Andras had a delicate balancing act to perform. Privately he might have agreed with O'Donohue that the place was a cancer that had to be excised, but publicly to pull the rug from under the college would make the government seem repressive and anti-youth. Andras hedged somewhat by calling for "ideas to rehabilitate the college" without foreclosing.

Andras would sustain this line for the next few months. He realized that Rochdale wasn't meeting its financial obligations and was a social problem, but he didn't accept that Rochdale was a high-rise Sodom and Gomorrah as critics such as Tony O'Donohue maintained.

The anti-Rochdale forces exerted considerable and constant pressure to close the building. William Scott, Progressive Conservative MP for Victoria-Haliburton, stood up in the House of Commons on June 2, 1971, and unleashed a vitriolic attack on Rochdale, the building "that was masquerading as an educational institution but is a haven for drug users, hippies, deviants of all kinds." Children were lured into Rochdale and kept there for the "depraved satisfaction of some so-called students."

For its part, the CMHC conducted a study of Rochdale's accounting system and considered its options. Besides the CMHC mortgage at a preferred rate of 5⅞ per cent over fifty years, Rochdale also had four other mortgages. To add to the financial straits of the college and the confusion of the entire financial picture, the Supreme Court ruled that the City of Toronto could not enforce the payment of the municipal taxes that Rochdale owed until the college's appeal was settled. That figure stood at $136,000 in 1970.

At City Hall, Rochdale became the hottest political football in years. Councillors like future mayor Art Eggleton joined Tony O'Donohue in crying out for Rochdale's hide. On the other side of the fence, reform aldermen such as Reid Scott and Karl Jaffarey emphasized that the college's mortgage problem was not City Hall's concern.

By May 22, 1971, matters were coming to a head as Mayor William Dennison, Metro Chairman Albert Campbell, CMHC President Herbert Hignett and Toronto medical officer Dr. Boyd met to discuss Rochdale's future. On June 24, 1971, Hignett, who was heading a committee of federal civil servants on Rochdale, released the group's findings to the press: if Rochdale was to survive economically, the government would have to subsidize it to the tune of $28,400 a month. If the government was not prepared to do that, it must foreclose.

By June 24, 1971, Rochdale was $330,000 in arrears on its CMHC-held mortgage. With all the mounting criticism and pressure to foreclose on Rochdale, the clock was running out on Robert Andras. The final word came on August 5, 1971. The federal government had decided to foreclose and take over the college. Rochdale had only paid eleven out of its scheduled thirty monthly mortgage payments. The owners of 341 Bloor Street West, Campus Co-op Residence Inc., were delinquent $450,000.

Andras stressed that this was not a moral judgement. "We are foreclosing," his statement went, "on a financial basis. This action directly involved the owners and not the tenants. It is not intended to make a statement about young people and their lifestyles." He went on to say that with the government in control there would be no mass evictions of present tenants, but the residents who remained had better get used to paying rent and maintaining "other normal standards of occupancy."

"We will set up no moral guardianship as managers," the government's press release read. "That is a matter, as in any other building, for local law enforcement."

Lost in all the noise about foreclosure was the vital piece of information that the actual ensuing legal action could take a couple of years. Andras tried to smooth the time factor element over by stating it would take only a "few months." In the meantime the government was to upgrade the building to the tune of $100,000.

Andras was still doing a tapdance around the "don't alienate the youth of Canada" issue when he appeared on CBC's "Weekend" program the Sunday after foreclosure and stated "that if this means the end of the Rochdale experiment, I really wouldn't be jumping for joy. I think there's something to be said for it." He said that if it worked out financially, the Rochdale experiment would continue.

Rochdale itself finally got to sit down with the minister at the Royal York Hotel. The college sent its king, some council members and a few residents. Nothing was really achieved at the meeting. If anything, Andras seemed even more determined not to compromise: there would be no reduced rates to try to save the project, there would be no plans to let Rochdale continue in half the building, and even mass evictions weren't entirely ruled out.

Rochdale's first reaction to the foreclosure was to flip the finger to both the government and society in general. By turning certain lights out in the structure and leaving others on, the building devised a plan whereby FUCK OFF would be spelled out. There'd be no mistaking The Rock's attitude toward the deal.

However, what took place on August 27, a week and a half after the foreclosure announcement, was closer to the spirit of what Rochdale was about. Syd Stern, "Papa Dope," flashed that ol' Rochdale never-say-die-just-dream-up-another-scam attitude. Here's how the *Toronto Telegram* described Syd's auction:

> The auctioneer warned the crowd that it wasn't going to be an ordinary auction.
> The location should have been one hint. The sight of a six-year-old boy casually lighting up his own marijuana cigarette in the midst of the crowded make-shift hall should have been another.
> Rochdale College sold off everything from empty wine bottles to Oriental rugs last night and auctioneer Syd Stern, 50, a college resident, was right—it wasn't your run-of-the-mill auction sale.
> If you didn't have cash, it didn't matter, or as Syd shouted from the top of his television set turned auction-block: "As long as you're going to pay sometime, it's all right."
> Where else could you buy a first edition of *Tarzan of the Apes* for $1.25? Or pick up a pair of nearly new skis for $6? . . .
> Although Rochdale officials were not sure how much money had been taken in, auctioneer Stern termed the event a success and guaranteed more auctions in the future.
> "All the merchandise was donated by building residents," he said. "And if the city and CMHC won't take our money, we'll use the proceeds to rent other buildings in the area."

College Vice-President Lionel Douglas sounded the Rochdale clarion when he proclaimed, "Rochdale is not dead. Rochdale has not failed." Those were not hollow words. Rochdale wouldn't go down without a fight, but it had outgrown the puerile defence built on throwing bottles and debris at a superior foe. No, this time Rochdale would use all of its accumulated wisdom and skill. It would do what it did best—use the system against itself. The first plan of attack was to stretch the foreclosure out in the courts for as long as possible. Instrumental to Rochdale's stalling tactic was Bay Street lawyer Joe Sheard.

By his own account, Sheard was "brought on to act for Rochdale in the foreclosure. I was supposed to delay the fore- closure because nobody had any enormous confidence, once the foreclosure action got to trial, that Rochdale would win. In fact when it did get to trial, Rochdale did not win. I did genuinely feel that there was a legitimate defence, although it was of a rather technical nature—the original authorization that gave rise to this huge mortgage loan had not been properly processed and that was essentially the nature of the defence, because there was no question that Rochdale was in arrears on its mortgage.

"The real question was whether the mortgage was a valid security against the property and that's where the technical argument came in. The case came before Madame Justice Van Camp—who I believe was given the file the morning before the trial—which is a tall order. I argued the case. She reserved on it for about three months and then she decided against Rochdale. That was appealed and the appeal was unsuccessful; when it made the trial stage it was unsuccessful.

"It was a tough one to win but I did feel that we had a chance; nobody likes technical defences, but they do work. But it was a lengthy process. I was instructed to stretch it out because during the proceeding Rochdale was going to stay alive and there was always some sort of expectation or hope that something would happen to save Rochdale. The foreclosure happened in the fall.

"I can't recall what I was paid at the time—it wasn't much. I think the biggest cheque I received was for a thousand dollars, but I was not waxing rich on the Rochdale account. I spent countless hours on the case. In fact my partner was a little upset at the time because I was devoting so much time to Rochdale's case. But I wasn't the kind of lawyer who added up every hour.

"The reasons for getting involved to such a degree? One of the reasons was it was an interesting case, and another was I liked the people at Rochdale. I thought Rochdale had a sociological validity and I thought there was a general predisposition to regard Rochdale as an undesirable presence in the community. People whom I knew expressed amazement that I was involved with Rochdale. But I didn't regard myself as a crusader, I had a job to do."

The length of the foreclosure litigation was a thorn in the side of Rochdale's sworn enemies. "One of the things," says resident Alex MacDonald, "that haunted Tony O'Donohue and the *Toronto Telegram* was why it took so long to close Rochdale. People screamed at the CMHC to foreclose the building. They did. And nothing happened except we stopped making even token mortgage payments. Then we got receivership and still nothing happened."

MacDonald goes on to say that, far from killing Rochdale, fore-closure "actually brought on the Golden Age at Rochdale. By that

I mean in the period after foreclosure in August of 1971 and before receivership in September of 1972 we felt there was no reason to pay our mortgage to the CMHC. Prior to foreclosure we had tried to pay as many installments of the mortgage as we could. That attempt drained all the available resources in the building. All the money went to try and prevent the foreclosure. After foreclosure and our decision not to make even token payments, suddenly we had a BUDGET!"

The money for the budget was generated by Rochdale's primary revenue source—rents. Occupancy was at an all-time high. The occupancy history of Rochdale's first few years was a roller-coaster adventure from the "empties" of the summer of 1969 (when only half the building was occupied) through the full house of early 1970 onto the ebb of the summer of 1970 to spring 1971 (when the figure was in the 60 to 80 per cent range). At the time of foreclosure, Rochdale was building up a healthy occupancy rate. In April of 1971 under the stewardship of treasurer Jay Boldizsar, a new, more realistic and businesslike approach to rentals was developed.

Karen Johnson, head of rentals, comments on the transformation: "I remember when the receiver Clarkson Gordon came in, they were genuinely surprised and confused to see actual offices with ledger cards, books, journals, financial records and statements. I think that they really believed we sort of had this great big bucket full of money and hands went into it as it was needed. They were genuinely surprised—'Oh, you have journals?' I came back for the summer of 1970; by that time we were a functioning office."

Under Boldizsar's guidance, the perennial double-occupancy drawback was dealt with and, by converting doubles into singles, Rochdale was made more attractive for single men. The addition of hot plates to the rooms, while hardly a major improvement, reflected a new attitude on the part of rentals. The disparity between the east wing's payment burden and the more favoured west wing was balanced. By the summer of 1971, Rochdale had once again achieved full occupancy. Not only was Rochdale full, the administration was collecting 95 per cent of the rent. By the spring of 1972, Rochdale was turning away applicants.

Perhaps even more important than the increased revenues was the internal evolution of Rochdale. Alex MacDonald, who came to Rochdale from the University of Windsor, claims he was "so dumb that I actually didn't understand that this place was weird, I mean I had so little life experience, I didn't understand this place was peculiar.

"Here's a great example of what I mean by the evolution of Rochdale. There was a lost kid about four years old. Now normally this wasn't a large problem at Rochdale because of the infrastructure. Everyone, certainly on security, knew what kid belonged where, what dog belonged to what apartment and so on. Now this kid was more than regularly lost, and a group of women just started to search the building from top to bottom and found the kid. He was off visiting a friend in another unit. That wouldn't have happened in '69—even though '69 was the time of flower power. In the period between '69 and '72, the 10 per cent stable population that was creative and put something back into its environment—more than party party party types—grew. When you have something to protect, the forces of law and order exert themselves—and it's not from on high, it's from within the community.

"Maintenance was also making gains in the '71–'72 period, and it was easily the largest force working on a single building in the city. It had a budget, a staff and social consensus behind it. Big chunks of the building were reasonably clean for extended periods of time. Rochdale became established; things were progressing nicely. There was internal regulation—an ostracism process plus the Eviction Appeal Board—that was a very important agency. You had to be genuinely sleazy and untogether to arrive at the point when Rochdale wouldn't tolerate you."

Still, keeping the building clean was never less than a major challenge, recalls maintenance chief Brian Lumley. "Basically, it was cleaning up the trash that was the hardest thing to do. Once a day, we had an elevator running for three hours straight as we took the garbage out of the garbage chute, loaded it onto the elevator and took it down to the trash bins. And the system worked only because we put such massive manpower into it—the thirty people who were working under me. Because of that, we had some mice, but never rats.

"And the dogshit! That was a horrendous problem—the number one thing the health department didn't like about us. The rules in the building were clear: 'Take your dog out, but if it does happen to shit in the building, you clean it up.' Well, that looked good on paper, but in reality, no one gave a fuck. Their response would be, 'Yeah, man. Great, man. Outasight, man. Fuck you.' "

With growing numbers of Rochdalians "settling down," and the increasingly domestic environment developing, we also see a concomitant growth in family-oriented concerns such as day-care—although Rochdale had from the very outset made an attempt at creating a co-operative family setting through projects such as the Rochdale Nursery School. Operating out of a fourth-floor Zeus, the school ran quite successfully until the provincial government shut it down because it was in contravention of some rule or regulation. The Rochdale kindergarten was in operation through most of 1969 and 1970. Kent Gooderham found Rochdale to be a decent place to bring up his brood of seven kids. His youngest attended the Rochdale kindergarten and learned some valuable life skills in the process (such as getting ice cream out of the storekeeper with imaginary money), while his oldest took a more traditional course of studies and operated a film projector and helped out as a librarian. All of the Gooderham children participated in the Children's Art Show and the "Roses For Rochdale" gardening project. Art shows, rose gardens, imaginary money—the picture Gooderham paints of family life at Rochdale is almost idyllic.

If not as idyllic as Gooderham's painting, the Darling children's (Justine, now eighteen, and Craig, thirteen) description of growing up at Rochdale is one of general contentment. "I don't recall any bad experiences at all in Rochdale," says Justine, "I was four or five. I remember playing on the roof and in the swimming pool. If you look at some of the newspapers of the day, you'll see us—Craig was a big smiling baby. We had our baby pool up on the roof—they had plants and flowers up there, it was quite nice.

"I used to go around and get made up all the time: 'Would you paint my nails?' 'Would you put some makeup on me?' People were always friendly and playful. There was this one guy who kept saying he was going to steal me because I was so cute and he was going to take me to South America and I'd live in a tree and eat bananas because I was so cute."

Rochdale's gradual domestication and concern for a good family atmosphere is reflected in the rise of the Acorn Daycare Centre. Judy Keeler felt that it was "ahead of its time and the women started it with nothing. They got it all organized themselves and they put in two dollars a week or something. They took turns taking care of these kids.

"For the most part, almost everybody's doors were open. If kids wandered in, it didn't matter whose kid they were, you just gave them a cookie and took care of them until their mothers came and got them. It was no big deal. And if they were there for a while, you took them down the hall back home. It was really nice that way, because it was a real neighbourhood.

"The actual daycare centre was set up in educational space by a group of about six or eight women. They organized it themselves, rummaged for toys, took turns taking the kids on outings to the museum. None of the women got paid for any of the work she did. All day long they took care of kids and they didn't get paid. The number of kids on any day really varied, from two or three to fifteen or more."

Not everyone at The Rock thought that 341 Bloor Street West provided the best atmosphere for child-rearing. Poet Victor Coleman wanted his children "to be free to go wherever they want" but after his five-and-a-half-year-old came home with a suspicious-looking pill Coleman questioned the building's attitude to drugs as it affected children. Rochdale lore is filled with stories of babies either born on drugs or brought into the world in a drug-ridden atmosphere, of kids who could say "give me a toke" before they could say "please" or "thank you."

Morality Squad Chief John Wilson's report on Rochdale contained an account of a shocking "conversation between a male and female tenant, in the presence of a ten-year-old girl and police, describing perverted sex acts that she had taken part in and would do in the future." This wasn't exactly Cap'n Crunch and the Saturday morning cartoons.

However, Rochdale remained a reasonably good place to raise children by all accounts and a pretty fair delivery room as well. Nicky Morrison, one of the founders of the fourteenth-floor commune, decided to give birth to her first child in Rochdale because "I was pregnant and I wasn't married at the time and I went to see a gynecologist and they sort of treated me like a slut—in those days if you were pregnant and not married and especially if you lived in Rochdale they looked down on you. So I had the baby in Rochdale."

Like more than one Rochdalian, Don Washburn was thrust into the role of spontaneous mid-wife. "It was no big deal," says Washburn. "This guy had four children, his wife was pregnant and having her fifth. They lived in the building, they were very nice people, an Italian couple. He had called an ambulance and came down to tell me to send the attendants up quickly when they came. I left another guard downstairs and went upstairs to see if I could help. The baby started coming. She was a real pro so it wasn't that difficult. I just helped the baby come out as smoothly as possible, making sure the head was out right. I didn't have that much to do really. It was a great experience."

Another area that Rochdale was far ahead of in its time was, according to Valerie Frith, the role and lifestyle of single mothers. "Single mothers helped one another, and in that way, it was very advanced. In fact, a lot of the people who stayed in Rochdale to the bitter end were single mothers who had worked out really efficient ways of living together. Probably today their case would have been better received by the establishment as a reason to stay there. But there was no general consciousness then about the reality of life for a single mother."

Another indication of Rochdale's maturing was the change in security. Alex MacDonald traces the history of Rochdale's security philosophy. "The period of September 1970 through February 1971 was a very important time. It was a time when the community made a decision to go through a transformation. It wasn't because a huge number of people left and a huge number of new people moved in, which is what happened in the summer of 1969 and early in 1970, and it wasn't because we got foreclosed, that is, because of external pressures. It was just that during that period there was the first recognition that there had to be some constraints on the private drug dealers. As those who felt imposed upon began to outnumber the people who felt they benefited, the social balance gradually changed, until 1971, at which time the CMHC intervened, and then everything changed.

"There were people who wanted to keep the dealing community, but that dealing community had to fall within certain regulations, so security as a result had to undergo a transformation. It started out that security was installed to control the unregulated flow of bodies into the building. Then it was there to thump speed-freaks. Later on, security was there basically to warn the dealers that the police were coming. Still later it started to have some actual regulatory function on the dealers. So it became necessary that security become smarter and have a bit more style. Security would have to contribute in a positive way to Rochdale's image. In the fall of 1970 security went twenty-four hours for the first time, and it stayed that way for four years. That meant it was always going to be the first thing the public met (be it a hostile public or not). So it was necessary to have a better image and also to have a strong personality who had the right credentials in the private sector to say, 'Hey, look, business will continue, we all know that, but we're going to have to change the style and anyone who doesn't want to go along with that is OUT—NOW!' That person had to have the muscle to back it up, and that person was Billy Littler.

"When you have a frontier environment—say an Alaska or a Wild West—you have an initial group of people who come through and you have huge enterprise and great success. Then as society develops you have more and more call for regulation. That demand isn't imposed from above, but comes from within the community. The nature of the regulatory force must change. It must become more sophisticated to handle the maturing society.

"Most people think that Rochdale security was full of actual bikers. But there never was a time when bikers—actual club members—were hired onto security. There were people who were ex-bikers and motorcycle freaks but never colour-wearing members. There was that image though, especially during the "blackshirt" phase during the speed-freak evictions and in through early 1970. These people did look like outlaws though, but that was part of their strategy—look bad and avoid trouble.

"But for security to truly function it had to have the social consensus of the community behind it. I'll give you an example. One night I was at the security desk at about three in the morning, just hanging out. These three guys wandered in off the street. There was an immediate tension. There were only two of us on the desk at the time. I had a baseball bat in my lap. Now I'm not bad by any stretch of the imagination. Yet as the confrontation grew more tense the elevator door opened and out came three residents, then in through the front door walked a couple more. And soon the troublemakers were flying out the door. That's social consensus."

Looking at a typical six p.m. to midnight shift by someone named Bruce we get the distinct impression that Rochdale Security was not there for show. Bruce's log entry for June 28, 1970, reads:

8:00   Evicted man trying to buy speed in 7th floor lounge
9:30   Took library acid freak out to Andy Wernick
10:15 Locked 3 crashers out of 611. Put them in 2nd

floor lounge since they are leaving for Windsor
tomorrow.

11:00   Evicted Jerry the Drano dealer for tracks
11:30   Lock out 3 crashers from 1215 at rentals
        request.

Billy Littler's background qualified him for the demands of
Rochdale security. "I was a former army brat and I lived in West
Germany as a high-school kid. I played around in West Germany,
playing around on the black market, selling cigarettes and liquor.
This was the mid-1950s, the reconstruction era in West Germany.
Then still being an army brat and still being a bit of a jerk, I ran off
to southern Florida in 1960 to join up with the anti-Castro
Cubans, so I was playing around Central America, Nicaragua,
Honduras with a bunch of the CIA people for about two
years.

"I used to hang around the original Yorkville scene. In fact I
first met Lionel Douglas at Webster's Restaurant. I used to deal a
little. I was a bit of a Messiah type. I thought drugs would change
the world. I also used to do some security for the various coffee
houses in Yorkville. I got caught trafficking $25 of marijuana and
$40 of hash and was sentenced. I got convicted and I was sent to
jail for four years, for $65 of drugs. I sat in jail saying 'My God,
what have they done for $65. This is pretty goddamned amazing.' I
served five months in the Don Jail and I served fourteen months in
Guelph. A total of nineteen months. I made parole after that.

"My first contact with Rochdale, although I didn't officially
move in till much later, was in November of 1968. I knew many of
the people there, in fact a friend of mine was "head of security"—
that is, he walked around with a construction helmet on his head
with the word SECURITY printed on it and a baseball bat in his
hand. I can recall him telling me to move in. I said, 'No, no, it's full
of speed freaks and rip-off artists,' and he said to me, 'Yes, but
we'll get rid of them.' But I didn't officially move in till a year and a
half later, the fall of 1970. The first place I lived was on the twelfth
floor. I shared it with a young fellow, a law student—David Fade.
He's a lawyer now.

"I thought in terms of atmosphere The Rock was pretty damn
exciting. There were people that I could call my own sub-culture,
counter-culture or whatever. They were trying to fight a losing
battle but their morale was pretty good. It was my belief that we
were trying to make Rochdale work. We were trying to make the

mortgage payments, clean up the building, get the responsible hippies in."

Littler explains he was called in after the drug referendum. "A chap named Lionel Douglas, who was the best friend I ever had in my life, was a political leader (although he would always prefer to be Cardinal Richelieu than Louis XIII is the way he defined it to me on several occasions). He said 'We need you,' and I said, 'Lionel, this is nuts. You've got a bunch of crazies in there,' but he said, 'Billy, you come to work on security. They all aren't crazy.' And he rhymed off the names of some of the people involved— they were all involved in the executive or in the administration. He said, 'If you come to work in security we'll turn this bastard around and everyone will be amazed.'

"My role as I perceived it was to throw out the hard drug dealers and the ones who were crazy—those literally open-door marijuana dealers. Guys who just sat there in a room with triple beam scales inside and loud rock music blaring down the hallway, saying, 'Acid, grass, hash,' that sort of thing. This wasn't what we wanted. We didn't want a Beirut or a Marrakesh in Toronto."

Once he assumed the helm of security, Littler began evicting the elements of Rochdale society that were undesirable. He did have a little help—from his dogs.

"My dogs were necessary. My dogs weren't attack dogs. I was never accused or charged under the Vicious Dog Act. No one was ever bitten by one of my dogs. They were trained dogs, that is to say, if I got into a fight they would defend me. There may have been that kind of stuff in the press—'Vicious attack dogs in the lobby,' that sort of thing—but the press was really trying to project the neo-Nazi kind of image. But I wasn't and the facts prove that. My belief is that a dog prevents violence to the person who is handling it. I was quite willing and able to walk into a situation where I was outnumbered six to one and have my way.

"A lot of times I would walk into a room with my dog. I would already know something about the room. Usually the rent hadn't been paid in two to three months, and as far as I was concerned it was vacant. I'd walk in and say, 'Hello there I'm security here and this room is vacant, there's been no rent paid on it in quite some time, I'm afraid you're going to have to leave.' They'd say, 'Aw, c'mon man, don't do that shit,' and I'd say 'No, excuse me you don't understand.' Then I'd walk over to the window, pick up the triple beam scales or the radio or something and throw it out the window. The guy would say something like, 'What the fuck are you doing, you fascist pig,' and I'd say, 'I don't have time to pack you up and I've asked you to move and you're not moving,' and then I'd throw something else out the window. They'd continue to mutter or scream at me, but eventually they'd grab their stuff and move out. Then I'd change the lock on the door.

"If the guy still wanted to argue about it after I'd thrown them out, I'd give them a notice whereby they could appeal to Rochdale's Eviction Appeal Board. The individual could possibly be re-instated but, let's face it, most of these guys hadn't paid rent in months."

While Rochdale security was actively involved in the eviction process, its primary duty was to control the flow of traffic in and out of the building. The front lobby security desk was the critical choke-off point, and Rochdale security was established to screen those who entered the building. "You had maybe 3,000 people come in on a weekend from Friday night at six until Sunday at midnight," explains security-man T.J. "These were almost all people trying to score drugs. It could get pretty wild at times, but I felt like I was contributing to this place I believed in.

"I was living at Rochdale and partying too much to make it to my regular straight day-job, so one day my roommate saw they were advertising for a security person in the *Daily* and he said, 'Hey, why don't you go?' I had mixed feelings. I said, 'I'm not into that brutality thing and the dogs.' I had kind of a negative image of the job, but I did need a gig so one night I went down into the front lobby to watch them work and I found that the security people were nice people and weren't mad dogs or violent at all. They were more or less involved in a screening process.

"We'd ask questions of the kids coming in. If they wanted to see so and so we'd ask questions like, 'What's his dog's name?' 'How many kids does he have?' 'How tall is he?' to try and trap them. We knew most of the residents, we knew if they had pets or children. We got to the point where we were very good at picking out the liars.

"We had a twenty-four-hour eviction for known needle users. I did it once by myself. There was this young kid from Mississauga—he was sixteen. I sort of took him under my wing. His parents had thrown him out and he had nowhere to go. He just got 'lost' in Rochdale, so I was looking out for him. One night he ended up in this guy's apartment and this guy shot him up. The next day the kid comes up to me and says, 'Look, I know I've just done something bad, and it happened in so and so's apartment.' I went up and evicted him on the spot. There was a minor battle with the residents because he was living in a communal area and the residents didn't want him to go. They were saying, 'He's not the only one,' but I just said, 'Yeah, but he got caught!' "

Party was Rochdale's middle name. In its prime it was a rockin' eighteen-storey house party out of control and it was this atmosphere that Rochdale tried to maintain in the dark days of foreclosure. By and large Rochdale's parties were drug-oriented; they were legendary in the underground dope world. As a result, one resident, Walt Houston, 'tended to avoid parties,' because he had given up drugs shortly after moving into the building "since I no longer had a taste for them. The parties were pretty raucous, including one where the Rochdale brewers commune made 500 quarts of beer that were consumed at the party. There was another party where someone—I think it was someone called Frank Fury—had what he called a 'dream machine.' It was an electric hash pipe. The people inside sealed all the windows and doors and just kept on toking and toking and toking. It was definitely a pass-out party. It was weird to see a roomful of absolutely gone people with the black lights on."

Bob Nasmith recollects another memorable party "where we had a grass-cleaning party. That was when Mexican came in bricks and it was kind of solidified and bricked with Coca-Cola or some kind of syrup that was sticky to hold it together. It would come in red, green or yellow wrappers depending on the grade. So we'd get a group of five to ten people together in a room and break open a package and clean out the larger stems and that sort of thing. Well, one day we just cleaned for hours and we took all the stuff and threw it into garbage bags and took it to the back patio to the barbecue pit and we put together some sheets, kind of stitched them together roughly to make a tent, which we put over the barbecue pit. And we burned grass for hours and people would just walk through this tent and breathe and walk out. Hundreds and hundreds went through this tent all day long. Breathing in pounds and pounds of grass that was burning there. It was wonderful. It was a generous, loving, and fun happening. Like the building itself at its best."

Ian Anderson cherishes the memory of yet another party that went down in Rochdale's annals. "They took an old hair dryer and rigged up a gas mask to it. They cut out the air intake on it and filled it with a big screen—the thing could take two to three ounces of pot at a time and they'd get it going and the thing burned on its own. Anyone who was foolish enough to put the mask on was in big trouble. Once they put it on you everybody held it there. It was freaky. You'd see four or five pairs of hands holding onto the mask keeping it on, and the person wearing the mask would just get absolutely wasted."

"The lights in Rochdale glowed all night long," recalls Don Washburn. The seventh-floor mescaline party was one of my highlights; it was particularly memorable. It was wall-to-wall hippies. Everyone was sitting in the rooms and hallways—just this endless line of stoned freaks passing pipes. The whole of the seventh floor was involved. It went on for a couple days straight."

James Johnson, the bopper suburbanite to whom Rochdale was "like Disneyland," says he and his friends "would hit Rochdale Friday afternoon and we would work our way up through the building. No kidding! Friday you start off on the lower floors, get into some dope, meet people—we'd do that for days. It could take you three or four days to work your way up and then back down. It was like a psychedelic snakes and ladder game. There was always a party happening somewhere in that place. You'd lose track of time. Like when musicians are in a studio. Day becomes night and night becomes day. It was great. Just one great big long party." Every December the 4th from 1971 on, Rochdale threw itself an upscale bash that came complete with a formal invitation straight out of a Hollywood costume epic:

I N V I T A T I O N

You Are Requested To Appear At The

Fourth Annual
EMBASSY BALL
Of The
EMBASSY OF MORGRABIA-BOULOGNIA

To His Majesty's Government
KING JAMES I OF ROCHDALE

On The Occasion Of
MAERSPRACHE DAY, WEDNESDAY, DECEMBER 4, 1974

Reception Will Commence At The Hour Of
8:30 PM
On The Fifteenth Floor In The
GRAND BALLROOM

B.Y.O.B & D   Medals Will Be Worn

The ball's centrepiece was "Maersprache"—that is, long-winded speeches, something the suitably cranked Rochdalians had a definite flair for. The Embassy Ball continued right through till the very end of Rochdale, a happy reminder that, despite its downfall, The Rock could still party.

Not all the parties were raucous affairs with mammoth drug consumption. Rochdale's seventeenth-floor roof offered some Rochdalians an oasis in their own urban jungle. Walt Houston "ran a refreshment stand on the roof and served beer for people who lay sunning themselves. It was actually a very quiet, peaceful place for people to lie around in the sun and do nothing. There was almost no noise and very rarely any music. To a large extent, it was family groups soaking up the sun and having a few beers. It was very pleasant. We put in a little wading pool for the kids. And there were flower baskets and buckets growing around the walls of the thing with flowers. One gentleman had a little brazier thing in the corner and made bamboo flutes. Once in a while, we'd have a barbecue or a keg party on Friday—have a keg delivered.

"We had a lot of non-building people come up, too. A telephone man came there almost every day for lunch. Two posties were there pretty much every day to sit around and chat and have a couple of beers. A lot of strippers came up because there were no clothing restrictions and they could get a good tan. It was mostly nude up there."

For resident Horst, waking up on the roof was an experience. "Walt Houston had a booze-can. He was sort of the roving bootlegger. On a hot summer night in Toronto when it was sticky we'd sleep on the roof, eight to ten couples. We'd wake up, somewhat the worse for wear, at about nine, ten in the morning and there would be Walt in his usual regalia—he was heavy into nudism at the time—screaming, "Ice cold Heinekins at outrageous prices!" And by eleven, Walt would be lying on his hammock and he'd have a fridge out of which he dealt wine and beer."

You can get an idea of the size of The Rock's thirst by the fact that Walt Houston made a living collecting empties.

Alcohol was an important part of the Rochdale social scene. Residents brewed their own potent spirits. Mention Mother Fletcher's to a roomful of Rochdalians and they'll smile knowingly, recalling what one resident claims "is the strongest fuckin' drink known to man; this stuff was beyond belief." The Pipe brand promised and delivered on its promise to "get you roaring drunk." Booze entrepreneurs like Walt Houston made wine-runs to Montreal where the quality and price were better than in Ontario.

Booze-cans—illegal liquor operations that sold without a formal liquor license—were strewn all over the building. As soon as one closed, another would pop up in its place. Howard Brenner still chuckles about one incident in which "a couple of girls were really strapped for money. Their old men were busted and they were trying to raise some money. So this wild booze-can gets together to get the girls to put on a little show. Everyone is passing along money and one of the girls is stuffing it down the front of her outfit but she has nothing on underneath so it's falling to the ground and this guy is scooping it up and passing it back to the crowd. Everyone was obviously pretty loaded. So these two do themselves, the whole routine, and split. And you hear them walking down the hall arguing about where the money is."

Rochdale also continued to have what Tony Phred calls "an active sex life. There was lots of sex. The clinic, well, let's say it was constantly doling out penicillin."

Honey Novick's comments demonstrate the population's casual attitude to sex: "It was really free. If two people hit it off and you were in a room full of people, you just excused yourselves. Nobody thought about the consequences of sex—AIDS or getting pregnant. It would be just a question of who could get you off the most. It was like a big fuck—open and free. You'd met somebody and often not too many words were exchanged. You made eye contact and slipped out of the room and fucked your brains out. It was great. A freer more beautiful time."

The lip-smacking lechery of Horst is more than evident when he says, "It was very very nice. Every spring a new batch of nubiles appeared on the scene. All of a sudden there were fifty eligible young women just hangin' out. Very nice."

From the teenage perspective of Alex Martin, Rochdale was a sexual wonderland: "Rochdale had a great sexual climate. There was a free and open mind towards sex. I wasn't a virgin when I came in (I had lost my virginity a few weeks before I came to The Rock) but when I came to Rochdale it was—well, the sex was as free as I could imagine.

"The second weekend I was there, this nineteen-year-old girl and I were talking and we went back to her place. She was amazing. She said to me, 'You're a virgin aren't you?' I said, 'No, but just barely'. She said, 'Well, we'll fix that.' And we spent this incredible weekend together. I went back to see her a few days later and she was obviously high. She says to me, 'You don't love me do you?' and I said, 'Well, no,' and she said, 'That's the last time we'll be together.' "

Teen runaway Bobbie Malone, who was one of the "exploited," offers her point of view: "Sex in Rochdale? Yeah, there was a lot of that. And yeah some of the guys in there did have a trip going with a whole bunch of girls. Almost like a harem—the big dealers had the money and the security. So it was a matter of survival. We got passed around. The worst part was getting a dose, but the clinic handled that. I'll tell ya one thing though it wasn't like no Charlie Manson trip or anything like that. We got it on, but it wasn't sick. It was part of growing up. At least then the worst thing you could do is get a dose. Today—Christ, forget it. I keep to myself today."

On occasion a particularly lascivious event would transpire. Horst notes one such occasion: "There was a pussy-eating contest once; it was a real international scene. The prize was the title. We got a bunch of upper-ranked people together. Xaviera Hollander was doing her number in Toronto at the time. We got her and ten other very eligible young ladies—they were going to be the judges. The idea was to eat out as many chicks as you could, get each of them off and then move on to the next. Whoever did the most and did the best would win. Xaviera was competing. The whole thing took place with the judges, the competitors, the audience, all of us bare-assed naked.

"There was this one guy, a Frenchie named Gaeten, and he was doing this one woman, a very beautiful girl and she was getting off, her ass up in the air. This Gaeten is doing it and then he couldn't take it anymore so he comes up behind her and zonk! He tried to stick it in. The last we know of those two, she was chasing him all over The Rock bare-assed, trying to cut his pecker off. Apparently he had really fucked her up and she couldn't concentrate on what she was doing.

On another occasion, during one of Reg Hartt's screenings, where nudism was encouraged by the lure of free admission, the Happy Hooker herself—Xaviera Hollander—made another personal appearance. And as Alex MacDonald tells us she got into the spirit of things. "The Canadian premiere of *Deep Throat* was held by Reg Hartt on the second floor. The admission was $10 or Cum Naked. Xaviera Hollander gave Nasmith a blow job as part of the presentation."

Part and parcel of Rochdale's free spirit was its attitude to nudism. "Tolerated" would be an understatement for an educational institute that listed Sun Worship as a legitimate course. More than one outsider visiting Rochdale was stopped in his or her tracks by the sight of a naked Rochdalian walking around taking care of routine matters. "There were naked people around all the time," says James Johnson, "but it didn't seem out of place. Nobody really paid it any mind. On the roof there was nude sunbathing, and if we came over in the summer we would definitely check that out. In fact our friends wouldn't believe us when we took them—there were all these nude women around. They were more than a little envious. There was this one fat guy, with long hair and beard. He was naked all the time, he walked around serving beers. He had this little shrivelled-up dick. And my friends and I just couldn't hold in and we'd break out laughing."

Rochdale was populated with all sorts of infamous streakers and nudists. Perhaps the most famous of them all was Smitty. Horst gives the background on this unique woman. "Smitty was this beautiful girl on a really different reality plane. She was also put together nicely, all the parts were there. Every time Smitty had an argument or a fight with her old man she'd take off all her clothes and go out on Bloor Street to direct traffic. This usually happened late at night, usually when there was a full moon. The secret was how she got out there. There'd be tire squealing and pandemonium out on Bloor Street at four in the morning."

For all the rhetoric and noise about "free sex," Rochdale, underneath its free-love surface, was actually a building that had its share of traditional relationships and attitudes. "By and large sex was a private matter," admits Howard Brenner. "There was a diversity, different attitudes, but you didn't have public sex, you weren't tripping over bodies in the hallways. There may have been some harbouring dreams of a giant building orgy, but, nah." Horst also admits that "at the porn movie screenings you wouldn't have widespread public balling. If a couple wanted to go at it they would just pull the blanket up over themselves. I don't think the building ever got together to fuck. There were a few quiet orgies here and there but it didn't happen in public areas."

Walt Houston noticed a definite relationship between one's attitude to sex and nudity and how high one lived in the building. "What I found interesting was that the heavy drug people from the lower floors almost never came up on the roof, and if they did, they wore bathing suits. The people who were involved in the building's government and the crafts tended to be far more relaxed than the people who were into dealing drugs. Sexual attitudes were fairly repressed on the lower floors—stereotyped one-man one-woman situations, with both individuals trying to sneak out and commit the equivalent of adultery. The upper floors were a lot more liberal but still not wide open."

One incident, the "What Do You Care Who Your Friends Fuck" controversy, showed Rochdale's conservative side. Lorraine Darling tells the story of a woman named Mary who cut quite the swath through Rochdale's manhood in three short months. "A bunch of women in the building got together to do something about this Mary character," says Darling. "She was running around ballin' every available and unavailable man in The Rock. A real nympho, or at least she certainly liked to ball. Anyway, the offended women got together to give her the word that she had twenty-four hours to get out of the building. There was this big meeting and debate with everyone carrying on. But you've got to give the woman credit; she faced her accusers and didn't back down. But it kind of showed you Rochdale wasn't as free-love, hippy-dippy as everyone outside thought it was. It wasn't ball your brains out with whoever you want!"

The "What do you care" debate was a rare show of solidarity and strength on the part of Rochdale womanhood. Rochdale was almost completely a male-dominated society. The male influence extended beyond the sheer weight of numbers (the population averaged around 70 per cent male). In creating his model of the "Cool Cat," the ideal that Rochdalians aspired to, anthropologist Kent Gooderham writes: "He is male. Rochdale is a man's world and many women play a role accurately described by the term "chick." On the other hand, a female can, if she wants, exercise her potential as well as any man without feeling the type of self-consciousness which would be present elsewhere."

Despite its progressive attitudes in many areas, Rochdale was often just as sexist as outside society, recalls Valerie Frith. "I always felt there was a big difference between the women themselves who lived in Rochdale and the notion of women that actually operated in Rochdale. And you can see this, as I did recently, by looking at a lot of old *Daily*s where pictures of female parts were used as filler. What you have is an enormous number of breasts and knees and things like this—an incredible number of images of women's bodies that are not complete. To see it now is quite dismaying, because it makes you think how unenlightened the community was, and there are hundreds of these images over the first few years of Rochdale's existence in all of its publications."

Despite its inbred, traditional attitude to a woman's role in society, Rochdale was not immune to the swirling currents of the time. Women everywhere were rising up and drawing attention to their dissatisfaction with their second-class citizenship. In fact, some women were instrumental to running Rochdale, but as Valerie Frith informs us, "There were years when there were just men on the council. I got elected to the council once, so eventually there were women on it. But certainly, in those first years there weren't. I always perceived it being run in my time by Lionel Douglas, Jay Boldizsar, Bobby Nasmith and Ian Argue. I worked with Karen [in Admissions], too, and she was very influential and important. But she wasn't there at night when the boys were meeting in their little smoky circles or when they were running down to the basement to find out what was going on down there and generally carrying on. They were the ones who had, or were thought to have had, absolute knowledge of what was going on in the building. And they let the knowledge out at their own whim. Karen would certainly have to be informed about certain things, but there were things she might never hear about. It was very much a man's culture."

For all the traditional role-playing there was an undeniable freedom for those Rochdalian women who chose to avail themselves of it. Judy Keeler elaborates: "I always felt there was a lot of room for any kind of behaviour. Anything was allowed. Everybody was into freedom. There were many variations. One particular lady, who's a good friend of mine, was one of the people instrumental in the daycare centre. She lived in a commune and had one child of her own at that point. She went to one of the Rochdale parties and painted her body in yin and yang—white and black—with a cape and nothing on underneath. She came in with this great big Renaissance hat and a feather, and then danced. So things like this were going on. You could be a mother and a whore all in one day—and a leader, too."

There was a nascent feminism in Rochdale. For example, the Women's Involvement Program created and produced a series of videos on women's issues. There were also attempts at formal consciousness-raising meetings.

Perhaps as an extension of their earth mother roles, women were also a creative force behind the Rochdale farm. As far back as 1969 a portion of the Rochdale population felt the need for a rural "retreat," a rural campus that Rochdalians could use to escape the pressures of urban existence and explore the benefits of the natural, rural lifestyle that was receiving so much lip service in hippie philosophy. Resident Bruce Maxwell began writing township clerks throughout Ontario, searching for cheap land where "Rochdale North" could be established, complete with domes and gardens. In early 1972, a general meeting of the building passed the resolution to buy a 350-acre farm near Killaloe, Ontario.

Jerry Neilsen gives an overview: "It was probably the worst piece of property that could have been found in the region. I was living in Killaloe when the crew from Rochdale came up to pick out a site for a farm. It was a party more than anything else, and people thought they were being scientific. But Lionel Douglas and Ian Argue came up there in winter with a GTL and no snow tires, and they ran off the road just down from my house. I got a friend with a tractor to help pull them out.

"There were communal meals in one large, fairly well-run kitchen. There were several bedrooms, a living room area, an outdoor two-hole crapper, a well and a big garden. There were other structures such as a dome, tents, a renovated barn and the Zome dome. People were busy with wood cutting, construction, gardening and cooking, depending on how many people were coming up for the weekend. It was a poor working farm."

Tony O'Donohue was irate. He told the *Star* that the $12,000 purchase of the farm while the college still owed $760,000 to the federal government was a "disgrace. Whatever money they collected," he fumed, "should have gone toward paying what they owe in mortgages and back taxes."

A perfect example of just how unprepared the Rochdalians were for the reality of farm life is illustrated by the way they handled the beaver problem. "Nobody wanted to hurt the beavers," laughs Howard Brenner, "so they wouldn't allow trapping. So the beaver pond grew and grew. They were still into the Greenpeace-hippie-brown-rice mentality and the beaver was, after all, Canada's national symbol. I guess they forget you've got to control the beavers or they'll flood you out. But the motivation for getting the farm was that a lot of people saw the writing on the wall. This was a chance to set up and carry on with a version of Rochdale North."

With a northern campus in place, and for that matter, with a generally active social life, Rochdale decided it needed a community vehicle. The choice—a 1951 Studebaker bus that went by the name of Wayne.

"Wayne had certain features most other buses don't have,"

offers Horst. "It had no floor, lots of boards, and one long board that went from the engine to the back that held a lot of plywood from falling out. You walked along that. You breathed a lot of exhaust, and the gas gauge never worked so we ran out of gas from time to time. There was no reverse. It worked only in second and third gear. You didn't want to get stuck anywhere because you couldn't back out. So we never got stuck. Or at least we were okay if we had enough people to push it.

"The bus never rolled out without an overload of drugs and alcohol. It was de rigeur—it was party time. The cops always had us under observation but they never really bothered us. When we were driving up to the farm they would hand us up the road, as it were. They tried busting us a few times but it didn't make any sense. What are a couple of country cops going to do after they've stopped this wild, very colourful blasted vehicle and this herd of people come stumbling out, their eyes sticking a mile out of their heads?

"There's this cop trying to write a ticket and someone is playing with the gun in his holster and a chick has got him by the balls, rubbing them. It's hard to write a ticket with ten people around you saying, 'Peace man, peace brother.' Cops would lose their composure and split. For one thing they never knew who was driving. We were always switching around. Someone would get paranoid while they were tripping and say, 'Hey, you can't drive, let me drive.' It was like a slapstick comedy. No wonder Wayne burned more oil than gas."

There was also a practical side to the purchase of the farm. "The farm was bought before foreclosure," says Alex MacDonald. "That was the time that sort of dispersing of assets was acceptable. In fact selling the farm to the people that lived there [Matrix] provided the income for the last round of legal challenges."

Whether it was psychedelic bus murals or freaky clothing or statement-making statues in front of The Rock, Rochdale had its own unique sense of style. That's style as opposed to fashion—Rochdale, like the hippie counter-culture in general, disdained the notion of fashion. With its belief in the virtues of the inner self over surface superficialities the movement was in a sense anti-fashion. However, "Rochdale was conscious of its own particular style," offers Karen Johnson. "You were in style, for example, if you wore jeans. You were out of style if you wore polyester pants or a suit. Denim was the preferred look, but even within that one type you had a sense of style—it could be your belt (they had some amazing ones that were actually functioning pipes) or the embroidered fringe on your jeans. It wasn't flashy but there was a sense of style at Rochdale."

Honey Novick suggests that "people were into looking good then. Men with their long hair, women too. It was a very sensual era. People took pride in the way they looked. It was a colourful, soft, swirling, sensual time." Hippies in general embraced an unaffected, natural kind of hedonism. Clothing, such as East Indian cottons or buckskins, was loose and unrestrictive. Furniture like beanbags or waterbeds (invented by a California university student in 1967) valued comfort over practicality. Food was light, digestible and natural.

Rochdale's masses were part of the growing "denim army," who wore denim almost to the exclusion of anything else. But there were some colourful characters around to add a splash of excitement against the sea of denim: "Popper" from California who wore a codpiece and a jerkin or Kim the Vancouver town fool who cavorted about with a flute. Even the heavy-duty Rochdale security boys with their black shirts had their own sense of style. In the process, security's wild-west desperado look, complete with gunbelts, gave more than one visitor to The Rock second thoughts about going in. Young women in Rochdale had the same mini-midi-maxi dilemma as young women everywhere.

Alex MacDonald remembers a Rochdale fashion trend that made a statement: "People running around in torn jeans and T-shirts, they hadn't bathed in three days. But they'd have these cases of money, full with $400,000 in crumpled twenties and they'd walk into the bank.

"One of the status symbols around Rochdale, for a while at least, was you'd see people with the standard Levi's cowboy jean shirt with the button-down front pockets (security wore black ones) and they'd have these huge bulges—these 'tits.' They would reach into their pockets and pull out a wad of thousand-dollar bills. People were into collecting: 'How many thousand do you have?' It wasn't just the money; I know people really liked the feel of the thousands."

As a self-contained community Rochdalians had access to a number of services and stores: a bookroom, a record store, a travel agency, restaurants, a grocery store and a bank. Though not specifically associated with Rochdale, the Canadian Imperial Bank of Commerce branch at 337 Bloor Street West was often referred to as "the Rochdale branch." Manager Tom Osborne claims that "there wasn't another like it in all of Toronto. Jay was our main contact. If we had problems, we were still a tenant of the building, of course, so they looked after us.

"There was an incident one winter involving the heater between the two sets of front doors. Both of them were closed, and they faced north but weren't insulated. So the heater froze and when the pipes burst, they let the hot water from all eighteen floors in the building flow into the branch.

"A mop-up crew came down from Rochdale—about twenty kids—and I just opened the branch totally to them. I phoned the alarm company and told them we were opening the vault doors, and these kids went in there and mopped it up. They cleaned things up, and they even tore the soggy carpet out of my office and dragged it outside. Of course, I kept an eye on what was going out the front door, but there wasn't any problem at all. They were just there to clean up the branch.

"The security people walked around with Dobermans in those days, and there were several instances of dog fights in the branch. It was very scary if you've never heard a couple of Dobermans go at each other.

"I seem to recall we once had a motorcycle race in the branch. I had very young staff. My wife and I went to the Canadian National Exhibition one year, and this chap came up to me in hippie-style dress and his hair down to the middle of his back—typical of the era. He said, "Hi, Tom!" and I wondered, "What customer would call me Tom?" It turned out he was my accountant, and all the time he worked at that branch he wore a wig over his long hair. I never knew it—and I didn't recognize this guy until I took a second look at him. My accountant was a day-time banker and a night-time hippie.

"I would be an absolute fool if I tried to say that we weren't aware of the drug trade in the area. We had a very high volume in U.S. dollar traveller's cheques and a very high volume in U.S. dollar cash—very high for a branch of our size—almost to the point where I was a foreign exchange clerk. So you'd be a fool to say that money from drug deals was not going through the branch. But how much responsibility is on a bank or on a branch or on a teller to say, 'That money looks dirty—I'm not going to take it?' Cash is cash."

Even though the bank was physically separated from Rochdale, some of the residence's tiniest inhabitants still managed to make their way into the vault. "The bank stores paper—tons and tons of paper," says Osborne, "and in order to store it, we have a central depot [for all branches at another location]. But the depot wouldn't accept shipments from Rochdale because of the bugs.

"So we had to make a deal with our central depository. A pest-control company would fumigate our paper for twenty-four hours with calcium cyanide before the depository would accept it. And I literally had to go down to the pest-control company and lock our vouchers in the company's vault while it was gassed. Twenty-four hours later, after all the gas had cleared, I had to go back and wait while they opened the doors so I could take our vouchers in a freshly cleaned truck to our central depository."

In this description of life at Rochdale it would be easy to create an unbalanced portrait of Rochdale as a fullblown mad house where nothing normal ever happened. That of course isn't the case. People did live normal, well almost normal, lives at 341 Bloor Street. Some even had straight jobs and faithfully worked from nine to five.

A shining example of Rochdale's "normalcy" was its hockey team—The Rochdale Roaches. Team member and frequent visitor to Rochdale Ian Anderson gives the details on the Roaches: "Most of the hockey team were big dealers. That's why they were playing hockey. It was hard to keep track of eighteen to twenty guys all getting into different vehicles and all carrying hockey equipment and meeting another group from a different part of the city—doing the same thing. A lot of hockey bags were exchanged. We played all over the city. Some weeks we played five or six times in different arenas. We had a regular Saturday night game at midnight at Varsity Arena. We tried playing the Metro police—they used to play at the arena Saturday night at ten but they declined our offer. We actually had a very good hockey team, we didn't lose often. One time we lost was to Satan's Choice. Once the fighting and stick smashing started we just skated off the ice. We weren't into that.

"The team played for about three years then a few guys got busted and eventually, as they were trying to get everybody out of Rochdale, the team fell apart."

Even at the bleakest of times when the College was enmeshed in financial and social chaos and plunging downward, there was always an element of the population that pushed for the active support of the education component. This segment of the population, as Alex MacDonald points out, grew throughout the years. "You see there was a high turnover of people who lived at Rochdale—up to 90 percent—but 10 per cent stayed and grew, and that figure continued to grow through the years. It means that over a period of time you build up a solid stable core of people with roots and commitment to the building and community."

The official organization entrusted to oversee education was Ed Con. Formed in January of 1971, Ed Con consisted of twelve members whose job it was to sort through the proposals for educational projects and to determine which ones were worthy of Rochdale's space and financial support. The board was elected by the Rochdale residents and, according to the Fall Catalogue for 1972, was "generally made up of people who expressed interest by attending meetings religiously." Anyone was free to submit applications, although only residents of the building could vote on the proposals.

Ed Con managed to persevere even while Rochdale was collapsing; it was still going strong as late as 1974. It had approximately fifty projects and well-attended open houses.

Ed Con, like its political counterpart, Gov Con, was a typical Rochdale body—chaotic, maddening, and unstructured. But, somehow, despite all of its flaws, it managed to fulfill its self-described mandate of "Encouraging Individual Initiative."

A practical and successful example of this philosophy was Rochdale's fourth-floor video studio, an innovative project run by Kevin O'Leary. "I was working in community-based TV—things like cable programming—when someone at Rochdale approached me and some friends about forming a studio at the college. They kicked in $9,000—a princely sum in those days—and we set up a small video-recording facility where we did a series of community programs.

"It was a fairly modest set-up, although we did smash down a wall in an adjacent bedroom to put in a window and use the bedroom as a control room. We had a two-camera set-up—porta-packs with half-inch tape and corresponding equipment, which was fairly primitive technology.

"But we kept busy. We made a number of contributions to a local Cabbagetown outfit that broadcast on Rogers Cable. I also did a tape on Gothic Avenue, a very nice west-end street that was under the developer's gun. We even showed that one at City Hall during the final debate on the issue. And there were a couple of pieces about Toronto Island during that community's struggle to keep its island homes.

"On the whole, my interests were more documentary than artistic. That's why we lent our equipment to a women's group to produce shows of interest to feminists. And there was a series of instructional films based on the work of the craftspeople in Rochdale. Even a couple of the daycare centres associated with Rochdale used the facilities to make public relations–type videos to help with their fundraising."

As one might suspect, Rochdale had a habit of supporting concepts and ideas from the less realistic portion of its population. Oddball schemes litter the history of the college's life including a grandiose plan to corner the maple syrup business in southern Ontario or the People's Institute of Aviation's plans to create ultra-lightweight craft like the single-seat Phantom Mosquito Helicopter for the Third World.

But underneath all the lunacy there was a genuine quest for knowledge, especially functional knowledge. Education at Rochdale may have been disorganized and frustrating, its courses may have suffered a high fatality rate, but it did deliver, at its best, what the Catalogue of '72 promised: "an intimate personal educational experience."

C H A P T E R 12

Riders
on
the Storm

Even after the Sixties had faded out of existence, echoes and aftershocks continued to reverberate through every corner of society. According to the idealists, the vitality and explosive energy were simply too powerful and abundant to die away, just because of an arbitrary change in the calendar. Indeed, dreamers argued that, to be concluded satisfactorily, the Sixties required nothing less than a twelve- or thirteen-year decade—a notion as delightfully outlandish as any of the cheerfully self-contradictory concepts spawned during that period. Cynics, on the other hand, claimed that the calendar really did bring the spirit of the Sixties to a close. And if any stragglers or remnants survived into the seventies, they were mere zombies—the walking dead, seemingly unaware that their time was already long gone.

By gradual degrees, changes were taking place that heralded the dawn of an unsettling interval of transition. Pierre Trudeau, who had personified the unassailable political vigour of the Sixties, returned to office as prime minister of Canada, but in a weakened, humbled position as leader of a minority government. By contrast, Richard Nixon regained the U.S. presidency in a landslide vote, but not before disturbing questions began to surface about a sinister break-in at the Democratic Party's national headquarters in the Watergate building. In Munich, the romantic aura of the Olympics was shattered forever when Arab terrorists killed eleven Israeli athletes and took nine others hostage. Even in the realm of culture, rock music meandered listlessly in search of the next trend, only to be transmuted by the Moog synthesizer or crudely yanked back to the fifties by the Broadway musical *Grease*.

So it was with Rochdale. By mid-1972, as foreclosure settled in with its inevitable grimness, a turning point had arrived. Tenants and officials of the beleaguered building clung bravely to the hopes and dreams that had seen them through the early years of audacious experimentation. But, in so doing, they failed to realize that the seventies had not only come knocking, but barged right in and taken up residence—much like that perennial nuisance, the crasher. Rochdale, formerly a harbinger of change, had ceded its vanguard position. Shock and outrage, emotions that Rochdale had once inspired in others, were now being generated by a less patient society and redirected back toward those within the eighteen-story cell. The war of attrition, which had been conducted in a haphazard manner by political and law-enforcement authorities, was now about to begin in earnest.

Leading the invading forces was John Biddell, the stern but soft-spoken president of the Clarkson Company, the receivership practice of the giant Clarkson Gordon accountancy firm. In previous years, Biddell had successfully handled a number of difficult cases. So it was hardly surprising that he was asked to consider involving himself in the particularly troublesome matter of a certain defaulted mortgage held by CMHC.

"I talked to some of my partners and decided that we would take it on," Biddell recalls. "But before accepting, I set two conditions. One was that I wanted to talk to the chief of police of Metropolitan Toronto. And the second was that I wanted to talk to the director of Legal Aid for the province of Ontario.

"I went along to see Chief Harold Adamson and told him what I'd been asked to do. I was ushered into the conference room at police headquarters and he had fifteen people there who were all senior police officers in the city. He asked, 'What can we do to help?' So I said, 'I know that attempting to gain possession of that building and trying to take responsibility for how it's run are going to involve a tremendous amount of controversy. What I'll need from the police department is, at a minimum, to have off-duty police assist me when required.' The chief of police answered, 'Well, we couldn't do that, but we do want to help you. Why don't you go and see Joe Thurston? He was deputy chief of police until he retired a few months ago to set up a private security firm. Go and talk to him, but be assured that we'll do everything we can to help.'

"Then he told me about some of the things that were going on there and some of the problems the police were having whenever they were called to the building. So I listened to those stories, but they didn't surprise me too much, because they confirmed my beliefs that we were in for a rough time when we took on that job."

For his part, Adamson was delighted to hear that an administrator with Biddell's expertise was seriously thinking about assuming part of the burden for Rochdale. "I thought that was fantastic and I certainly encouraged him, because he didn't seem very enthused about it. Obviously, he had some reluctance, because the place was an armed camp. Deputy Chief Ackroyd came to the meeting, too, and we encouraged him jointly to take it over."

Next, Biddell approached the director of Legal Aid with a request. "I said, 'I'd like an understanding with you. There are people whom I may decide I have to evict in order to operate Rochdale properly. When you're approached by them, before you automatically give them a Legal Aid lawyer, I want you to allow me to tell you whether they've got a lease and whether or not the rent is paid and what reasons I have for wanting to get them out of there. Because of the way landlord-and-tenant law is administered, if you're going to give a free lawyer to anyone who asks, I'm going to be fighting every one of those people and I'll have an impossible task.'

"And the director said, 'If somebody comes along and asks for legal assistance and they can't afford it, they're going to get it.' So I said, 'Well, won't you at least inquire as to whether or not they have any vestige of rights of tenancy in the building at all?' And he said, 'No, we won't inquire.'

"I walked out of there and was I fuming! Nevertheless, I decided to accept the job that day in September, 1972, because I realized that the problem, from a community standpoint, was even more serious than the newspapers had made out. Rochdale was, by then, the drug-dealing headquarters for Canada, and the police had made several attempts to go in and apprehend people, but the place was just short of having a shooting war. It was becoming impractical from the standpoint of preserving law and order in the city. So, around our firm, we felt an obligation to the community, and we thought we should do what we could."

Biddell also took Adamson's advice and hired the Community Guardian security company, founded by Joseph Thurston. "Joe was just a super fella," says Biddell. "He told me that he had not been long retired from the force and most of his people were ex-members of the Metro Toronto police force who had decided to retire or resign and come to work with him. And he said, 'Look, there's no way you can go into that place unprepared. You just don't realize what you'd be facing until I can train a staff.'

"I met some of the senior staff people, including the senior psychologist. And he explained to me that we would need, as our security force, a staff with very special training to put up with the circumstances that they were going to face. So I agreed and he set up a training program for the people we wanted to have on staff around the clock. They all had had police training, but they had to realize what they were going to face and be emotionally prepared to live with it. He was concerned about using people who could go in there and withstand terrible treatment from that horde of young people. And when we finally went in, all his predictions came true in spades."

On September 13, 1972, the Supreme Court of Ontario granted the Clarkson Company permission to take possession of Rochdale, operate it, pay its bills, collect its rents and profit financially from the deal within certain limitations. This order was to remain in effect until Rochdale's entanglements were resolved by the courts.

Later that day, in a gesture of diplomacy and appeasement, Biddell announced at a press conference that he would operate no differently from any building manager and that he had "no intention of interfering in the private lives of the tenants. But if they interfere with the lives of other tenants, then we'll have to take some action, just as we would in any other building. I'm not going in there with any preconceived notions. I've got no mandate to clean the building out. I do have a mandate to clean the building up."

Understandably, this did little to comfort Rochdale's nervous populace. In a hastily prepared one-page newsletter, Council President James Newell admitted that the court's decision "was not unexpected," but that didn't mean the fight was over. He urged the community to demand a voice in the management of the building and to insist that space for the educational program, the offices and the workshops be maintained. An accompanying message by Bob Nasmith concluded, "We may have been fucked, but we will not be buggered."

Biddell also arranged a meeting with Rochdale's governing council and got what he recalls as "a pretty frosty reception." But Jay Boldizsar, who accompanied Biddell on that first visit, remembers the encounter in somewhat more frightening detail.

"We went up to the fifteenth-floor commune and the meeting started out congenially, but got increasingly heated. It was 'What about this?' and 'What about that?' Biddell became more and more upset, until he determined that it was time to leave.

"As he was going into the elevator, 'Commie' Charlie Taylor slipped in with him. Now, Charlie was an intelligent man, but he was one of the militants who had taken too much LSD over the years and he had some strange ideas. Of course, Biddell was visibly nervous because this was not in his management handbook. And as the elevator was going down, Charlie whispered in his most menacing voice, 'Biddell, I could slip a knife between your ribs right now.' Whoosh! Biddell was out of there so fast you could see him bolt across the Medical Arts parking lot and burn rubber through the intersection. It certainly confirmed any suspicions he had about Rochdale."

Not surprisingly, when the Community Guardians set up shop in Rochdale on September 14, it was Thurston, and not Biddell, who supervised the operation. The seventeen Greenies—nicknamed for the colour of their crisp, long-sleeve shirts, ties and trousers—established a sort of headquarters in the reception area. But no amount of training could have prepared them for the punishing harassment they would face in the coming days.

"We were going through psychological warfare with the Community Guardians," recalls Tony Phred. "When they got to Rochdale, it wasn't at all what they were expecting, because the information that the people on the outside had about Rochdale had nothing to do with reality. They were geared up for a building full of armed drug dealers. And on the first day, what they ended up with was women and young girls coming up to them and playing with their balls and such. They couldn't handle it and left after about three hours.

"Then we got an ultimatum: 'Either you let these people stay or we bring in the police in large numbers and on a full-time basis.' Naturally, we opted for the Community Guardians. But we still ended up with police officers part-time and in uniform at the front desk. It was that kind of game."

The pressure also continued to intensify, as relations between Greenies and Rochdalians deteriorated. "It very quickly turned into pretty much of a nightmare," sighs Biddell. "The security people spent all their time surrounded by waves of these inmates, both male and female, who were attempting to get them to leave. The attempts involved everything from standing there and screaming at them at close quarters to bringing down chamber pots of urine and throwing it over them. Nobody actually attempted to beat them up, but I guess they probably would have liked to. It was just psychological harassment of the worst order."

"We were never really bad with them," says resident Sandra Littler, "although we did drop eggs out the window on their heads and other juvenile things. It was fun and they played the game. Mind you, since they had to keep coming back to work, they had no choice but to play. It was pretty bad because there were some pretty bizarre Community Guardians. Some of them used to be cops and couldn't keep from being cops. Others were old, retired guys who really didn't care what was going on.

"It was no party for them. They had orders not to interfere or cause any trouble, so we went down and caused them all kinds of problems. People were constantly doing things to them. I was never into the vicious stuff—y'know, the ones who were in there stealing files. That was not my scene—just the taunting and teasing and just generally making life miserable for them."

Biddell himself never suffered harrassment at Rochdale since he was not present on a regular basis. "But there was a significant number of threats. In the early stages, I got a lot of phone calls anonymously waking me up at three in the morning. They'd swear and curse and call me whatever. So I arranged for twenty-four-hour surveillance of my house and my young children, but there was never any incident or damage. There were just the phone calls for about three months, and they eventually stopped."

Not all residents approved of such a strategy. In a newsletter dated September 15, Jay Boldizsar may have spoken for the majority when he advised his friends that "the amount of guerilla tactics available to us is limited only by our collective imagination." But in the same circular, James Newell announced he was resigning his presidency of the council for various reasons, including personal opposition to violence. "I learned that lesson in the summer of 1970 when I saw hundreds of police and Rochdale residents confronting each other on the front plaza of what I still consider to be my home. I think that the only outcome of last night's talk of 'throwing the interim receiver out' or of 'staging a rent strike' will be violence. If you cannot learn to live with another human being, then you are acting as less than a human being yourself."

Reg Hartt, Rochdale's long-time movie exhibitor, today says he agreed with Newell's stance. "When Clarkson Gordon took over the building, I told the others, 'If the government had wanted to wipe you out, then they would have sent in the army. It would be that simple. They wouldn't play games. What they're doing right now is trying to give you a second chance.'

"Clarkson Gordon never said, 'We have our security, but you can't have your security.' The two security systems functioned together. They did not do things like trying to intrude on the dealing community. But the dealing community started to do things like dropping acid into the Greenies' pop, and stuff like that. And they began to threaten the Clarkson group, so defensive measures had to be taken.

"There was simply no understanding that Clarkson Gordon could be sincere. One time, I left a tape recorder overnight in the security office that was run by Rochdale. When I came back the next day, the tape recorder had vanished. So I asked, 'What happened to my tape recorder?' And someone in security said, 'Aw, well, we don't know, man.' So I ran my silent films without music for six months until I had the money to get a new machine. And when I had to leave the new one overnight, I went to the Greenies and said, 'Do you people mind if I leave this thing here tonight?' And they said 'No. That's fine. We'll take care of it for you.' And they did. So I'd leave film and projectors and other equipment overnight in the Clarkson Gordon security office because I knew that it was secure there, and the next day I would find my stuff there.

"In fact, when I ran the Wet Dreams Film Festival, it was the Greenies who told me, 'The police have called up to find out what's going on. And we've explained to them that you're not charging admission. So the police said, 'Fine. That's okay.' As long as you weren't trying to profit by it and as long as the program was sincere, the police weren't going to move in and bust you. And the Greenies made that clear to the cops.

"So I knew from my own experience that they were trying to help. But try to explain that to the rest of the Rochdale people. They'd just say, 'What are you? Some kind of turncoat? Some kind of spy for them?' So I'd say, 'No, I'm just trying to survive in here and instead of looking at them as a threat, maybe you could look at them as an aid to what you're doing.' "

Not only was Hartt's approach not adopted, but the intensity of the harassment increased. And only a week after the Clarkson forces had moved into Rochdale, Biddell reluctantly concluded it was time to declare war and launch an all-out assault on the Bloor Street fortress.

"After a lot of discussion with Joe Thurston and my associates,

I came to the conclusion there was no way we were going to be able to handle this thing by ourselves. So I went back to see Jack Ackroyd and told him that there appeared to be little likelihood of let-up of the sort of thing we were faced with. So we set up an operation to actually clear the building. It was discussed in great detail with the police department, because only they could do it. They planned to use twenty busloads of police officers and they were going to go in there and take everybody out early one Sunday morning, late in September of '72."

Ackroyd says he and Adamson were under the impression that this proposal was illegal. But officials of the provincial government assured them that as long as a court order for police assistance was requested by and issued to the receiver, the assault could go ahead as planned. "So we did an extensive amount of planning. We were going to go in around four-thirty or five in the morning, occupy the lobby with our SWAT teams and our emergency task force, and we were literally going to put X-number of police officers on every floor and take control of the building. We've never talked about that publicly. In fact, this is the first time we've talked to anybody—the news media or a reporter or a book writer—about this.

"On the weekend of the operation, Harold and I cancelled all the days-off. And, God bless him, [*Toronto Star* crime reporter] Jocko Thomas just about went crazy because he couldn't find out why all the leaves were cancelled. Nobody twigged to the fact that what was really going to happen was we were going to go into Rochdale that weekend." In fact, an article in the *Star* said that an 800-man emergency assault team had been assembled because of rumours that "police expected trouble from Black Power groups or a clash over the visit of a foreign dignitary, perhaps from Israel."

But, says Rochdale lawyer Joe Sheard, plans for the invasion were not kept entirely secret. Ackroyd began to experience grave misgivings about the distinct possibility of serious injury or even death in the ensuing riot. During an informal conversation with Sheard, he suggested there might even be a way of avoiding the bloody showdown. What the police wanted, said Ackroyd, was information that would enable them to carry out a series of arrests of specific individuals within Rochdale. "In that way," recalls Sheard, "the purpose of the assault would have been achieved, but in a much more civilized manner. The upshot of that conversation was that I agreed to talk to the Rochdale people and set up a meeting. But I stipulated that Ackroyd come alone in an unmarked car and that the meeting be non-antagonistic.

"So we all met in the living room of my nice, old home in aristocratic Rosedale. Jay Boldizsar was there, and so were Alex MacDonald and Mike Randall and this one fellow who was dressed in an unusual outfit—a Canadian Indian outfit complete with a ceremonial feather. He sat cross-legged in front of our fireplace. In contrast to this group was my daughter Sarah who was attending Branksome Hall (a private girls' school) at the time. She came in to serve us coffee, complete with the Branksome skirt.

"It was a rather awkward and long meeting. The purpose was to forestall this dreadful concept of the assault by giving the police the specific names and apartment numbers of certain people in Rochdale. I understood that the names belonged to individuals who weren't really a part of the Rochdale community, but were opportunists who just used the building. They were really foreigners to the Rochdale concept and they were in the business of dealing narcotics. The main problem, though, was that turning them over to the police was contrary to the Rochdale philosophy.

"It finally ended up with several people going into the dining room and quietly writing down some names and handing over the list to Ackroyd. But it was extremely awkward because it was so contrary to the fundamental philosophical tenets of Rochdale."

Ackroyd was not the only one with serious doubts about the scheme. John Biddell had been mulling over the plan, "and as the invasion day got closer, I became more worried, because the police had told me they believed there were guns in there and they believed there would be shooting and people would get hurt. Finally, on the Saturday, twenty-four hours before this raid was supposed to happen, I phoned Jack to call it off. I said we'd never had a riot in the city of Toronto or even in Canada—at least not in my lifetime—and I wasn't going to be the one responsible for having it here. We were better off just seeing if we could live through it somehow."

Ackroyd agreed whole-heartedly and, at a last-minute meeting with Adamson and Biddell, the operation was finally cancelled. It was only then that the press caught wind of the aborted raid—a scheme that the *Star* said had been scrapped because the crucial element of surprise had somehow been lost. Another popular

rumour, says Jocko Thomas, was that "Ackroyd was afraid of
Pierre Berton whose daughter was a resident of Rochdale. There
were sons and daughters of other prominent families living there,
too. And the theory was that the police were afraid of the
derogatory opinion of what might happen if they went ahead with
the raid."

Today there is near-unanimous agreement that the decision to
scrap the invasion was a wise one. "If we had gone in there just
to kick some ass," says Adamson, "we would certainly have
accomplished that mission, because we were in a position to do
those things. But we would only have escalated something that
was already volatile, when the name of the game was to close
Rochdale and let tranquility return to the community. Naturally,
there were some police officers who were unhappy about our
position and some of them even told me so. But in the final
analysis, you've got to take a mature, effective stance to correct
these types of situations. And that's what Jack was doing."

"Let's say we'd had to occupy Rochdale," continues Ackroyd,
"and there had been an all-out war between the residents and
police, and people were killed. You people would not be writing a
book about bringing Rochdale down without a whimper. You'd
be talking about the bloodbath that went on in there. And I don't
think that twenty or thirty years from now, people will be sitting
back and criticizing Harold Adamson and Jack Ackroyd for the
foresight of closing that place without serious injury or death.
After all, we had an eighteen-storey powderkeg just sitting
there."

Even from a tactical point of view, the operation was nearly
impossible believes community relations officer Dean Audley.
"First of all, you'd have needed a thousand men, but I don't see
how you would have gotten much above the first floor because the
stairwells could be blocked so easily. Over the years, the residents
were able to close off parts of that building and make them
absolutely inaccessible. Tactically, one could never get a strike
force up to the twelfth floor, for instance. It was physically just too
high up. You'd have to get a cherry picker and stick the officer in
through the window—and I'm still not sure if that would have
done it. There was such a mass of humanity and such a chain of
communication that physically it would have been impossible."

"I think it was a wise desision to call it off at the last minute,"
agrees drug squad officer Dan Marshall. "Can you imagine—here

you're raiding a building where you don't know how many drug addicts you're going to run into, you have no idea how many people are in the building, you have limited intelligence of what's going on, you don't know how many guns there are, you don't know how many bikers are in the place—you don't know an awful lot of things."

It was not as if the police lacked opportunities or excuses to launch an invasion. Ackroyd chuckles as he remembers the time when Phil White—mayor of Metro Toronto's Borough of York and a member of the police commission—decided he wanted a first-hand look at the notorious high-rise. "So I drove him over there and I said, 'Now look, if you're not out of there by 3:30, we'll come in and get you.' Sure enough, he was half an hour late and I began to get a little worried. And everybody joked that that would have been a great time to pull a raid because we could have said we were going in to rescue the mayor. But we didn't. We just walked upstairs to look for him, and there was the mayor calmly sitting and having tea with the council."

By the fall of 1972, as jubilant Canadians celebrated Team Canada's hair's-breadth defeat of the Soviet national hockey team, a pall was descending on Rochdale. And although cancellation of the massive police raid may well have prevented serious injury or death, it made day-to-day life considerably more difficult for those who had to keep tabs on Rochdale. Much of this burden fell to Sid Smith who had been hired by John Biddell to manage the property for the Clarkson Company. Smith's duties were to see that rents were collected, apartments rented, the building kept clean and the books balanced.

"When I got there," says Smith, "I went to see the people in charge of Rochdale, and they had nothing—no books whatsoever. They were all destroyed. They knew we were coming in, so they destroyed all the books. We had no idea who was in the building, who was renting, who was paying any rent. There was no staff payroll. Nothing at all. In other words, a line of battle had been drawn of them against us.

"I was there every single day, usually from 8:30 in the morning until 4:30 or 5:00. I had an office of my own in there, which [Community Guardian] security was not happy about. They felt I should have sat in their office with them. But I said, 'No, if I'm going to get to those people in Rochdale and bring them into our line of thinking, then I've got to build up a rapport with them. I have to have my own office and they have to feel free to come in and talk to me.' My office was on the main floor next door to the security office, facing Bloor Street. At that time, in October of 1972, the Community Guardians weren't allowed to go past the second floor because the Rochdale residents wouldn't allow it. But after they got to know me, I was allowed to go all the way to the top floor to the different apartments and speak to people.

"I would go around to each and every apartment, knock on the door and find out if there was anyone in the apartment. And I could tell whether it was empty, so I'd get a key and go in. Then I made my own notes of who was renting. And you had all sorts of stupid names on the rental records. They were calling themselves Pasha or the King of Egypt or the Prince of Arabia. It was just a farce—there was no question about it. It was just impossible to keep track of who was living there. One day you'd have one guy living in some apartment, and another day, you'd have ten people living in there."

As the months wore on into 1973, Smith increasingly found that Rochdale was sapping his patience and peace of mind. But a sense of responsibility to his employer and his community kept him from quitting in frustration. "I used to go home on Friday and, quite frankly, take all weekend to try to regain my sanity to go back on Monday. I wasn't actually frightened to be there. I mean, I'd been in the army for twenty-five years, so I wasn't easily frightened of things.

"But I was threatened—there was no question about that. The police had to watch my house and Jack Biddell's house, because both of us were threatened with abduction. I got threatening phone calls once or twice a week. They'd say, 'If you don't get out of Rochdale soon, you may not live the rest of the week,' and stupid things like that.

"It was a very nervous time for my wife, as well, especially because we never knew what could happen at home. When we went on vacation, there would be police watching the house for us. As it turned out, there was never any damage, but there were lots of threats, lots of phone calls. Parcels were left at our door and I wouldn't touch them. The police would pick them up and find nothing in them. It was just harassment—nothing else.

"Wherever I went, it was a conversation piece. Whenever we went out to dinner with some people, they'd say, 'Oh, you're looking after Rochdale. Tell us all about it.' So I was at the centre of all these discussions. My wife used to tell me, 'You're crazy. You'll never have a rapport with those people.' And I suppose I could have refused the job, but it was a challenge to me, even if it meant endangering my life.

"I remember one time there was a knock at the office door and this guy walked in. He was spaced out, I think, and he had an old army great-coat on. I said, 'What can I do for you?' So he opened the army great-coat and he had this gun. And he said, 'Have you ever had one of these between your eyes before?' And I said, 'Oh, yeah. Many a time. I was in the army for twenty-five years and I saw lots of those things.' 'Oh,' he said, 'you're a smart motherfucker, are you?' I said, 'No, no. I'm not smart.' And for some reason, he just turned around and walked out. I had a buzzer and I pressed it to let the security people know there was something wrong. They got the guy with the gun, and it turned out to be fully loaded.

"Another time, I went to the maintenance room where there was a sink and mops and stuff like that. And I thought it was rather strange, because there seemed to be a new lock on it. I even tried it with my master key, but it still wouldn't budge. So I knocked and the door opened. The place was only about four or five feet square and there was a guy standing there with a shotgun. And he said, 'Look, if you don't shut that door right away, you'll get a blast.' What else could I do?

"Then there was the time I walked into this two-bedroom apartment and the only thing in it was a small, four-drawer cupboard. I thought that was rather strange. So I started pulling out the drawers and there must have been at least $50,000 or $60,000 in there in cash—tens, twenties, fives, twos, ones, all in old bills. Drug money, probably. So I immediately shut the drawers, locked the apartment door and went down for the security. Two of them came up with me less than ten minutes later. The cupboard was still there, but the money was gone! The Clarkson people, as ex-policemen, were more security-minded than I was and they found a trip-wire on the door that went to an apartment further down. Obviously, they knew I'd discovered their money and they came and got it when I left the room.

"I also remember this guy walking into my office one day and saying, 'Where's your briefcase?' I said, 'Why would you want to know?' And he said, 'Well, you usually put it at the side of your desk.' I said, 'That's right', and I looked and my briefcase wasn't there. So he said, 'Look, is this it?' And he held up a briefcase and I said, 'Yeah, that's my briefcase.' 'All right,' he said, ' all I want you to do is take this briefcase out of the building in the normal way when you go home. Now, open it.' And there was $50,000 in cash. He said, 'All you have to do is walk out with this briefcase which looks exactly like yours. And just before you get off the subway train at the Davisville station to go home, someone will switch briefcases and you'll get yours back.

"Well, the reason for all this was that, at the time, the police were stopping and searching everybody going in and out of Rochdale—except me, obviously. And this guy wanted me to get his money out of the building for him. But I refused. Otherwise, I'd have been gone for life. Luckily, though, I eventually did get my briefcase back with all my papers and everything. It just turned up, out of the blue.

"Even the little things about Rochdale got to be annoying after a while. You had fellows and girls walking around completely naked. It was nothing to get into the elevator on a summer's day and find it full of naked girls and guys going up to the roof to sunbathe. The girls would come over and pull my zipper down and feel all around and make a sort of joke out of that. And I'd just stand there, because there was no use resisting it. You're only asking for trouble when you start resisting."

Among the most creative nuisances was "Commie" Charlie Taylor who, as Horst recalls, "would make long distance calls from the Greenies' phones. He phones Moscow and tells them he's a KGB agent stuck in Rochdale and could they please come and rescue him. Then he phones the White House and does the same thing, except he's a CIA agent. Five minutes later the RCMP call back and raise hell. Once, he actually called the Pentagon and demanded to talk to Alexander Haig. And sure enough, we had these characters in suits and ties show up a few days later. They were hanging around for four days, looking for this guy. The shit Charlie could raise was unbelievable."

Embattled residents were also feeling the pressure of the ongoing tax assessment dispute with the City of Toronto. By the spring of 1973, Rochdale owed at least $750,000 in back taxes, but refused to pay on the grounds that it deserved exemption as an educational institution. During testimony before the Ontario Supreme Court, Jay Boldizsar admitted that only about one-quarter of the building's 550 remaining inhabitants were students. But he added, "They are still fully involved in Rochdale and think of it as an educational community."

At the same time, court-ordered evictions were proceeding at a steady but restrained pace. John Biddell announced in a May press conference that a hundred eviction notices had been issued to non-paying and drug-trafficking tenants. Court action was also promised to enforce the orders against any who had not yet left. And, perhaps mindful of the aborted invasion the previous fall, Biddell added: "The receiver believes that some of the residents are armed and that any attempt to evict all or a substantial number en masse would lead to a riot in which a number of people would be killed or injured, possibly among them some of the younger children."

"Very few people in there had a lease," says Biddell today. "Most of them never had one and very few people were paying rent. That happened because a handful of young lawyers moved in and knocked on doors and suggested to the residents, 'Give me a hundred dollars and I'll see that they don't kick you out for X-number of months.'

"Very few left voluntarily and we had to grind through the courts and get eviction notices. But they'd be appealed, so most people got another six months of free living there. But eventually, we managed to clear them out.

"During the course of that, I had many friends and quite a number of acquaintances call me or come up and speak to me when they'd see me on the street. They'd say, 'Do you know so-and-so in Rochdale?' And I'd say 'No', and they'd say, 'Well, that's my son'—or daughter or nephew or niece—'and they're in there and we don't know what to do about them. We sure hope you can get the place straightened up.' "

Where possible, resistance to Biddell's tactics was attempted. For instance, lawyer Paul Copeland tried in vain to prosecute Clarkson Gordon for violation of the Post Office Act for refusing to allow delivery of mail intended for Rochdale's residents. But evictions continued to be handled in a very rough way by the police. "I remember going down one day and taking the part of the young people who were screaming at the police," says Rev. Edgar Bull. "Some girl who was out of it had been put into the back of a paddy-wagon in a fairly rough way. She was in tears and her friends were sobbing. So, sentimental me, I was on their side at that point and not the police's."

But despite the considerable moral support of neighbours such as Bull, irresistible and continuous pressure was exerted by Biddell and his team. And so, by the end of 1973, about one-third of the building stood empty.

The New Year, 1974, dawned in much the same way as the previous one had begun—with yet another inquest. Once again, the coroner investigating a fatal fall from an eleventh-floor window damned Rochdale as "a festering cancer, dirty, disreputable, intolerable." And once again, the jury called for evictions of everyone within Rochdale.

But this time, there was reason to believe that the jury's recommendations would be carried out—perhaps not in 1974, but eventually. In February, the courts gave formal possession of Rochdale to Central Mortgage and Housing Corporation. And in March, another court decision granted the Clarkson Company permission to evict the building's remaining seven hundred residents, including all 408 legal tenants. By May, more than 80 eviction notices had been served, followed by at least 150 in June.

Property manager Sid Smith was present at many of these evictions, since he had the master key that permitted access to Rochdale's apartments. But, he recalls, a single key was rarely enough to get the job done. "The sheriff's officers brought wire cutters and other tools because people used to put their own locks on the doors—bolts and things. And, of course, the press used to come. It was murder! And the screaming! Oh, it was terrible. Really terrible."

"Yeah, I went in with the sheriff's guys," says *The Globe and Mail*'s Donald Grant. "One of them asked me if I was interested in getting inside. And I jumped at the chance because the Rochdale people didn't allow any newspaper guys in unless you passed their security. We used to go charging in at night to grab people. One time, I was up on what I think was the twelfth floor where they had all the gambling and the drinking rooms and the drug rooms. It was just like a speakeasy during the Prohibition era—unbelievable.

"I figure I must have been in on about a dozen evictions. Once you're through the lobby and into the elevators, the elevators never stop on the floor that you want. Eventually, you get to the floor that you're after, and by that time, they've got the dogs up there. People are pushing and shoving and screaming—a fight all the way.

"Six or seven of the sheriff's people would be in on a typical eviction, plus police. So you're looking at probably ten or twelve people. They'd have sledge-hammers, too, because no one would ever voluntarily open the door. Once the sheriff's guys got into an apartment, there weren't too many fights, because these people weren't fighters. They were peace people and half the time they were so mellowed out that they couldn't do anything. After we were finished, the police had to padlock the door, but the padlock only stayed on until we got to the elevator or to the stairs. By that time, somebody else would be back in the room."

With officers finally able to fight back as they'd always wanted to, the police department found itself facing a mounting list of claims of excessive force. In one incident, two Rochdale tenants—a twelve-year-old youth and a twenty-year-old member of a Christian commune—were stopped on the way to church, searched without justification and verbally abused.

In another highly publicized case, Rochdale resident Richard Hemingway submitted a written complaint to Metro Council's executive committee. In it he stated that he had been stopped by police near Rochdale and taken without cause to the 52 Division station. "I received various forms of physical abuse causing the dislocation of one of my ribs and the hearing of my right ear to be impaired temporarily. A blank was fired in a pistol approximately two feet from my ear. Sawdust was forced into my mouth and a barrel of a gun was placed to my forehead. The officer threatened to shoot."

In their own ineffectual way, Rochdale's residents mounted an occasional counter-offensive. On one eventful day in July, two police constables who had made a drug arrest were mobbed by a hundred angry tenants and prevented from leaving their prisoner's apartment. Only after they had shouted for help from a tenth-floor window did other officers rush up to rescue them and disperse the crowd. Later that same day, frustrated Rochdalians turned fire hoses on six Community Guardians, barricaded them in a second-floor office, carried their security desk out of the lobby and burned it on the front plaza.

But outbursts such as these only served to tighten the vise. By early August, two policemen were stationed in Rochdale for the first time on a round-the-clock basis. And a month later, Etherea Natural Foods was shut down and padlocked because its owner was more than $4,100 behind in his rent.

No matter how inevitable Rochdale's demise seemed, a small core of residents—those who still clung to a vestige of the building's founding philosophy—refused to submit without resistance. But all they had to do that August was look south to the United States to realize that even a supposedly immovable object—namely, President Richard Nixon—had finally been compelled to give up when confronted with the irresistible force of hostile public opinion.

"We knew that no matter how much we fought, Rochdale was going to go," says Judy Keeler. "But the people who were left near the end were the ones who truly believed that, no matter what, this was a better way to live than what they had ever known. Unfortunately, there were also some freeloaders and hit-and-run artists and hangers-on and crashers who ruined it for the rest of us. That's what made it so difficult, because those people were really irresponsible, and they just wanted a place to mooch off. So they mooched off a sinking ship.

"But when the building was falling apart, that belief in its ideals really brought people together. And we realized that what was happening to us was really wrong. On one hand, it's true the books didn't balance. But what the authorities did was so low-down and dirty and so ugly and horrible! It makes you realize that when somebody really wants to get rid of you, they'll find the means. And, if nothing else, Rochdalians became highly politicized because of that. We learned not to trust authority in a blanket way, which is a good thing—not that authority is always wrong, but we shouldn't place complete trust in it without questioning what those people are doing.

"It was terrible living there in the end, because the [Clarkson] people running the place used to sabotage the elevators. So children and parents with baby carriages sometimes had to walk up seventeen flights of stairs with their groceries. Then they'd turn off the hot water on us for a day, or the washing machines didn't work. And we knew it wasn't because the washing machines couldn't be fixed. They were doing just enough to make it uncomfortable for us to be there. It was a process of wearing us down.

"The last days were very sad. It was a feeling that the dream had really ended, of 'What did it all mean?' There was also a feeling of desperation because some people were simply not psychologically prepared to move out after having been so cloistered in Rochdale for so long."

One final, fruitless attempt was even made to sell the building and, as Jerry Neilsen recalls, "We actually found a few people who were interested in investing. But what happened was Rochdale's mortgage-holder scared them off and told them it would be very hard to pick up the building because of the financing. They were also scared of the name. I mean, we got along fairly well with people, but when we had them walk into the building and look around, we got quite a few odd responses.

"It was also difficult finding other properties we could afford. There would have been a profit turned on the building, but not as much as there should have been. And the new version wouldn't have been the same. In a property of one-quarter the size of Rochdale, you wouldn't have had the same sort of collective that was at Rochdale. It would have been more like some artists' studios downtown. It would have been a spinoff of Rochdale, but it wouldn't have been Rochdale. Rochdale had to live and die. It didn't need to continue—we continued. There was no reason for the monolith to continue."

Ironically, the end of 1974 saw the election of one of Rochdale's most loyal political allies—Allan Sparrow, one of two aldermen representing the downtown Toronto ward that included Rochdale. While hardly in position to reverse the tide of opposition, Sparrow believed the building could meet a dignified end without police harassment or violation of landlord-and-tenant regulations. "By the time I got involved," he says, "a lot of people had already moved out of the building for one reason or another or had been harassed out of the building. I was perceived by the people in Rochdale as the politician who would respond to their concerns and who would look into the legality of certain things that were happening. It was (Alderman) Dan Heap's ward, too, but we tended to divvy things up. I was more into landlord-and-tenant issues and he was into labour.

"My first actual contact was when I looked into some arbitrary evictions after I was elected. Some of the residents still had the idealistic notion that Rochdale could be salvaged and fulfill its original purpose. Others were so wrapped up in the persecution by police that that became their sole purpose. Still others branched out to become amateur lawyers in terms of their interpretation of the law. But in the end, it boiled down to the die-hard people who wanted to make the thing work and who had been through all the ups and downs.

"I believed an elected official should follow the law of the land and protect people who were being mistreated or being dealt with in an arbitrary fashion. That was clearly happening in Rochdale, although it was clear in my mind that the notion of Rochdale College was no longer viable. There were people living there legally who were being harassed and mistreated, and it was their choice to hang in as long as they wanted to. Instead of being harassed by the police and the authorities, they should have had full protection in dealing with the landlord. But by that time, the police had such a vendetta against Rochdale that it became an obsession on their part to clear the building out. And in my view, they resorted to any steps—legal or illegal—to achieve that purpose."

With the dawning of Rochdale's final year of existence, Sparrow found himself scrambling to ensure that measures undertaken by the receiver in 1975 would not result in the injury or accidental death of any of the remaining tenants. On a number of occasions, he had received telephone calls from frightened residents who worried about the authorities' practice of welding fire doors shut and failing to replace burned-out light bulbs in certain parts of the building. Such tactics, he was told, were implemented to isolate the tenants from one another and to make living in the building as uncomfortable as possible.

"So I went over and tried to get in to check the situation out for myself and I was met by a group of police officers. That was my first exposure to police being in the building. So I said, 'What the hell are a dozen police officers doing in this private building reading comic books?' Then I said I wanted to see a particular person in the building, but they said I couldn't come in. I asked if that person was there and they said they couldn't tell me. I was really outraged that there were legal tenants living in the building and that they'd called me, but police were saying I couldn't even communicate with them. It was like holding them hostage.

"So I went through the routine of saying I was the alderman for the area and I had a constituent complaint and I wanted to go in and see person X. And they still refused to let me in. So I phoned police headquarters and got the duty officer of the day and explained what was happening. We had a long discussion, after which I went back and produced my assistant-to-the-fire-marshal card, which I had by virtue of the fact I was a member of the committee on Toronto Council that looked after the fire department. But they still wouldn't let me in. So I again went and talked to the duty officer at headquarters. He suggested I get someone from the fire department, and that would allow me to gain access.

"So I phoned the deputy fire chief at home—this was on a Sunday—and he sent over a platoon chief. And when he came over in uniform with the gold braid on, the Red Sea parted and the cops let us in. He trailed around the building with us, taking notes and documenting all the fire hazards. I went to the police commission with complaints about that episode, but I never got any satisfactory answers."

For Judy Keeler, the end came quietly one morning in January, 1975. "They just put a piece of paper under my door saying I had to leave. And I didn't have any money, so I had to get Legal Aid. But we were all very skeptical of these lawyers, because they were only doing it for the publicity. It was a really hot thing to be involved with and we questioned whether it was something they wanted to be involved with at all. But my lawyer turned out to be okay.

"I had lived in Rochdale rent-free for almost a year and I knew that it was getting close to the end and that I had to start looking for another place. I wasn't exactly sure when the end was going to be, but I certainly was sure I didn't want to be there right until the end because morale was so bad. So I moved out in January and was probably one ot the last fifty people to go."

Surprisingly, Keeler managed to find a sunny, spacious, inexpensive apartment on the top floor of a house on Washington Avenue—a one-minute walk around the corner from Rochdale—where she has lived since her eviction. "I could practically have thrown my stuff out of my window at Rochdale and moved into my new home," she laughs. During the course of living in Rochdale, I really came to love the neighbourhood—even the little parkette next door that's still called Dogshit Park. I didn't want to live in a high-rise or rooming house, so I visualized the place I wanted and got it to a 'T', including the rent. It was just coincidental that I found it around the corner from Rochdale. I knew the girl who had lived in this apartment, so when she left for Montreal to live with her boyfriend, I moved in.

"Living so close to Rochdale in its dying days wasn't really much of a problem. What was hard was that I missed the sense of community. Rochdale was the first time in my life that I'd ever felt such a strong and positive sense of community."

Numbers dwindled, but not the antagonism. In one celebrated, February incident, council vice-president Kevin O'Leary re-occupied the old administration office after insisting that the Clarkson Company had never produced the proper legal documentation to seize it. "I was holding the office," he says, "when they actually bashed the doors down. A bunch of cops—four bull sergeants, one on each limb—dragged me away by force while I was quoting wildly from the court's receivership decision and from tomes on common law and property rights. I was charged with assaulting police and breaking-and-entering and a few other assorted odds and ends. As far as civil rights were concerned, we didn't have any."

O'Leary's ace-in-the-hole was a relatively new technological marvel—a home video camera that he had used for several projects at Rochdale. At the time of the occupation and arrest, the unobtrusive camera was recording the entire incident in and around the administrative office. "The trial was a delightful experience," remembers O'Leary's lawyer, Joe Sheard, "because we had a complete videotape recording of the whole event. I was apprehensive about the situation because videotape was a bit of a novelty back then—at least from an evidence point of view. So I informed the judge that I had this tape and I was prepared to play it, depending on how the evidence went during the trial. Well, that did it! In my entire career, I've never seen witnesses give more perfect, accurate, unexaggerated evidence. So in the end, it wasn't necessary to play the tape. And, of course, Kevin was acquitted."

"Even so," adds O'Leary, "the police accomplished their end. Sure, the whole thing was a joke, but they had the territory."

And that territory fell increasingly into the hands of the receiver and the police. On February 19, the Supreme Court of Ontario ordered a judicial sale of Rochdale for $8.6 million. Two months later, CMHC purchased the building outright with a vow to evict the remaining tenants and a hint that conversion to a senior citizens' development was being considered.

All the while, sledge-hammers continued to smash through apartment doors, as residents were cleared from the building in an uninterrupted stream. The last, great push came during the final week of May, 1975, when several dozen residents were ousted by a team of two dozen uniformed and plainclothes police, seven sheriff's officers and the Community Guardians. Perhaps as a result of the O'Leary incident, several officers even circulated through the building with video cameras and recorded the evictions for what they claimed was a police training film.

What the cameras and curious bystanders saw were tenants, many of them wearing only housecoats, being escorted to the street. Evicted residents milled around in front of the building, shouted obscenities, and picked through heaps of belongings that had been piled on the plaza.

"I was there the day of the last mass evictions," says Bill Littler. "I was asleep and hung over and someone came running down the hall screaming, 'The police are in the building! Lots of police everywhere in the building!' So I locked my door and I started to pack my things up. That included two German shepherds that I put into a couple of collapsible air-freight cages. Every once in a while, I would peek out into the hall to see what was going on. I knew they were throwing absolutely everyone out and they would eventually get to my room. So I tried like hell to sober up because I was really hung over—the bile-in-the-throat kind of hangover. And when they walked into my room, I said, 'All right, somebody help me carry the dogs out.' I knew it was over.

"I'll tell you, the dream for me ended about six months before the final eviction. I was just playin' out the string and I wasn't paying rent at that time. I did pay earlier, because I was one of the responsible ones. But at that point, they wouldn't have accepted the rent even if I had offered it. I wasn't even living in a room registered under my name. It was just a place to stay. There was no final stand, as it were."

For the lucky few, the end came with little fuss. Sandra Littler, for instance, happened to be spending two weeks with friends in Calgary when she heard that Rochdale had nearly been emptied. "A friend of mine rescued most of my stuff, so it was all right. I think we must have heard about Rochdale on the radio, because we knew what had happened.

"How did we feel? That it was amazing that Rochdale stayed open as long as it did. Also, we couldn't believe it. But it was kind of a relief, too, because it had fallen to such a terrible state. And it was sad because everybody was so disorganized. Most of the people who were left were there to fight the system, as opposed to carrying on and having other goals in life. It was the hard core that stayed till the end—which I would have been, had I not been away."

As summer melted into fall, all that remained in Rochdale was the odd straggler or squatter. "One of the last people to be evicted was a guy named Chips," says *The Globe and Mail*'s Donald Grant. "I remember going up to his room alone when the rest of the building was empty. He let me in and his girlfirend was lying on a box spring entirely nude. She never made a move to grab a sheet or clothes or anything. This guy also had three or four cats that kept jumping on him, and that's the way we did the interview. It went on for an hour or so and the girl never made a move.

"Then a couple or three bikers came bouncing through the door quite suddenly to make a delivery of some kind. They saw me, but Chips said, 'Forget him.' And the girl still never moved to put her clothes on. Finally, these guys, who were a little high, ended up in the shower with all their clothes on."

It was not until late September, 1975, that Rochdale was truly empty. The last resident to leave was "Animal" Dick Barnes, the eccentric part-Indian and Korean War veteran who cared for

Rochdale's pets. Because of ill health and confusion over Rochdale's collapse, Barnes needed help to move—and he found it in two old friends, Walt Houston and Judy Keeler.

"We had trouble getting into the building," explains Houston, "because the police and the Community Guardians didn't want to let us in. It took fifteen or twenty minutes to talk our way past them and convince them we were really the movers and we had no intention of coming back there to live. It was interesting that Dick was the last one out. Seeing as how he was about fifty-five or sixty years old in a building that had been a symbol of youth."

"We went up in the elevator," remembers Keeler, "and it would stop automatically on every floor empty. And what a sight! It was just awful. People had abandoned blankets, animals, clothes, beer bottles, hash. You could tell they were angry about being thrown out because they'd thrown cement down the toilets.

"Dick, on the other hand, didn't want to throw anything out. At first, Dick was very unemotional about it. It was done with relative ease, and I think it was very important for him to have me help him, because he was a dignified sort of person and having me there gave a sense of civility to the occasion. But finally, they closed the doors and locked up after us. What else could we do but have a cry about it?"

And so, seven years to the month after ushering in a new age of freedom and joy, the dream was dead and only the battered hulk of a tower lingered on.

C H A P T E R   13

After
the
Gold Rush

By the time the last resident had moved out, what remained of Rochdale was not so much an empty building as a seemingly bombed-out, high-rise ghost town. The stillness, so welcome after years of fire alarms, deafening screams and splintering doors, was broken only by the sound of flies buzzing through the scattered heaps of animal and human excrement and rotting garbage.

"I can remember going in when they finally had everybody out," says *The Globe and Mail* reporter Donald Grant. "Jimmy Gifford, the guy from the sheriff's office, gave me a guided tour of the whole building. We went up into what I call the speakeasy area where he happened to open up one of the fridges. Out of it came this cloud—a cloud like smoke, except that it was all bugs, just a mass of bugs. I remember the two of us just taking off—getting the hell out of there—as if we'd been near a bomb. We'd sprayed ourselves earlier with disinfectant and insect repellant, and I was thankful for it, because the place was absolutely filthy."

Newspaper stories by Grant and other reporters painted a sad, sickening picture of a once-proud tower that had been despoiled and vandalized in its final months and days. The roof sagged dangerously under the weight of earth-laden bathtubs that had been used to grow marijuana, flowers and vegetables. In one of the communal lounges, an entire wall had been demolished to provide more space. Rooms and corridors were strewn with shattered liquor bottles, plaster dust, ground-in dirt, yellowing papers, old clothes, dog hair and the ever-present cockroaches. Ceilings had been damaged by leaking water beds on upper floors. Pipes were blocked with hashish oil. Some of the walls were blackened and fire-scarred, while others were spray-painted in garish colours or solid black. Official CMHC stickers had been relettered to read "Cannabis Marijuana and Hashish Corporation." Appropriately, one apartment still sported an old Alice Cooper poster emblazoned with the words "Welcome To My Nightmare."

As chairman of Metro Toronto Council, Paul Godfrey briefly toured the building to acquaint himself with the property that the municipality was thinking of buying. "The damage was horrifying," he shudders. "There was broken glass, holes in the wall, toilets were cracked and not functioning, and it smelled.

"It was a really eerie sensation walking through the catacomb— it was in terrible shape. People had defecated on the floors. There were wrappings for bales of marijuana. Tenants had abandoned stereo sets and furnishings—just left them and walked away. Obviously, these people had made a lot of money and didn't care, or had used the rooms as a front for drugs."

"I couldn't believe that what was, for all intents and purposes, a new building had gone so far down," sighs Toronto alderman Tony O'Donohue. "It appeared to me that it was a building that had been inhabited by a group of people who had no use for modern life whatsoever, but lived in the jungle or lived in their own squalor. They didn't have any regard for anything at all. It was just a total shambles."

That Rochdale needed cleaning up was obvious. What to do with it afterward became a matter of debate. Many politicians favoured conversion to a senior citizens' home, while a vocal group of neighbourhood ratepayers argued that a mixture of seniors and other types of residents would be more suitable.

Uppermost in his mind at the time, says Paul Godfrey, was finding some way of "removing the black mark of Rochdale from the map of Toronto. There were those who professed that the only way to really get rid of it was to demolish the whole building and write it off. But, to me, that seemed like a silly thing to do. Even though the inside needed extensive renovation, the shell was very appropriate. You'd have to be crazy to demolish it and build almost a duplicate thing there.

"You could turn it over to the university for another residence, but then you'd always have the stigma of young people attached to it. You could make it into an office building, but at the time the federal government was on a kick of supplying housing. And since Metro Toronto was really determined to change it dramatically, it seemed logical to put seniors in there."

And so, in August, 1976, a year after the last Rochdalians had been evicted, federal Urban Affairs Minister Barney Danson announced that Rochdale would become a seniors' building. Since negotiations were proceeding smoothly with Godfrey, Danson expected an agreement within weeks and a grand opening by early 1977. As it turned out, he guessed wrong by nearly three years.

"Discussion started early to change Rochdale around," says Godfrey. "But as I recall, it seemed to take forever because of the legalities that were involved in this thing. I remember that for government to get full control, there were various court decisions that had to be made. We knew what we wanted to do, and the provincial and federal governments were totally co-operative. But it was the untangling—string by string—of the legislative nightmare that had to be accomplished in order for us to get control."

First, the courts granted Central Mortgage and Housing full possession of the building. Then, in September, 1976, Metro Toronto formally bought Rochdale for $9 million, with most of the money borrowed from CMHC itself. "We knew we had the federal government on the ropes," chuckles Godfrey. "The federal government gave it to us—gave us a mortgage for 90 per cent of the value of it. The government also fixed the building up to our standards and then helped us pay 50 per cent of the costs to operate an existing building. And Metro Toronto got most of the credit. You know, I sometimes can't believe the way the federal government acts. They're the ones with the problem, they want to dispose of the problem, so they sell it to you, but with their money. Then they fix it up with their money. Incredible!"

Despite the early successes, opposition was steadily mounting to what was perceived by critics to be a potential senior citizen's ghetto. "It took a lot of political in-fighting, public hearings and mobilizing the community to push forward the idea of Rochdale as a model mixed-use building," says Allan Sparrow, who was alderman for the area in the mid- to late 1970s. "That was actually a fairly radical proposition, because the government usually built only senior citizens' housing or assisted housing. The notion of a combination was unheard of, although now it's a reasonably normal proposition. So even in its dying days, Rochdale ended up being a pioneering building."

Controversy, so much a part of Rochdale in its heyday, was also a prominent part of its aftermath. While Metro Toronto and Ottawa kept pushing their plan, vocal community groups urged the city's housing committee to refuse to re-zone the building for residential accommodation until Metro agreed to a mixed-use formula. The protests were finally acknowledged in November, 1976, when Toronto Council's executive committee sided with

Rochdale's neighbours. Three months later, Metro capitulated and agreed to make a substantial number of units available to the general public, with priority given to people over fifty, those with disabilities and those referred by social agencies.

A major obstacle had been cleared, but still the delays persisted. Postponements were announced with irritating regularity because of unforeseen renovation costs and difficulties in bringing the building up to standards suitable for seniors and people with disabilities. In addition, every window needed to be replaced with the double-glazed variety, all the communal rooms had to be redesigned as regular apartments and almost all the tubs, toilets and counters had to be ripped out and new ones installed. One of the few remnants from Rochdale's psychedelic era was a portion of the free-form mural that was allowed to grace part of the lobby and the elevator area. Final price tag for renovations and repairs: $4 million.

The new name, proposed by Paul Godfrey, was the Senator David A. Croll Apartments, in commemoration of the man who had represented Rochdale's downtown ward as a Member of Parliament, had served as mayor of Windsor and is credited with having introduced the welfare system into Ontario while a member of the provincial cabinet in 1934. "Naming the building after Senator Croll meant that the black mark of Rochdale would be eradicated by the sunshine of the Croll name—and I think it worked," says Godfrey with a smile. "You ask people on the streets of Toronto today about Rochdale, and they'd have to be in my generation to remember it."

Further obscuring Rochdale's colourful heritage was the burden of years and the constantly shifting perspectives in politics and culture. By the time the Croll Apartments opened in December, 1979, the Vietnam War, which had traumatized and radicalized an entire generation, was already fading from memory, along with the presidents who had fanned its flames. An aging generation of baby boomers slowly began to succumb to the pangs of domesticity and materialism—yearnings that would soon earn them the tag of Yuppies. Meanwhile, those who tried to retain their youth sought refuge in the upscale, musical posturings of disco or in the hip, after-hours satire of TV's "Saturday Night Live." The tones of respect and awe that had once been reserved for such ground-breaking musicians as Jimi Hendrix and Jim Morrison were now being applied to a new wave of innovators, including Bruce Springsteen, Elvis Costello and Talking Heads'

David Byrne. And Rochdale? It was totally eclipsed by the elderly generation against whom its youthful residents had rebelled.

"I still go by it today and think about the irony of it," says Julian Fantino, a member of the police's drug investigation unit during the Rochdale years. "The people who are in there now and needed housing way back then are the ones who should originally have had the use of the place—not a bunch of people who drove the thing into the ground. It gave Toronto a black mark, and Rochdale became synonymous not with any education it was structured to provide, but rather with the illicit drug scene. To this day, I think it caused an awful lot of grief and aggravation."

Still, its absence was felt just as keenly by some of those who had valued Rochdale as a refuge and a community of friends. Among the neediest was "Animal" Dick Barnes, the last resident to be evicted in 1975. "By 1986," says Judy Keeler, who had helped Barnes move out, "Dick was living in a subsidized-housing apartment building at the worst corner in Toronto—Queen and Sherbourne. Even though he had no money, he remained a very refined person, but living in this building with welfare bums and boozers and really rough people was not his style.

"The week before Christmas in 1986, Dick had chest pains. He'd been diagnosed as having a heart condition, but I don't think anybody expected him to die. I was in school at the time, taking courses in law, but I was on holiday and went down every day to visit him at Mount Sinai Hospital. I was listed as next of kin, because I was the person closest to him—he had adopted me and I always had taken care of him in Rochdale. So when he died, I got the phone call. I had to get a funeral together really fast, but co-incidentally, another ex-Rochdalian named Shane Clair happened to be around and she helped me arrange the funeral. Billy Littler also showed up and took me out to a wonderful dinner when I really needed it after being under so much stress in arranging things.

"Dick went out like a king. The service was held at the Cardinal Funeral Home on Bathurst Street, across the street from Toronto Western Hospital. He got buried in his only British suit in pinstripes. His whole casket was strewn with Rochdale memorabilia, including pictures of his dog and his friends.

"And, you know, it gives me a funny feeling when I go back to Rochdale to visit. When I went up in the elevator, I kept having flashbacks of where the murals were and other things. And my feeling was that the politicians and civic officials had to leave it empty for so long to exorcise the ghosts. I've always had the feeling that, spiritually, that corner of Bloor and Huron is very empowered."

On rare occasions, however, the two worlds meet—if only briefly. In 1985, for example, Coach House Press needed room to expand, so Stan Bevington arranged to rent space in the Croll building. "We put our software company there! No problem! Nice people running the place. We did some really creative work and set up some great deals. We outgrew it again, though, but I don't mind.

"I never wish the building could be the way it used to be. But I look forward to visiting ex-Rochdalians there someday as a retirement home. I'm quite confident we'll have reunion parties there and they'll be wonderful opportunities to reassess the idealistic values that caused it to grow."

The host of those get-togethers might well be Major Domo, who lived in Rochdale from late 1968 to early 1969, but returned to take up residence when the building reopened in 1979. Just to be on the safe side, he keeps his identity as an ex-Rochdalian a secret from those who run the Croll Apartments.

"Getting back in was a co-incidence, pure and simple," Major Domo says with a shrug. "In the fall of 1979, I was living at a friend's house, but it went up for sale and I had to move out. While looking for a new place to live, I happened to be walking by Rochdale and saw a sign that said, 'Rental information inside.' I walked around back and there was a hubbub of activity—people signing leases. So here I was walking downtown to do some shopping, and I signed a lease instead! I signed right on the spot, and bang! I was in Rochdale again! It was a one-year lease, and I sign a new one every year. I moved in December of 1979 and was one of the first ones in. I started on the third floor, because I thought, 'Never trust those elevators.' But now I've moved up to the fifth floor.

"It's a great place to live—lovely!—a great location on the intersection of two subway lines. It's fun and there's also a bit of romanticism to it. It's nice that they've left the mural on the main floor and it's good to remember the past and the lessons of the past. I don't really have anything to flash back about, though. I remember the good things and don't remember too many of the bad things. I just like to keep my eyes open and recognize opportunities when I see them. And this was an opportunity that I saw. But I don't know if I want to pay rent all my life, although

I love the neighbourhood—I love the Annex. I still even go to the U of T; I'm working on a graduate degree.

"I'm certainly not nostalgic for the way Rochdale was. It would have been nice if it could have been what people wanted. And that's why it's so frustrating. What it finally boiled down to was the loss of an opportunity to do some very progressive things."

CHAPTER 14

Won't
Get
Fooled Again

If you ever feel the perverse desire to wound or enrage an ex-Rochdalian, just declare—purely and simply—that Rochdale failed. As devil's advocate, you might even adopt the extreme position of Toronto Alderman Tony O'Donohue, who vehemently condemns Rochdale as "a total disaster. If it had a silver lining, I'd sure as hell like to know what it was. I think it was a very negative thing for any city to have, because people committed suicide or were just totally derailed. There was no medical attention. There was no psychiatric attention. There was no attempt to help people. It was 'do your own thing.' If you feel like pissing up against a wall, you do it."

Having stated that opinion to the former Rochdalian, prepare to hear a passionate, sincere and, in many ways, sound rebuttal. It will touch upon Rochdale's contribution to the arts, its role as a haven for the abused and the maladjusted, its experiments with alternative forms of education. Also expect a heated refutation of factual errors in the O'Donohue tirade, especially his claim that medical and psychiatric attention—indeed, help of any kind—was entirely lacking.

But don't overlook the kernel of legitimate criticism that O'Donohue aims at the do-your-own-thing philosophy. In fact, similar sentiments have been echoed, albeit less harshly, by dozens of "alumni," including some of Rochdale's staunchest supporters. They point out that, as a microcosm of society, Rochdale captured not only the idealism and vitality of the late Sixties, but tolerance for and acceptance of virtually any concept, no matter how high-flown. This outlook was instrumental in transforming such fringe issues as civil rights, opposition to the war in Vietnam and concern over the ecology into matters of mainstream concern. But in its most radical form at Rochdale, it also resulted in a deliberate and debilitating breakdown of the administrative mechanism that had brought the building into existence. Even generally reliable organizations and individuals, such as Campus Co-op and several of Rochdale's founders, adopted an uncharacteristic attitude of "laissez faire" when firmness was needed most. And those who facilitated the dismantling of authority cannot escape responsibility for what Rochdale eventually became, or failed to become.

However, to go so far as to blame these same people for their tragic naivete or excessive liberalism is as senseless as denouncing the whole of Canadian or North American society for being mesmerized by the heady atmosphere and dizzying changes of the late Sixties. Rochdale was no more and no less than a product of its times, and it was accorded both the blessing and the curse to encompass the best and worst that those times had to offer.

"We were too easy and loose," says Campus Co-op developer Howard Adelman. "The Co-op should have kept total manage-ment control and total financial control, instead of handing it over to Rochdale's council. But once you enter a new world and aren't self-critical, you make mistakes. What we were asking for was an amateur, nineteenth-century university where there weren't any professionals or rules. But I had no idea at the time that we were really talking about that kind of throwback—the camaraderie, the lack of defined roles, operation by good will, the religious and moral flavour. The difference was that in the nineteenth century, they didn't have esthetic or social reform. That was pure Sixties. And it was a crazy mixture.

"The key factor [in Rochdale's evolution] was that the new culture took over the building. But we were responsible for allowing it to happen, and the question is why we allowed it. I think it was because there was a romanticism in what we were involved in—a dream that wasn't well enough grounded. It was a dreamy time, I guess. We thought anything was possible. And then the romanticism actually got taken over by romantics. We in Campus Co-op were romantic about it, but we weren't true romantics. And when the real romantics took over our dream, it became unreal."

Even after Campus Co-op surrendered most of its authority, a good deal of adminstrative power still resided in the education committee that had co-ordinated the activities of the Rochdale Houses. But this, too, fell by the wayside and enlarged the vacuum, says Rev. Ian MacKenzie. "We in the education committee had had a continuous existence for three or four years and we were afraid of being seen as occupying the same position as a university lecturer or teacher who supposedly knows it all. It wouldn't have been in keeping with the idea of people coming to Rochdale and determining the form and content of their own educational process. So the only way for us to be true to our principles was to disband and have each of us do our own thing. But that was a major error, I think, because life is not like that. People do not do their own things. Life is inter-relationships and community."

Instead of gaining an adequate opportunity to flourish, Rochdale's fledgling community was eroded by the huge influx of crashers and by a scarcity of checks and balances. "There were simply too many people who didn't know each other," says council member Pamela Berton. "And in any community where you get too much turnover, nobody has time to learn the rules. We can pretend there weren't any rules at Rochdale, but there were a lot of rules—unwritten rules. And any community that doesn't take the time to absorb that and to integrate people into the community will have social problems."

There were many occasions, says architect Malcolm Wells, when compassion for certain residents was the true motive behind the council's apparent irresponsibility. But that made the dilemma no easier to solve. "The question that inevitably arose was, where was the greater right? Was it more right to meet your obligations to your mortgage payment or to provide a roof over the head of a handicapped student who was trying to go to school and didn't have the fees? Those are the kinds of questions that were debated, and ultimately Rochdale wasn't able to meet its financial commitments. At that point, it became the victim of real authority—the people who wielded the money in a society, who said, 'We don't want this kind of thing going on in our midst.' "

Dennis Lee believes Rochdale might have had a fighting chance "if there had been some organic process of growth over three or four years, with ground rules and precedents and common law, but without all the other stuff in the Bloor Street building. Then, perhaps, the quantum jump into the building could have been managed. But that never happened to begin with. So it went from mild and troubling but amiable chaos to chaotic disorder.

"If you take away all orientation points for people and throw them into something that's virtually structure-free and ask them to respond, it seems clear that the reaction will be panic. That was the sort of free-floating process that went on. And on. And on.

"To make matters worse, the Bloor Street building was just too big physically, and people couldn't acquire any sense of history in it. Every month, there'd be hundreds more people who had some involvement in Rochdale, but they knew nothing about it except the instant media mythology. So even in the short life of Rochdale, you'd see generations go by in three- or six-month periods. I myself became a dinosaur within six months."

Poet Victor Coleman feels that basic structure and some sort of continuity could have been maintained during Rochdale's early years, if more of the founders had persevered. "The idealism of Dennis Lee and his cronies went like this: 'This ideal, which we five or six or twelve people have, we want you thousand people to live out for us.' From their attitude, it's obvious that Lee and these other people were not living in the Sixties—maybe the 1860s, but not the 1960s. But then Dennis Lee says, nose in the air, 'I don't wish to do this any more.' And that was too bad, because he was a powerful influence. Campus Co-op had pretty much disavowed it, so when Lee pulled the rug out, what was left? A lot of inexperienced people running Rochdale—bikers and a bunch of people from the States with large dogs. And because people like Lee failed to maintain some sort of association with the place, anarchy followed very closely upon the heels of their departure."

Lee acknowledges this criticism and admits, "I should have realized at least a year earlier that this was not the right place for me to be and that I wasn't the right person to be there. I regret helping to contribute to a milieu where some people came with exaggerated expectations but felt woefully let down by the reality. During my second year, I was staying there while my real impulses were carrying me somewhere else."

Magnifying the anomalies of the psychology, sociology, philosophy and politics of Rochdale was the non-stop headache of dealing with that colossal, eighteen-storey slab of concrete. "When we actually got around to taking possession of the building," says executive member Paul Evitts, "it was like an albatross. More and more of the energy of people in leadership roles got sucked into trying to figure out how to manage this thing."

Science fiction anthologist Judith Merril also realized that whatever advances Rochdale made were often achieved in spite of, and not thanks to, the building itself. "I was extremely impatient with people who were determined to cling to that chunk of masonry. I argued very hard during the second year to move out of the building, and a bunch of us were saying that the proper kind of space [for an education program] was a block of small houses and adjoining back yards.

"I was really disgusted with myself and with everyone else for having been conned into the idea of that building and the notion, with all this rhetoric, about creating your own environment. I had nothing against the concept of a high-rise, but that place was built to be a student residence, a rental residence. It was not built to be either an educational centre or a space for people to learn how to live together."

And so, in the true, unfettered spirit of its era, Rochdale was allowed to stagger from crisis to crisis. A succession of governing councils appeared, each with the initial radiance of a rainbow in a summer shower—and each just as fleeting. Dissenting voices were usually accommodated, while the will of the majority too rarely held sway. "No one ever took charge," complains filmmaker Michael Hirsh. "Rochdale started in the most anarchistic year of recent history—1968-69. And they made a bold statement in *Time* magazine that said, 'We're gonna be the most liberal, anarchistic college around, and we want people to come from all over.' And that's what happened, people came. They came before the building was finished, and they came with no money, and they lived in closets, and they lived in the incinerator dumps.

"So the legitimate residents who were paying rent no longer really had what they'd been sold. And there was no one in charge who said, 'Everyone who's living here for free has to get out.' They'd have these open and direct democratic meetings, and people who were crashers would come and vote. So management would be stuck. And since there were more crashers than rent-paying people, the rent-payers didn't feel like paying, and slowly but surely, many of them stopped. But whenever anyone tried to establish a set of rules, everybody challenged it because they were against rules. So you had an organization that proudly proclaimed itself as anarchistic, and it fell apart precisely because it was an anarchistic organization."

Some individuals foresaw the potential for trouble, but because they were part of the much-scorned Establishment, their warning went largely unheeded by those in nominal control of Rochdale. "There isn't any operation that can go on without rules," says Police Chief Harold Adamson, "and I expressed that concern at the outset of the thing, because the people in the federal government made it abundantly clear to us that this was an experiment where people did their own thing without accountability to anybody. But it just reinforced my thoughts that there have to be rules for everyone, or else we end up in a barbaric situation. And that, actually, to some extent, is what happened."

Robert Crampton, one of the earliest police officers in Rochdale, adds that he and his colleagues "alerted Rochdale Council of the potential for violence, the potential for drug abuse, the potential for harbouring of wayward children, the potential for the market for contraband. But they did absolutely nothing about it. And that disappointed us immensely.

"The people who were running Rochdale just didn't want to become involved. They thought we were over-reacting. They thought the police were biased. They could have nipped it in the bud by literally declaring the people involved [in undesirable activities] 'persona non grata' and evicting them. They had the power to do that in those days, but they decided not to do it for whatever reason."

But, Howard Adelman believes, advice and assistance from the Establishment would have been welcome, if it had come at an early stage from the right source. "I blame the University of Toronto for not lending us any guidance. Here was a creative group of people [Campus Co-op], and what was the university doing? Expropriating and not giving a shit about us and saying, 'Go find another place to build.' Here students need housing, and what does the university do? It builds New College that occupies a whole block at a cost of $12,000 a bed, while we were building at $5,000 a bed. All the university had to do was provide guidance and work with us.

"I also think of society's irresponsibility—the abdication of guidance and the failure to see a creative thing and support it. I really believe the rule of institutions is to foster creativity and give it guidance with controls and boundaries."

Matt Cohen agrees there were "positive things that could have happened but didn't, that weren't Rochdale's fault. I think the university or Central Mortgage and Housing should have seen what was positive in it, stepped in and subsidized the whole thing. Look at the situation now. There's a great housing shortage at the University of Toronto, and it would have been really valuable if Rochdale were somehow part of the solution. The university is poorer for having jettisoned it. It's a real opportunity that's been missed, and it's typical of Toronto, in a way, because there was no foresight."

Ignored by some institutions and mistrustful of others, Rochdale reasoned that it had no choice but to operate as an independent entity to as great a degree as possible. That, too, proved to be a fallacy, says registrar Jack Dimond. "You can never really check out of society, unless you literally go out into the wilderness and are self-sustaining. And if you don't have the kind of organizational network that society develops through experience, then you simply replicate all the problems of society without any of the safety nets."

Adds former Toronto Mayor John Sewell, "They saw themselves as a counter-culture, an alternative culture–'We're doing something outside the political mainstream,' and all that sort of stuff. But the point is that none of that survived. It was a brave, new world that these guys were trying to establish, as were many other people. But they suffered to the same extent as everybody who went to the country to found their own little farm. You just can't get away from the world. So, at the time, my impression was that Rochdale was having a very, very small effect on the political world that I was operating in–the world of urban politics, of trying to stick things together."

Inevitably, Rochdale became the hothouse for a strange, new environment where even the most basic of social conventions somehow crumbled. "Owning things was rather odd at Rochdale," recalls ex-resident Carol Shevlin. "People weren't normally willing to let you keep anything you had. Something would disappear because somebody else perceived that they had a need for it. And they just couldn't imagine that the reason you acquired it in the first place was that you yourself had perceived the need and had gone out and bought the item.

"But it went deeper than that. All of these kids came from homes where they'd always been supported. Hardly any of them had any life experience–and anyone who did was set up as a wild guru with followers. So these sheltered people expected that things would come to them, the way things had always come to them. Food would be there. A place to sleep would be there. If they needed something, it would be provided. And they were completely sincere, but they were also being completely unrealistic about what life is.

"Another example is that, for a while, you couldn't go out onto the second-floor balcony because people would throw down garbage and other things—not because it was easier to get rid of your garbage that way, but because it was an anarchistic act. It was an expression of freedom.

"Originally, people acted as if there really was authority there. And the place always looked like it would eventually get some authority, but it didn't. The anarchy just continued to grow, because it became obvious that if you did something, you could get away with it. More and more people who weren't there for any kind of intellectual stimulation kept walking into the building. So the ones who were there for better reasons walked out."

"There were some terrible things that took place there," sighs Bryn Waern, "because some people came in with a big chip on their shoulder and nothing to offer ideologically. I remember speaking at a council meeting against people who came in with the drug/crasher mentality that killed the whole idea of Rochdale. It meant that even if there were a hundred people respecting their surroundings and taking care of everything, all it took was one person to break the fire alarm or put up some graffiti, and there it was—the essence of Rochdale. And somehow, we allowed that. There wasn't a solid enough authoritarian mentality that said, 'Hey, this is killing the building.'

"There were some really psychopathic-type people there or people who just didn't care about the welfare of the building. Every person who ever threw garbage in the hallway or let their dog poo in the hall and didn't clean it up—those people should have been thrown out. But because they were there, it somehow meant that they had established their validity, and what they did was okay."

What's so dismaying in hindsight, adds Rev. MacKenzie, is that this extreme insularity was not only accepted, but embraced. "In effect, what we did was remove all the structures, and that was done consciously. The theory was that when people graduated from high school, they were so directed that, in order for them to break out, you had to remove all the structures and give them a chance to find out for themselves who they really were. What that meant in practice was that people immediately began to do what they knew, which was what they'd been taught. Within a month, they discovered that that really wasn't any good, so they went through an immense and rapid learning experience. Some of them survived and went on to do great things. But many of them got caught up in the drug scene and it was a very, very destructive event."

It was not long before excessive drug use and trafficking, fostered by the free-for-all atmosphere, became the most visible and the most censured of Rochdale's sins. The disapproval of police, politicians and straight society is well documented, but even former residents such as Patsy Berton were repulsed by this "grisly side of Rochdale. There were some people who were very strung out on drugs and there was always that element of people living on the edge. For me, that was a real eye-opener because I hadn't really associated with people who were down-and-out in such a depraved way.

"I don't think Rochdale would have been such a peculiar place, if not for the drugs. It had the potential to be something pretty amazing, but I think the drugs made it different from what it started off to be. I'm not totally down on drugs—don't get me wrong. A little pot and hanging around and listening to music is great. But there was a side of it that attracted people who were desperate—the speed freaks and the people who jumped off balconies. I don't know where those people were coming from, but they seemed to have less in life. And their coming to Rochdale turned the building almost into a den of iniquity."

"The down side of it was definitely the drugs," agrees resident Jerry Neilsen, "and that's really what killed it, even with the bad economics and the lousy construction in the beginning and poor financial strength. You couldn't live with the drugs, because it was too negative politically. A few of the dealers were really part of the community, but even they realized that drugs were destroying it."

"I don't know what it would have been like without dope," says video artist Kevin O'Leary. "It might not have had any meaning whatsoever. It might never have existed, but it was dope that killed the place for sure. The city fathers, I think, would have put up with the other strangeness and we could have made a deal economically. But the dope dealing—well, they just couldn't handle that. And that's what killed us."

What Rochdale needed, believes American poet Allen Ginsberg, was not just stronger leadership and a basic set of rules, but "something like what we have in Boulder, Colorado—the Neropa Institute. It's a school founded on communal principles with everybody co-operating. But the key to it is that everybody meditates—basic, classical, Buddhist meditation. And perhaps some of that was needed in Rochdale for grounding and to provide everybody with a common ideological space or a common emotional space to resolve their nervousness.

"You need some sort of minimal organization to maintain the organism. Otherwise, it just isn't an organism. And it isn't the organization itself that's so bad. It's the tendency of the bureaucracy to become solidified and to lose its sensitivity, its humour and its gentility."

In the absence of such an all-encompassing principle, residents were forced to find their own solutions. For the lucky few, this meant learning to balance Rochdale's hedonistic, anything-goes lifestyle with the day-to-day discipline of earning a living. For instance, Stan Bevington, founder of Coach House Press, partook of many of Rochdale's delights, but never forgot that his publishing company would flounder without a steady hand at the rudder. "We at Coach House had the Protestant work ethic to start with, and that's something I'm grateful for. I was working with something that didn't revolve around a building, but around a group of people and a certain consciousness. Our concerns weren't and aren't building-focused—and I'm really glad that we surpassed that goal of building-focus and moved on to other things."

Reg Hartt, too, discovered at the outset of his career that he could either indulge in Rochdale's excesses or teach himself to become a knowledgeable movie exhibitor—but not both. "The key thing that kept me from getting totally absorbed by the drug culture inside the building was the fact that the discipline required by what I did was too severe to allow it. I had to design posters, put those posters up, maintain the continuity of the program, meet my bills to anyone I was doing business with and arrange the screenings. I had to be able to guarantee that any prints I used would go back in the same shape they came down in. Consequently, because I did meet those guarantees, I had an extremely co-operative situation [with film distributors] for a very long time. What it meant was that there just wasn't time for me to freak out or be casual or disintegrate."

And so, just as it had reflected the wide-open attitudes of the late Sixties, Rochdale closed its doors amid the increasingly conservative mid-seventies. Lacking the necessary authority and responsibility of its own, it was unwillingly forced to accept the strictures of a society that had long ago lost patience with the antiquated credo of "do your own thing."

"Its time was over," says former Toronto Mayor David Crombie. "By the seventies, it had become a place from the past, a place from some other era. It was clear by then that there was no way it could continue. There was simply no one with a strong enough argument that it ought to continue. It couldn't continue in the name of 'This is what co-op housing is about,' because that wasn't what it was about. And it couldn't continue in the name of 'This is what student housing is about,' because there were other kinds of better student housing. So, in a sense, the only thing it had left to offer was itself—and by then, that was just not enough.

"It was an interesting experiment, I suppose—but I don't even know that for certain. It was just one of those things that happened as a consequence of a lot of forces in the early Sixties. And it was an opportunity for expression for a particular group of young people. But because of the way they ran it, it meant that if one day they were content to go off and do their own thing, then the next day they would be gone."

C H A P T E R   15

Right
Place
Wrong Time

In evaluating Rochdale, we must inevitably ask certain questions: What went right? Did it succeed? What went wrong? Did it fail? From a certain point of view, the questions aren't even relevant because Rochdale was not, according to Bob Nasmith, "particularly goal-oriented."

We cannot approach the subject of the evaluation of Rochdale with a scorecard mentality; the scale weighing the positive and negative aspects of Rochdale cannot be precisely balanced. Rochdale was like a maelstrom, drawing its residents from everywhere and scattering them each with his or her own sliver of the experience.

By 1975 thousands of people had lived at Rochdale and hundreds of thousands had passed through its doors. In a way the spectre of Peter Turner's statement that "to write the true story of Rochdale you would have to write the story of every individual that ever lived there" has haunted the writing of this book. Ultimately, Rochdale's legacy is carried around by all the individuals who experienced life at The Rock.

For some Rochdalians, like Jim Garrard, talk of "the noble experiment that failed" is unnerving because for Garrard, Rochdale worked. "Maybe you could say it was a noble failure. I say it was a noble success. When people start talking about the fact that Rochdale could have worked I get nervous, because to me it worked perfectly. The building was the perfect place for what was happening, but it came and went."

Rochdale exerted a profound influence on the personal development of those who lived there. Even someone like Dennis Lee finds that, despite abandoning the project when he did, Rochdale did play an important role in his evolution.

"It had some effect—good and bad—on a personal level. I was an overachieving, academic, would-be writer in my mid-twenties then. Rochdale gave me exposure to a whole range of ways of being human. But much of the hassle and psychic bloodshed and people's feeling of betrayal or disillusionment—enough of that comes to one in life, and right then there was more than I was able to handle.

"Then again Toronto had never had a heady, adrenalin-racing, iconic place before, and it's good in itself that that happened. But it's a shame that it so quickly got turned into a caricature."

Paul Thompson was one of those who acquired real work skills that stood him in good stead in the outside world. "It's given me a very good understanding of structures," claims Thompson, "and how human dynamics work. It's also given me a really good money sense. Until Rochdale, I had never had to run the financial part of an organization before. So I dug in and learned how to balance the monthly statements. But I think I understand structures quite well, and a lot of that came from Rochdale.

"I sat on the Canada Council's advisory arts panel for three years, and this was a pretty structured and organized group. I would say that the tactics of human dynamics that I learned at Rochdale—the way to have a fruitful interplay of debate and how it all has to end up with a certain practical response—served me in great stead there. Rochdale gave me the ability to rethink how to solve problems."

For Parachute Club drummer Billy Bryans, who came to Toronto in the late Sixties, Rochdale was very important. "It gave me a footing here in Toronto. Through working with Downchild and Rush and the others I learned about the recording procedure and process at Sound Horn. Plus, I didn't know anyone when I came here, and at Rochdale I started meeting and developing my social contacts and music business associations."

Don Washburn feels he was exposed to a stunning breadth of experience that he couldn't have been in touch with anywhere else. "How many people can say they've looked down the barrel of a shotgun? On the other side of the coin, how many can say they've delivered a baby? Both those happened to me at Rochdale, and every other kind of experience in between, from finding a jumper's body on the concrete to taking part in the decision-making process of an entire community. It was all there at The Rock. I learned so much there; in a way I'm still absorbing it today."

Teenage runaway Alex Martin is emphatic in his belief that "it changed me for life. I tell my kids not to do what I did, but I don't know if the circumstances are the same these days. I don't think another Rochdale could exist.

"I did more in six months at Rochdale than many people do in decades. I had to make my own way and my life was so varied, things were always changing, you never did the same thing two days in a row."

Martin's assertion that he somehow had an accelerated upbringing at Rochdale is echoed by a multitude of Rochdalians. Carole Popkey, for example, believes that "Rochdale was an acceleration of the evolution within myself. I was introduced to a lot of new things very, very quickly. I think a lot of people would say a part of their life was on super-fast-forward because there was just so much input. It's had as much effect as all of my university education because it was so concentrated. And the social relationships were so complicated that it was like Peyton Place in a geodesic dome, which I've never run into before or since."

Rochdale was in the vanguard of the creative revolution—although, unlike a learning environment such as Black Mountain College, it never became an intellectual centre, nor did it become a vital arts centre. Rochdale may have conducted sculpture classes, staged arts festivals, and been the site of an occasional recording but it was no Left Bank. For example, despite all the literary types and writers who passed through her halls, only two books were published under the Rochdale flag: Peter Turner's tome *There Can Be No Light Without Shadow* and the Victor Coleman-edited *Book of Flophouse Poetry*. Turner himself feels that this was because "if you look at what Rochdale accomplished in terms of individuals you'll find that most of them accomplished things after they left; while you were there the building absorbed all your energy. Rochdale was like a constant stimulus, it was like constant daylight in there. People like Dennis Lee, Matt Cohen, Judith Merril found they couldn't produce in that structure and a lot of them hated the structure for that; but, I wonder if they looked back at it now whether they wouldn't see that the building gave them that stimulus, that extra edge."

Merril disdains comment on the influence Rochdale had on her work, saying only, "I will leave it to literary critics and their little string games to decide what had an effect on my writing. But on my life, certainly Rochdale had a tremendous effect. For me in particular, my world had completely come apart. And there was terrible desolation for me in having to surrender essentially within my own mind any hope for the United States. I had to say, 'I simply will stop being an American, rather than thinking I can do anything to change what's happening.'

"Rochdale was possibly the only place I could have gone. Wherever I went, I suppose I would have worked through these things. But Rochdale was the place where people of many, many ages were in some similar condition. It was the place where you were allowed to go in disaster and be in disaster, and mill around with no expectations from anybody, and find out which way you were going to turn after that.

"There was a kind of ethic and intent and hope for humanity that I was totally comfortable and happy with. There was all kinds of shit and annoyance and trouble, and physically things were often inadequate in one way or another. But socially, they were marvelous.

"There was a sense of existing in a—these words don't do it, because as soon as I say 'love,' it's going to be like 'peace and love, hippies and flowers,' and that's not what I mean. I think I can express it best by saying that the first year I was in Toronto I was totally celibate, partly because Toronto men are really slow—I mean, it takes a long time for them to do anything emotional in this town—and partly because I was an older person in a young community. But toward the end of the year, I remember being in a discussion and hearing myself say, 'I don't miss sex, because I'm getting so much love and so much touching.'

"There was enormous tolerance of people for their idiosyncracies and foibles and carelessness and sloppiness. There was a great deal of honesty, but no sense—or almost no sense, ever—of maliciously motivated criticism. If you were being criticized, it was because somebody cared about you. On the few occasions when we had the sense of somebody operating out of hostility, it was extremely shocking."

Rochdale may not have been the creative fount that many have claimed it to be; however, the College did play an important supportive role for the local and Canadian arts scene. Michael Hirsh of the Nelvana film company feels that Rochdale was a catalyst and energizer for Toronto's artistic community.

"The energy level that permeated the scene—whether in film, drama, painting or whatever—a lot of that energy for the next decade came out of Rochdale. It was a great idea, and the sad part is that it only really survived one season. The most rewarding thing was the synergy of people—the tremendous number of interesting and good people doing some of the most interesting stuff around, all in this contained space that was slowly going mad around them. And these were people who were often on the edge of madness themselves, so it was bizarre. I remember having a very good, short-lived time there."

One gets an idea of how important artistic expression was to some Rochdalians by some of their acts. Honey Novick recalls the time the entire building became an empty sheet of paper. "This one guy started writing this one word all over the building—like the poem went all over the building—and he asked each of us to participate. He would write on the floor and it was continued wherever he went. It started out with one word and then progressed and progressed all over the building. At first, I thought, 'This isn't right, he's destroying the place,' but then I saw that he was turning the whole building into a poem, the building was his paper—it was brilliant—great."

Rochdale's internal publication—the *Daily* (or at least that was the best-known of the various editions of the newspaper)—provided an outlet for the building's writers. While no major talent emerged from its ranks, it did send people, such as the Juno Award—winning album-cover artist Bart Schoales, into the world a little better prepared.

Many of the institutions and organizations that sprang from the Rochdale womb dissipated with the end of Rochdale the building in 1975. They were, by their very nature, suspect and contrary to the prevalent "go with the flow" philosophy of the day; people on drugs generally didn't have the sustaining power and attention to detail that institutions need to endure.

However, two examples of the opposite spring to mind—the clinic and the Indian Institute. The clinic began as a one person operation that dealt with "bizarre people and freak-outs," progressed into a birth-control information centre and then developed into a full-fledged, full-service clinic treating tens of thousands of Torontonians who otherwise wouldn't have received medical attention. Clinic originator Ann Pohl (Auntie Flo) has mixed feelings about her time at Rochdale, although she does recognize that her experience there did help formulate the present direction of her life and career.

"Eventually, I came to the conclusion that there was no point trying to help individuals. What I had to do if I was serious about trying to make conditions better for individuals was to change society. That's a part of my personality and the way I operate and the reason I do what I do. That's why I haven't done any nursing work since then.

"Now I work on peace issues. That includes human rights and Third-World development and Central America and nuclear disarmament and South Africa. So I have a very broad definition of peace."

The Indian Institute had already been in existence for six years prior to Rochdale's involvement. For the two years that the Institute spent on the seventeenth floor of 341 Bloor Street West, the College provided a base of operations and support for Wilf Pelletier and the other Native Canadians' cause. The Institute carries on to this day as the Nishnawbe Institute.

A more traditional expression of Rochdale's artistic drive came in the form of Laurie Peter's lobby mural. Her Diego Rivera–influenced work depicted the faces of the tenants in an attention-grabbing manner and still remains in the lobby, the last remnant of a vanished civilization.

One of Rochdale's most visible and successful associations was with Theatre Passe Muraille. As the theatre's founder, Jim Garrard points out that "Rochdale gave Toronto a leg up as far as Passe Muraille was concerned, because it supported a great many of the directors who went on to do fairly important things and to change the face of Canadian theatre. Certainly, Paul Thompson, Ken Gass, Martin Kinch—those people either had their rent paid or their work supported in some way."

Coach House Press, a superior publishing operation, was another creative endeavour, and writer and resident Sarah Spinks feels that Coach House Press represented what Rochdale was striving for. "The whole building speaks of sensuality and a love for the work being done. The people who come there every day want to be there. The usual split between work and pleasure is absent. In the melding of the two, a very radical sense of art and business grows."

In its seven years, Rochdale was associated with and played benefactor to a number of artistic organizations: the Canadian Filmmakers Centre operated out of the second floor for almost two years; the Canadian Whole Earth Almanac was published from its Rochdale base for a number of years; the Alternative Press Centre housed its operation under the roof of 341 Bloor. Rochdale's support could be a one-time affair (as was the case when The Rock hosted the inaugural meeting of the League of Canadian Poets), a brief association (as when the iconoclastic arts group General Idea had its genesis at Rochdale) or a long-stand-ing relationship (as it was with Coach House Press and Theatre Passe Muraille).

Reg Hartt, The Rock's premier film impressario, offers this comment on the benefits of Rochdale in his life. "What I wanted in the beginning was to study film and what I got in that space was the opportunity not only to study the history of film, but to learn how to run, manage and maintain a theatre—how to design promotion, how to take something that nobody had ever heard of and make something of it.

"Rochdale gave me the opportunity to develop those ideas and find the ways and means to make those films succeed as entertainment—to put that element of pizzazz or that extra thing into it. As a creative space, it was the most important space I could walk into because there was a sense, at that point in time, of 'Look, you're doing something that is helping us. You're not going to make a lot of money out of this, we realize that. As long as you take responsibility for the bills, that's fine. Don't come to us and ask us to help you with that. We can't help you, but as long as you're willing to take responsibility for it, then you can do whatever you want. You've got freedom.'

"I could have gone anywhere else in town and attracted a larger audience, and I knew that. There were people who came up to me on the street and said, 'Look, we like what you're doing. We just wish you'd do it someplace besides Rochdale because we're not going to go into Rochdale.' What I tried to explain to them was that Rochdale was giving me the creative freedom that I couldn't have elsewhere. At Rochdale I could get up and introduce the film and perhaps even alienate the entire audience, if that's what it meant to follow a particular path of ideas."

As has been noted earlier, it was in the crafts part of the artistic spectrum that Rochdalians excelled. Rochdale turned out more than its share of leatherworkers, beltmakers, tailors, woodwork-ers, sculptors, weavers, printers, and hash-pipe manufacturers. It wouldn't be surprising if there were leather pouches and belts and sandals from the Rochdale era still floating around the continent.

"I learned the basics of business and the art of wheeling and dealing," says Walt Houston. "I learned several important skills—cooking, for one. I used that to survive up north later in my life. I learned how to brew beer in the brewer's collective. There were a number of firsts for me at Rochdale."

Although many of the Rochdale's founders, such as Dennis Lee, bemoaned the fact that the college had abandoned its original ideas and degenerated into a "Yorkville social agency," the second generation of Rochdalians felt that, in fact, that was Rochdale's true achievement.

According to Valerie Frith, Rochdale was a valuable socializing force in the community. "Lionel Douglas once described Rochdale as 'the babysitter to the post-hippie sub-generation.' There was this out-of-town deluge of underaged teens pouring into the city and Rochdale. The social services people were very worried about them. They found a home in Rochdale. It wasn't that they were in one place at Rochdale and therefore could be watched, but, more important, that their lives improved at Rochdale, they were socialized at Rochdale. That to me was the key thing about Rochdale, learning that there were certain things that happened within communities and that there were certain, well, laws.

"That was a discovery—as was, say, what happened to people's characters on security. Those changes—I didn't think they could happen in the counter-culture.

"Now, the other side of that was these pasty-faced kids who were coming in from places like Bridgewater and Thunder Bay, places where they had bad drugs and where what they thought was acid was really some circus animal tranquilizer. They had no money, they were on welfare. They came to Rochdale completely asocial and they learned that within that community they could actually make things happen. We saw that all the time.

"Call them the lumpen-proletariat, the vagrant masses, whatever. They'd stay there for six months, but they left in better shape than when they came in. They left understanding that you can work within a system. All you needed was the belief that if you find the right switches and the right levers you can make it happen. I believe that's also true of the people who left Rochdale and went on to become successful and prominent—that belief that you can work a system."

During its positive-press days, Rochdale continually tried to make that point. The *Star*'s Tom Hazlitt interviewed college leader Ian Argue, who told him, "It's really like a small town in which kids who are often very alienated learn to build a community and are judged by their peers. The process causes problems. Often very serious problems. But in the process of problem-solving the basic alienation is often reduced." Argue went on to describe an individual named Bob, an orphan from birth and a ward of the Children's Aid Society. When he came to Rochdale he had lost touch with reality, had delusions that he was Christ, had adopted homosexual mannerisms and had no idea of his role in society. "After he had been here for a while," continued Argue, "he learned to relate to people. In a situation of complete freedom he learned who he was and what he really wanted. And perhaps because of the sexual freedom he found that he was a man, indeed a man. I call that important."

Walt Houston speaks for many Rochdalians when he says, "Rochdale was a haven for a lot of people, but I think of it more as a therapeutic community. There were a lot of people who could not have survived without the kind of support they got there. A lot of people—literally hundreds of street kids—were emotionally disturbed and would have had a very difficult time surviving on their own. They picked up social skills in the building that allowed them to survive later on.

"If the kids had stayed on the street, they would either have gone into the heavy drug network on Madison Avenue and Huron Street or they would have gone into prostitution. In either situation, they would have been dead within a few years. As it was, many of them found their way into the skilled crafts or into the arts."

Rochdale's role as a valuable social agency is supported by some of the medical people that were involved with the college. Dr. Lionel Solursh feels that "Rochdale saved a lot of psychiatric bills. "I can recount cases where I think significant growth occurred. In other cases, it was acceptance of and reinforcement of behaviour that would, in the broader community, have been dealt with under the criminal justice system or treated psychiatrically.

"For some people, it was often a chance to pull away from society and to drop out to grow at a pace that they could handle. Some people definitely were able to survive and grow, who seemingly wouldn't or couldn't have otherwise."

It seems that the only official body that heard and recognized Rochdale's plea to be seen as a viable social agency was a 1970 Grand Jury. Its report recommended that "the feasibility of maintaining Rochdale College and its present environment as a publicly supported social research project should be explored. This recommendation is quite consistent with Premier John Robarts's announcement on April 22 that a fund of $20,000 will be allocated for the purpose of studying ways and means to investigate the drug problem of today's youth. Part of this allocation should be used to initiate similar research at Rochdale."

If Rochdale did work as a social agency it was because of the "us-against-them" solidarity. The bond between everyone within the building, whether spoken or not, was that they were in this thing together. Tripper strikes the appropriate image when he says, "Rochdale—that was the time we decided to go into the fort and draw our wagons around and make our stand. Rochdale to me was like the scene in *Yellow Submarine* where every time John opened a door some fantastic creature would come out. Rochdale was like that—behind every apartment door there was another world, another Pandora's box. It was a trip. But it was OUR trip—that was the whole point. Take dope for instance—the Sixties generation wasn't forced to deal dope. But it was more than money, the money was just a bonus. We didn't do it as an organized crime thing, we just sort of fell into it. Drugs were part of our army, they were our ammunition in this battle of consciousness that we were engaged in. They were what kept us one. Them and our belief in peace and not war. And Rochdale as the drug centre became an important symbol for the struggle everywhere in Canada. There was a camaraderie there; in fact there was a camaraderie among the youth of the day that you don't see today. Maybe it's because they have no place like The Rock to go to."

To many, Rochdale's anarchic style of participatory government ultimately led to its downfall. Founder Howard Adelman is adamant that Rochdale was doomed the moment the college severed relations with its parent, Campus Co-op. Rochdale's self-government strategy backfired and "Campus Co-op should have kept management control, total financial and management control, instead of handing it over to council."

Had that in fact been the historical case, Rochdale would have perhaps run more smoothly, but it would have been far less an experience. By adopting an interactive form of self-government that truly tried to do the will of the people, Rochdale went on to one of its greatest triumphs as an institution—that of providing freedom.

What made Rochdale so different from so many other "hippie projects" was its bold attempt to take on the concept of a free and open society and to deal with its implications. Rochdalians were not merely paying lip service to some ideal pie-in-the-sky notion of freedom; they were actually rolling up their sleeves and plunging headlong into the void to see what would work and what wouldn't work in their own community. Yes, Gov Con could be childish, irresponsible and just plain lunatic, but in its own way it was an heroic attempt to put philosophy into practice.

Tony Phred recreates the feeling of wide-eyed awe that an American felt upon entering Rochdale for the first time. "I looked around and there's all these crazy hippies running around and I said, 'Hey this is an eighteen-storey HIPPIE SKYSCRAPER!' I had never seen anything like this. I went on every floor and everyone I ran into said, 'We own this place.' And I'd say, 'Yeah, right, you own this place, but who do you pay your rent to?' And they'd say 'Rentals is Rochdale.' I'd say, 'Ah, Rochdale owns this place, who owns Rochdale?' And they'd say, 'We own Rochdale.' "

His brother Pat picks up the story. "When we first came up here we couldn't understand why the building was still standing. We thought, by our standards, in the States, that the building would have been levelled long ago. You didn't run across very many places like this in the States. It was—to use an analogy from a past life—like walking out of the woods and seeing Venice for the first time.

"It was amazing to see a spontaneous form of government. There was no way you could evoke the normal standard logical order in that situation and structure. But this spontaneous form of government that took place at Rochdale responded to critical situations, and those situations were handled with adeptness.

"With all of today's problems I think The Rock should have stayed open. Sure it had a lot of problems but the authorities shouldn't have got it back. That building did serve a purpose—whether it was runaways or the clinic. There was a lot to feel good about at Rochdale. It was a real, live incredibly interesting experiment, and a different sub-culture really. We found so many alternative ways to handle so many critical situations that it was, and this may sound funny, it was closer to Saint City than Sin City."

Alex MacDonald's eyes well up with genuine tears as he leans over the table to say in choked-backed words, "You see I love democracy . . . and I learned to love it at Rochdale." He breaks off for a moment, collects himself and continues, "Rochdale was, for all of the chaos and faults, a real live walkin', talkin' goddamn' democratic experience. Maybe Gov Con didn't have the powdered wigs and rituals of the normal legislative body, but it did fulfill its mandate of providing a forum for people who had something to say, it provided an outlet for the voices in the community that had something to say. A Rochdale meeting could not be used to control dissent.

"You had these drug-crazed twenty-three-year-olds who were in a technical sense executives of a multi-million-dollar corporation involved in substantial litigation. We learned a lot—or at least those of us who participated learned a lot. I've always believed there are people who whine and people who do. You see in Rochdale the grand slogan was 'We've got to get it together' and 'Somebody should do something.' Well some of us did and we're the richer for it."

For his part, Walt Houston found Rochdale to be "a lesson in politics, economics, sociology. There was no better school than Rochdale for a crash course in how a community works and interacts with society. You got the newspapers and you saw what they said and you understood the parts that were true and the parts that were not. You saw what the courts were doing and what the police were doing and what CMHC was doing with the financing and what the government was saying. You talk about an education—it was one hell of an education in what went on in Ontario for a time."

College President Peter Turner, who ultimately left Rochdale frustrated but still clinging to his democratic ideals, was amazed at "the openness in politics and administration. There wasn't a single thing you could propose at Rochdale that couldn't be opposed, and you had to supply the answer.

"At the most critical phase in our existence, when we had just started to convince CMHC that they should take another look at us, along comes Don Black and he asks, 'Why do we need a vertical structure, why do we need horizontal structures, why do we need a governing council?' And as a result of the ensuing debate, for weeks on end there was no government functioning in Rochdale. But we had to go through this whole process and let events prove that we did need a governing council. In Rochdale you learned by that kind of process."

In its courage to be open, in its willingness to become the embodiment of Walt Whitman's open-armed philosophy—"I am large, I contain multitudes"—Rochdale exhibited a willingness to take risks. That risk-taking mentality informs the entire history of the building. Even a relatively conservative outsider like former Toronto Mayor David Crombie believes that one of Rochdale's benefits was "that it gave the younger generation of students a sense of being able to test themselves." American poet Allen Ginsberg, though only a casual observer, notes, "I think it was an experiment. There are a lot of experiments that need to take place to see how things will work and what you need to do. It was a success in that people tried out different modes at a time when they needed to try those modes.

"Also I think that to think in terms of success and failure is to get involved in the New York Stock Market type of thinking. Those reference points are slightly dehumanizing, because I'm sure a lot of people learned from it."

For Paul Evitts, the constant risk-taking was a character-builder. "The things that I've learned at Rochdale that have turned out, as far as I'm concerned, to be generally true are how to experiment, how to be playful and how to survive in the kind of world we live in. And the skills that I learned one way or another at Rochdale have been skills that I've utilized in all the things I've done since then. I see this playfulness and willingness to take risks, this willingness to make mistakes as the really big thing. I got confidence out of that. A lot of the intellectual skills I've got I also acquired at Rochdale."

Rochdale's openness was founded on a fundamental tolerance for alternate lifestyles. In a broad sense this tolerance was grounded in the psychedelic revolution's re-ordering of perception—if reality itself was so multi-layered and nebulous, who was to say one way of living was right and another way wrong? If people were to reach their true potential and infuse the world with peace, love, brotherhood and creativity they would have to learn to tolerate other approaches to life and living. Rochdale's concept of freedom, like that of John Stuart Mills, was founded on the idea that one was free to pursue one's own course as long as harm was not done to others in the pursuit of that freedom.

Brian Lumley summarizes his Rochdale learning experience: "I learned tolerance. Everyone had their own way of life and you had to accept that if you were going to make it at Rochdale. Anyone could live in any fashion they chose as long as they weren't hurting and interfering with anyone else's lifestyle. You had all kinds in that building. Some people went to normal day-jobs, the party people got up in the afternoon, the night people only came out at night. You had all these different rhythms and lifestyles and you had to be comfortable with that."

Lorraine Darling found Rochdale to be a supportive community and "a good place to bring up kids." She is also proud of the fact that her children's upbringing in The Rock opened their eyes to all kinds of different human beings and situations. Her eighteen-year-old daughter, Justine, explains: "Living there as a kid you saw sights and different things that normal people didn't see. For example, you met different kinds of people who you just accepted. If you were in a more normal middle-class family, you know, it would be, 'You can't talk to THEM.' But we know crazy people. It's not their fault what they do. Some other people might look at them and go 'Hmmm,' but to us they're okay. They're just different. Nobody has grown up the way we have—all the interesting people we know and the places we've lived—plus we still know the people who lived in Rochdale and it's like one big family."

Craig Darling relates that one of the benefits of being part of that extended Rochdale family is the protection offered to him by bikers like his "Uncle Bobby" Lattice. "It's the same with any kid from Rochdale. Bobby says, 'Anybody bothers you you just tell me.' I did it once. This guy was beating up my friend and because this guy was an adult beating up on a kid I went and told Bobby and he came over to take care of that—threw the guy's face into a wall and that was that."

Rochdale, for many individuals, was a catalyst for a personal metamorphosis. Karen Johnson, who ran Rochdale's rental department, marvels at how far she came. "When I lived in one of the original Rochdale houses before 341 Bloor Street went up, we actually had a house meeting to discuss evicting a person because two other people *thought* this person was using marijuana. I cringe to think of it today, but it's true. We didn't have any evidence, we just suspected it. When I first came to work at Rochdale as my summer job, I wore these little white gloves because that was what proper young ladies wore to work in those days. Somehow those proper white gloves seemed out of place in The Rock. By the time I left I was a devotee of nude sunbathing. I felt very strongly that I had been saved from a middle-class white picket fence existence by having been exposed to Rochdale and its people—saved from a very dull existence, one without a critical point of view.

"It was very sad leaving Rochdale. And it wasn't a philosophical sadness—you know, the good idea gone bad. It was the attachment I felt to the people I had met there. I feel lucky to have met the variety of people that I did. Good solid friends.

"It was such a high-powered concentration of people. They could satisfy every possible whim you had, from crazy spaced-out philosophical talk with others who could party and have a good time to every conceivable other kind of interaction. There was an incredible range to Rochdale's people. And I was sad—I felt I was losing access to these people."

For Sandra Littler, Rochdale was "like running away to the circus and then getting back to the real world. You long for that freedom and those days after responsibility rears its ugly head. Oh, yeah, I still long for it. I realize I've outgrown it, and if it were there to do again, I wouldn't do it now at this age. But it was just tons of fun for somebody who wasn't basically prepared to cope with society or reach the goals that were set for me.

"I suppose I felt that I didn't fit into the society I was brought up to fit into. I found a niche to fit into and it made me feel very comfortable that way. It spoiled me—it did! Life was so easy. It was fun. Nothing's been quite as good since. It was a real fantasyland.

"I can't say I would want my kids to go to a Rochdale. But I wouldn't panic and freak out like my parents did. I would hope they'd have enough sense to protect themselves from harmful things. Not that I did, but I don't feel I was damaged by it in any way. My mother said, 'How can they have interviews with people from Rochdale? Half of them can't even talk.' 'If they couldn't talk at the end, Mother, it's because they couldn't talk at the beginning.' She sees them as drooling people who don't know how to wash. We all got involved in this conspiracy together and we all got away with it, so there's a lot of camaraderie there."

Undoubtedly the most frequent response to the question "What was Rochdale's positive influence upon your own life?" is "The people I met while I was there." Bob Nasmith counts among the benefits he derived from Rochdale his reawakened interest in theatre, but even more important than that was "the people that I met. My closest friends to this day, fifteen to twenty years later, remain the people that I knew at Rochdale. That's important because so often in your life you leave behind people that you knew and grew with as you move on to something else. That didn't happen with the Rochdale people, at least the core. I still keep in close contact with everyone. Now they're accountants, lawyers, computer people, teachers, what have you. We've had that cross-pollination. And through them I keep in touch with ideas that I wouldn't normally be exposed to."

"Uncle" Joe Sheard, Rochdale's foreclosure defense lawyer, tells the story of his grandfather's watch as an example of the community's sense of ethics. "I had a cousin who was living in Rosedale and while he was away someone broke into his house. They took his sound system—the usual toys—but the one thing that concerned him was that they also took a gold watch that had belonged to our common grandfather. He was really upset. Now he had heard somehow that the thieves had taken a taxi to Rochdale where they had auctioned the stuff off right in the front lobby. He called me late that afternoon and asked if I could help. I phoned Jay Boldizsar directly and Jay, very helpfully, managed to get some people together, and lo and behold my grandfather's watch turned up. That was only about an hour or an hour and a half after my call. I came down to Rochdale and the guy who had bought the watch didn't even want to be reimbursed, he just gave it to me. He was also very apologetic—'Shit Joe, I didn't know it was your grandfather's watch.' After dinner I went over to my cousin's house. He was a very excitable fellow, he was pacing back and forth, chewing his mustache, cursing the thieves up and down. He poured me a drink and I produced the watch. He looked at me and said, 'How the hell did you get that?' I just smiled and said, 'If you have any other problems just let me know.' But you see that was another side of Rochdale."

Even police officer and "mod squad" member Dean Audley admits that, despite all of the problems, Rochdale did have some worthwhile individual residents.

"Some people were absolutely destroyed by the use of drugs. But a lot of the people who I thought, at the time, were going to be total write-offs came out of it okay. Now there are people in government who lived in Rochdale. There are people in big business who lived in Rochdale. I've done fairly well, and I spent a hell of a lot of time in Rochdale. So I guess it was just part of the times, although at the time it seemed to me that it was the end of the world in many situations. My life was in danger many times. But I came through it, and a lot of other people came through it. I can't think of any specific things that were good about Rochdale. But I did grow to like some of the people I met there."

For many of Rochdale's residents its true mark of success was its development of a sense of community. Resident Murray Campbell experienced the "sense of being part of something larger. My wife, who grew up in the working-class Parkdale neighbourhood, thinks I got sucked in by the hippie patina more than was sensible. She thought hippiedom was basically a bunch of middle-class kids who always knew they could go home and shower on the weekend.

"I was sucked in to an extent, I guess. I was at a perfect stage in my life when I was ready to be sucked into a non-family experience. And people were talking good games then. Though it had its dealers and speed-freaks and scary, fun-house characters, Rochdale attracted lots of very ordinary, conventional, middle-class kids. And that's because there was a sort of energy to it. You could really convince yourself you were a different generation from your parents and you felt like you were part of a new groove in life and had shed all this baggage."

In a more immediate sense, community also meant Rochdale the building, the radical experiment in urban co-op living. If nothing else, Rochdale was a valiant attempt to come to terms with the growing alienation and depersonalization of life in the modern urban environment. At Rochdale you knew your neighbour, you got involved with others around you to help shape and direct your environment. At Rochdale you were no longer a replaceable pawn in the game. Your voice mattered, at least in the immediate Rochdale community. Whether it succeeded or not, whether Rochdale was or wasn't "the small town in the big city" ideal that many thought it was, the mere attempt to try and humanize the urban living experience has to be considered a triumph.

This sense of immediate building community reached its zenith with the communes. There was a reason that official tours of the building immediately went to one of the commune floors—be it the fourteenth, seventeenth, eighteenth or, in the post-dealing commune days, the sixth floor. These communes were showcased to the press and government officials because they were dramatic proof that Rochdale could work, that in fact Rochdale did work when the circumstances and attitudes were right. The right balance between good, solid citzenship and a free-form but supportive environment could be struck. Ex-residents like Alex MacDonald feel strongly that "the communes were our crowning social triumph." The attempt, as Frank Cox put it, "to live together rather than apart" in its own way paved the way for rethinking the modern urban living environment.

To this day Rick Waern still dreams of living in the Rochdale co-operative lifestyle. "One of the things that I've been wanting to do," offers Waern, "is buy a factory building and turn it into a loft space. I'd like to live in a situation that is in a sense like the floor I was living on at Rochdale, with other people involved."

Rochdale not only nurtured this community ambiance, but the Rochdalians themselves were ready to fight attacks from the John Birch Society, bikers, policemen or crusading politicians. Rochdalians were like a mother bear when it came to defending their own turf. When asked why he chose to stay on security all those years, Tony Zenker answers laconically, "I believed in the building and the people in it. I saw the good aspects. It was worth fighting for. To me Rochdale was an experiment rather than an abnormality."

Rochdale also deserves credit for its role in developing an awareness of tenants' rights in the city. The Toad Lane Tenants' Association, formed in March of 1973 to collect rent and then use it as a bargaining tool against the receiver Clarkson Gordon, was more than a flashy way to anger the overlord; it taught tenants in the building that they did not have to accept passively whatever the landlord dished out, that tenants had rights too. Rochdale was also one of the charter members of the Federation of Metro Tenants Associations. In general, through its front-page publicity profile, Rochdale helped focus attention on the issue of tenant rights.

In the same manner The Rock also had an important role in the battle for legal rights, especially as they concerned "street people." Carrying on the work of the Yorkville organizers, Rochdale was instrumental in informing and educating those who needed advice. The college was always printing pamphlets and newsletters to "tear down the myths that surround the police and the courts."

Rochdale didn't pioneer the concept that education existed beyond the classroom, nor did it originate the idea that there was substantial value in the practical application of a "course of studies." However, Rochdale was one of the few educational experiments in North America that tried to put these concepts into action. "It was a meeting place for people that was unlike college," says Stan Bevington of the Coach House Press. "Here we were, on the edge of a university campus, but the most important college in terms of changing our attitudes at that time was

Rochdale. It was exceptional that around the U of T, you could have a college where the topic was drugs and draft dodgers—the real issues of the times—and that they were being dealt with right then."

Another positive legacy of the Rochdale experience often referred to by the college's graduates is the Rochdale way of thinking and its perspective on the world. After surviving any length of time in the building, residents found themselves "thinking in the Rochdale way." If it were a recipe you might start off with a healthy dose of scepticism, add a touch of absurdity, a good measure of compassion, distrust of authoritative figures, belief in the individual self and in the power of communal solidarity and, finally, throw in a handful of primo grass or hash.

"Rochdale gave me a rock-bottom certainty about the relativity of opinions," says Nelson Adams. "Rochdale also instilled in me the ability not to confuse my own common sense with somebody's else's common sense or reality."

There is, of course, another way to look at the "positive legacy" of Rochdale—that is, as negative-aversion therapy. More than one Rochdale survivor points to the fact that he or she learned what NOT to do at Rochdale. Victor Coleman considers that "all in all, Rochdale was a positive experience for me. I felt it allowed me to confront the worst aspects of hippiedom and post-hippiedom, which a lot of so-called hippies weren't able to do, because they were so isolated in their ivory clouds. But I was able to see the worst aspects of it—the speed freaks, the bikers, the bad drug deals—and I was actually able to help people. In a way it was like confronting myself as I had been a few years earlier. I think that the first couple of years were, overall, quite healthy. A lot of flowers and plants grew out of the dirt. It was chaotic but healthy."

For Hare Krishna devotee Bill Charnell, Rochdale underscored the fact that he had made the right life decision in opting for the spiritual path. "Because I was an ex-hippie-turned-Hare Krishna, it was a good thing for me because it helped me with my convictions. It was good to get out of the hip thing before it turned ugly. Rochdale itself pointed out to me, more than anything else, that the die-hards who were attached to so-called freedom were going nowhere fast."

As for filmmaker Michael Hirsh, despite the positive artistic legacy Rochdale helped instill in him, "the flip side of what I learned is that, despite one's ideals that anarchy should rule or that democracy works, Rochdale was positive evidence of the failure of those ideas. It taught me the importance of structure and organization and rules. I've never seen an organization fall apart faster or more completely, and that was a telling experience."

Drug dealers were also the beneficiaries of Rochdale's shelter. Fortunes were made. Rumour has it one of Rochdale's biggest dealers is currently residing in a castlelike villa on the cliffs overlooking Negril beach in Jamaica. Places like Rochdale helped a new breed of entrepreneur arise. It seemed as though overnight various hand-to-mouth types were suddenly, as the result of their dealing, very rich. The dealers filled the gap between the ever-increasing demand for drugs and the availability. It was straightforward supply-and-demand economics. And while the dealers did amass fortunes, their money inevitably trickled down through all layers of the community. Because money didn't mean much in and of itself, the hippies' idea of luxury goods—Navajo rugs, Persian jewellry—were being provided by boutiques that sprang up everywhere, mostly backed by the drug money. If nothing else, Rochdale proved that the drug economy was indeed a self-contained, viable economy.

From the police's point of view Rochdale was a first-rate "classroom." Police Chief Adamson feels Rochdale was a valuable lesson in "learning how to handle a situation like that in the best possible way. Rochdale was a powder-keg. It could have blown up, but it didn't, and I think that our closing it down in the end without the cost of human life was a valuable lesson for the police force."

From a "nuts and bolts" perspective, the local police force, according to Dan Marshall, was able to assume some of the responsibility of drug enforcing. "Rochdale caused a great deal of change on our force. Procedures were changed—not just procedures for our local force but federal procedures. It used to be that whenever we made a seizure, we had to hand over our seizure to an RCMP drug squad officer. And they'd get called out in the middle of the night to make a seizure of one marijuana cigarette. Well, it got so the seizures became more and more frequent, so the feds let their grip of that go a little bit and allowed us to handle our own exhibits. So we set up our own procedures and formed our own drug squads, which didn't officially take place until 1975. Although we had men out doing drug enforcement, they weren't officially recognized by the police force as being a drug squad until 1975, believe it or not."

Certainly the Rochdale experience was an eye-opening one from the point of view of community relations. "Mod squad" member Ross Prasky believes, "If you look back at it, we weren't necessarily that sophisticated when we started to deal with that problem. But in the end, we got quite sophisticated in handling it, in the sense that there were no big confrontations. Let's face it, the whole country was looking at us. And the United States was looking at us, because Rochdale was a big deal in the United States, as well. Its West Coast had Haight-Ashbury, its East Coast had Greenwich Village and Canada had Rochdale. In terms of what was happening elsewhere, it was a very sophisticated approach that the Toronto police force used.

"You can say about our initial attempts that we banged our head against the wall of that building for perhaps a year or so. But then we realized there were some really different and creative ways to work. We didn't lose anybody—there were injuries, but no cops were killed in there. And police didn't go in and shoot anybody, although on a number of occasions we were shot at.

"Going in there certainly opened your eyes, not only to the other side of the fence, but to the ideas that people were trying to express. We got to do some community work with some very forward-thinking and intelligent individuals. So as police officers, we got taken to a very different aspect of policing—for instance, the meeting rooms where policy was decided.

"It influenced me positively, because it let me see that there was another side. It took me out of my law-enforcement box and put me in a big, big room with a lot of ideas bouncing off the wall."

Police Inspector Robert Crampton believes that Rochdale helped "point out the inadequacies of Canada's immigration policies. A lot of people came into this country under a lie. They came in ostensibly to evade the draft. A lot of people had some good and moral reasons for not going to fight in another man's war, and one respects them for that. But a great deal of people slipped in under the net who were nothing but hoodlums. We missed them, and the seeds that they planted are still with us today."

Perhaps, ultimately, the mere fact that Rochdale was attempted is its greatest legacy. "This is something that didn't and couldn't happen anywhere else," offers Tom Shevlin. "It was the Pierre Trudeau era, at least before his arteries hardened—Pierre was the symbol of the 'Swinging Sixties.' The federal government was handing out money to all sorts of hare-brained schemes and Rochdale was one of them. Having said that, it was still wonderful while it lasted. Just the fact that something like this could happen and that it was tried was great and may be in and of itself enough."

C H A P T E R 16

The
Long And
Winding Road

The following are the real names of individuals interviewed for *Dream Tower*, except where an asterisk appears to denote the use of pseudonyms to protect both the innocent and the guilty. Information is correct to spring, 1988.

JACK ACKROYD served with the Metropolitan Toronto Police Department as deputy chief of field operations from 1970 to 1980 and as chief until 1984. He is now chairman and chief executive officer of the Liquor Control Board of Ontario.

NELSON ADAMS has spent all his time since Rochdale as a typesetter and jack-of-all-trades at Coach House Press in Toronto.

HAROLD ADAMSON served with the Metropolitan Toronto Police Department as deputy chief of field operations until 1970 and as chief from 1970 to 1980. He is now vice-president of security for the Ontario Jockey Club.

HOWARD ADELMAN helped organize Operation Lifeline in 1980 to bring the Vietnamese boat people to Canada. He is a philosophy professor at York University's Atkinson College in Toronto and is director of York's Refugee Documentation Project.

IAN ANDERSON, non-resident but frequent visitor to Rochdale, is a licensed steamfitter. He is married, has two children and owns his own home in Toronto, but feels he hasn't changed much since Rochdale.

DEAN AUDLEY is an inspector with the Metropolitan Toronto Police Department and is the officer in charge of 41 Division in Scarborough.

"ANIMAL" DICK BARNES moved to a subsidized-housing apartment building at Queen and Sherbourne in 1975. He died the week before Christmas in 1986.

PAMELA BERTON is a nature tour organizer for the Federation of Ontario Naturalists in North York.

PATSY BERTON is a Toronto homemaker and mother.

PIERRE BERTON, one of Canada's most popular writers and broadcasters, works in Toronto and is the author of *The Last Spike, The National Dream, Vimy, Klondike, Hollywood's Canada, The Invasion Of Canada, Why We Act Like Canadians* and other books.

STAN BEVINGTON continues to own and run Coach House Press on Huron Street, around the corner from the building that used to be Rochdale College.

JOHN BIDDELL retired in 1982 as chairman and president of the Clarkson Company, the receivership operation of Clarkson Gordon. He is now a private consultant in Toronto.

JAY BOLDIZSAR, as chief budget officer for the Association of Canadian Community Colleges, administers financial aid to Third World educational projects.

HOWARD BRENNER provides transportation for various movie projects in Toronto.

* BRUNNEL has returned to university in Canada as a doctoral student in computers and education.

BILLY BRYANS is co-founder and drummer with one of Canada's most popular rock bands, Toronto's Juno Award-winning Parachute Club.

Rev. EDGAR BULL retired in 1978 as rector of St. Thomas' Anglican Church. He now serves as chaplain at Toronto General Hospital.

MARTIN BURNS is a Toronto accountant and the father of ten children.

MURRAY CAMPBELL is sports editor for *The Globe and Mail* in Toronto.

BILL CHARNELL (known as ROCANA during the early 1970s) was a member of the Toronto Hare Krishna Temple during the 1970s. He is now a Winnipeg businessman who adheres to his earlier religious beliefs, but no longer takes an active role in formal temple life.

TOM CLARK has worked as news anchor for Toronto's CFTO-TV (flagship station of the CTV network), as co-host of the CTV current affairs series "Hourlong," as CTV's correspondent in Beijing and as news anchor on the network's "Canada AM" show. In 1987, he was appointed political editor of CFTO.

MATT COHEN has written several novels, including *The Sweet Second Summer Of Kitty Malone*, *The Spanish Doctor* and *Nadine*. He lives in Toronto, but has taught at the University of Victoria and has been writer-in-residence at the University of Alberta and the University of Western Ontario.

VICTOR COLEMAN is a Toronto-based poet whose publishing credits include *From Erik Satie's Notes To The Music* and *America*. He is involved in various projects, including *Earlick*, a series of performance pieces based on songs with lyrics by Canadian poets. He is also working on a song cycle based on William Burroughs' *Naked Lunch*.

ALICE COOPER was in semi-retirement until the mid-1980s revival of shock rock, of which he is the acknowledged founder. He is still actively recording and can be found mutilating dolls and simulating suicide on concert stages around the world.

PAUL COPELAND, a practicing lawyer in Toronto, is vice-president of the Criminal Lawyers Association of Ontario and a former bencher of the Law Society of Upper Canada.

FRANK COX is a self-employed title searcher who also dabbles in real estate in Toronto.

ROBERT CRAMPTON serves as an inspector in the trials preparation unit of the Metropolitan Toronto Police Department.

GEORGE CREASE has served with the Metropolitan Toronto Police Department since the early 1950s and is now a sergeant in North York.

DAVID CROMBIE was elected alderman for a north-end Toronto ward in 1969 and Mayor of Toronto in 1972. As a Progressive Conservative, he became Member of Parliament for the riding of Rosedale in 1978 and served in cabinet as Secretary of State and the minister responsible for multiculturalism. He retired from politics in 1988 to head an inquiry into the future of development along Toronto's waterfront.

* JOHN DALTON is an engineer and is thinking of following in the political footsteps of his father who was an Ontario cabinet minister in the early 1970s.

LORRAINE DARLING is a sculptor who continues to raise her two children, high-school students JUSTINE and CRAIG, in Toronto.

JACK DIMOND completed his Ph.D. in humanities at the University of Toronto after his association with Rochdale. He has held various administrative positions with the U of T since 1969 and has been secretary to the university's governing council since 1980.

LIONEL DOUGLAS was killed in a motorcycle accident in July, 1979.

PAUL EVITTS has been a Toronto computer consultant since 1980, with specialties in systems analysis, feasibility studies and strategic planning. He is also developing a plan to increase the use and effectiveness of computers in Third World countries.

JULIAN FANTINO serves as an inspector for the Metropolitan Toronto Police Department in Toronto's 55 Division.

JIM FLAHERTY is an environmental health supervisor for the Toronto Department of Public Health.

VALERIE FRITH spent three years in the 1970s as literature officer with the Ontario Arts Council. She was also an editor at *Quill & Quire* magazine, started the Banff publishing workshop and is currently a freelance editor and writer in Toronto.

JIM GARRARD is a Toronto playwright and director whose scripts—including *Cold Comfort, Getting Even* and *Peggy's Song*—have been produced in theatres across Canada, including Theatre Passe Muraille, which he founded. He has been resident director at the University of Toronto and Simon Fraser University, playwright-in-residence at Montreal's Centaur Theatre and a board member of the Playwrights' Union of Canada.

ALLEN GINSBERG is a New York poet of international stature and author of *Howl And Other Poems*, a seminal work of the Beat generation. *Collected Poems*, a volume of more than 800 pages that span 30 years of his work, was published in 1985.

PAUL GODFREY was a North York controller who became a delegate to Metropolitan Toronto Council in 1970. He was elected chairman of the council in 1973 and served until 1984, when he became publisher of the *Toronto Sun*.

DONALD GRANT is an assistant city editor for *The Globe and Mail* in Toronto.

REG HARTT is a movie exhibitor and manager of Cineforum whose avant-garde programs are screened regularly in the Cabana Room of the Spadina Hotel in Toronto.

DAN HEAP was elected to Toronto Council in 1972 as an alderman representing the downtown ward containing Rochdale. As a New Democrat, he has served as Member of Parliament for the riding of Spadina since 1981.

MICHAEL HIRSH is a partner and co-founder of Nelvana, a Toronto company that has produced feature films such as *Rock and Rule*, *Burglar* and *The Care Bears Movie*, and TV series such as "The Edison Twins."

* HORST lives on and off in the Killaloe area near Ottawa and has undergone career changes from social worker to drug dealer to restaurateur.

WALT HOUSTON spent five years on and off in the Canadian north after leaving Rochdale. In addition to currently working as a clerk in a Toronto book store, he salvages and sells discarded books.

* JAMES JOHNSON became a disc jockey after Rochdale and spent most of the 1970s in various Prairie cities. A radio journeyman, he is now one of Canada's best-known commercial voices and works in southern Ontario.

KAREN JOHNSON moved from Rochdale to a communal house in Toronto, where she decided to study law as a mature student at York University's Osgoode Hall. She has had her own Toronto law practice since 1980, but plans to move her family to Lake Skugog, Ontario and continue her legal work in Port Perry.

JUDY KEELER is a freelance publicist in Toronto and the author of two novels.

TIMOTHY LEARY, former LSD guru and psychedelic visionary, travels the North American lecture circuit to discuss LSD, the 1960s and the new age of enlightment heralded by the computer revolution.

DENNIS LEE won the 1972 Governor-General's Award for poetry for *Civil Elegies*. He also writes children's poetry—his most notable work is *Alligator Pie*. He has written lyrics for the Muppet TV series "Fraggle Rock," worked as consulting editor at Macmillan of Canada, served as literary adviser for the poetry program at McClelland and Stewart, been writer-in-residence at the University of Toronto and Trent University, and in 1984 received the first annual literary prize at the Harbourfront International Authors' Festival in Toronto.

GEDDY LEE is bassist and co-founder of Canada's most popular international rock band, Rush. The group's multi-platinum-selling albums include *2112*, *Signals* and *Moving Pictures*.

BILL LITTLER lives in a tent with his dog in the Vancouver area and travels across Canada to co-ordinate security services for carnivals.

SANDRA LITTLER is a waitress, mother and home-maker in Guelph, Ontario.

BRIAN LUMLEY left Rochdale to work as an illusionary engineer and animal trainer for magician Doug Henning. He then spent four years in Northern Ontario building canoes for the Bear Mountain Canoe Co. He has developed a system of movable insulation for windows, patio doors and skylights. He now builds movie sets in Toronto.

ALEX MACDONALD works in the computer field and acts as informal contact and nerve centre for dozens of former Rochdale residents.

GREG MACDONALD has worked in the electronics industry and is now a technician for Bell Canada in Toronto.

Rev. IAN MACKENZIE is archdeacon for the 450,000-square-mile Anglican Diocese of Caledonia in northwestern British Columbia. He has lived in the area since 1974.

* MAJOR DOMO works for a Toronto computer company and has lived since 1979 in the building that used to be Rochdale College.

* BOBBIE MALONE worked as a stripper and is now a waitress in Toronto.

DAN MARSHALL serves with the Metropolitan Toronto Police Department as sergeant in charge of the hit-and-run squad.

* ALEX MARTIN was dragged home to England by his irate parents, after living in Rochdale as a runaway for six months. He spent several years hitch-hiking through Europe and joined the British army, resulting in combat duty in Northern Ireland. He is now married with children and lives in Toronto.

JUDITH MERRIL is an award-winning science fiction writer, anthologist and resource person at the Spaced Out Library in Toronto's public library system.

BOB MILLER is a partner in the Bob Miller Book Room in Toronto.

NICKY MORRISON works for the CBC in Toronto, is married to Ian Argue and is still raising Brendan, often referred to as Rochdale's first baby.

BOB NASMITH is an actor who frequently appears at Theatre Passe Muraille and with the VideoCabaret theatre company in Toronto. He also earns a living in the dry-wall construction trade.

* JERRY NEILSEN is an energy consultant who designs heating and air-conditioning systems for commercial buildings and high-rise residences in Toronto. Together with Alex MacDonald, he developed a computer program for replacing heating systems in apartment buildings.

JAMES ("ISRAEL") NEWELL is a Toronto computer programmer.

HONEY NOVICK was part of the circle in General Idea, one of Canada's most popular avant-garde performance art groups. She is an accomplished improvisational singer who lives in Toronto. Her credits include a scat-singing performance at Carnegie Hall's recital hall.

TONY O'DONOHUE has been an alderman on Toronto Council for most of the time since he was first elected in 1966.

KEVIN O'LEARY works in the home renovation industry in Montreal and is still involved in the film world through his girlfriend's association with the Soleil Film company. Their most recent project is a movie about a female guerilla fighter in El Salvador.

TOM OSBORNE has been employed by the Canadian Imperial Bank of Commerce since the late 1960s and is a senior inspector in the bank's credit department in Toronto.

* TONY PHRED and his brother PAT were active in the anti-war movement in the United States in the late 1960s and have maintained an impeccable reputation for fairness and honesty in Toronto's soft-drug community.

ANN POHL is a Toronto peace activist and homemaker.

WAYNE POLLOCK is a senior inspector with the Etobicoke Department of Public Health.

CAROLE POPKEY lives in Toronto and has been trained as a teacher of English as a second language.

(HARRY E.) BUD PORTER is a senior sales representative for an interior design company in Toronto.

ROSS PRASKEY serves as staff sergeant in the communications bureau of the Metropolitan Toronto Police Department.

* VAL R. spent two years in jail on drug charges in Toronto and continues to deal drugs.

* "RED" REBEL is a former school-teacher and American draft dodger who is currently one of Canada's most stylish purveyors of the blues. He can be found working in steamy, smoky nightclubs across the country.

ROBERT ("ROSIE") ROWBOTHAM was tried in 1977 for conspiring to import a ton of hashish into Canada. In May, 1982, while on parole, Rowbotham was again arrested. The subsequent trial before the Ontario Supreme Court was one of the longest and costliest in Toronto history. But in a dramatic reversal in March, 1988, the Ontario Court of Appeal set aside the convictions of Rowbotham, who still remains in Collins Bay penitentiary near Kingston, where he completed studies toward his BA from Queen's University.

JOHN SEWELL was first elected to Toronto Council as an alderman in 1969, served as mayor from 1978 to 1980 and returned as an alderman in 1981. In 1984, he became an urban affairs columnist for *The Globe and Mail* and, in 1986, was appointed chairman of the Metropolitan Toronto Housing Authority.

JOE SHEARD worked as a Bay Street lawyer in Toronto and, since the late 1970s, has been an Ontario district court judge.

CAROL SHEVLIN is a certified general accountant in Toronto.

TOM SHEVLIN is a radio system design engineer for the Canadian Broadcasting Corporation in Toronto.

LARRY SIMMONS was a leading North American amphetamine dealer in the 1970s and served five years in a federal penitentiary for possession of a pound of heroin. He left the Satan's Choice motorcycle gang and has worked as a film editor at CBC-TV and on the Brian Linehan interview show for CITY-TV. He is now employed in the construction industry in Toronto.

SID SMITH is a registrar for the Supreme Court of Ontario in Toronto.

Dr. LIONEL SOLURSH treats combat-related stress disorders at the Veterans' Administration Centre of the Medical College of Georgia in Augusta, Ga.

ALLAN SPARROW served as an alderman on Toronto Council from 1974 to 1980 and now runs the Domicity computer management consulting firm in Toronto.

SYD STERN, now in his seventies, was one of Rochdale's leading drug dealers and currently lives in British Columbia.

* T.J. is involved in security operations for various Toronto clubs and concerts. He was manager of Toronto's Hotel Isabella for about two years in the mid-1980s.

ELMAR TAMPOLD is a Toronto architect in partnership with J. Malcolm Wells.

JOCKO THOMAS has been a police reporter for *The Toronto Star* for more than fifty years.

PAUL THOMPSON was artistic director of Theatre Passe Muraille from 1970 to 1982 and is now director-general of the National Theatre School in Montreal.

* TRIPPER is a part-time bouncer, part-time screenwriter, part-time drug dealer and full-time bon vivant in Toronto.

PETER TURNER is active in the Liberal Party of Ontario and works for the University of Toronto.

Dr. TY TURNER practiced family medicine in Toronto for ten years and, from 1982 to 1986, ran Canada's first psychiatric patients' rights program. He is now a resident in psychiatry.

BOB WADDELL, as a result of the astounding arrest record that he and his late partner Peter King amassed at Rochdale, was promoted to sergeant in 1974. He retired from the Metropolitan Toronto Police Department in 1980 after sixteen years and is now director of security for National Trust in Toronto.

Dr. BRYN WAERN is a family physician who practices psychotherapy, psychiatry and nutrition in Toronto.

RICK WAERN renovates homes in Toronto and dreams of creating a Rochdale-like commune patterned after the successful eighteenth-floor set-up.

MICHAEL WAITE is a Toronto-based musician and producer who owns his own record store. He has produced albums for Nash the Slash and FM and has released an album of his own.

* DON WASHBURN has been employed by General Motors of Canada in Toronto since the mid-1970s. He is married with children and coaches little league baseball.

J. MALCOLM WELLS is a Toronto architect in partnership with Elmar Tampold.

(A.E.) TED WHITESIDE is manager of environmental health and inspection services for the Toronto Department of Public Health.

TONY ZENKER used the leather-making skills he developed at Rochdale to produce products for Toronto musicians such as Ronnie Hawkins, the Good Brothers and Subway Elvis. He is currently involved in the home renovation industry in Toronto.